# NEW AGENDAS FOR WOMEN

3

*Also by Sylvia Walby*

CONTEMPORARY BRITISH SOCIETY (*with N. Abercrombie, A. Warde, K. Soothill and J. Urry*)

EUROPEAN SOCIETIES: Fission or Fusion (*co-editor with T. Boje and B. van Steenbergen*)

GENDER SEGREGATION AT WORK (*editor*)

GENDER TRANSFORMATIONS

LOCALITIES, CLASS AND GENDER (*with L. Murgatroyd, M. Savage, D. Shapiro, J. Urry, A. Warde and J. Mark-Lawson*)

MEDICINE AND NURSING: Professions in a Changing Health Service (*with J. Greenwell, and with L. Mackay and K. Soothill*)

OUT OF THE MARGINS: Women's Studies in the Nineties (*co-editor with J. Aaron*)

PATRIARCHY AT WORK

RESTRUCTURING: PLACE, CLASS AND GENDER (*with P. Bagguley, J. Mark-Lawson, D. Shapiro, J. Urry and A. Warde*)

SEX CRIME IN THE NEWS (*with K. Soothill*)

THEORISING PATRIARCHY

# New Agendas for Women

Edited by

Sylvia Walby
*Professor of Sociology*
*University of Leeds*

Foreword by Clare Short, MP

First published in Great Britain 1999 by
**MACMILLAN PRESS LTD**
Houndmills, Basingstoke, Hampshire RG21 6XS and London
Companies and representatives throughout the world

A catalogue record for this book is available from the British Library.

ISBN 0–333–74558–2 hardcover
ISBN 0–333–74559–0 paperback

 First published in the United States of America 1999 by
**ST. MARTIN'S PRESS, INC.,**
Scholarly and Reference Division,
175 Fifth Avenue, New York, N.Y. 10010

ISBN 0–312–22242–4

Library of Congress Cataloging-in-Publication Data
New agendas for women / edited by Sylvia Walby ; foreword by Clare
Short.
p.   cm.
Includes bibliographical references and index.
ISBN 0–312–22242–4 (cloth)
1. Women's rights—Great Britain.   2. Great Britain—Social
policy—1979–   I. Walby, Sylvia.
HQ1236.5.G7N49   1999
305.42'0941—dc21                                          98–53534
                                                              CIP

This book is printed on paper suitable for recycling and made from fully managed and sustained forest sources.

10   9   8   7   6   5   4   3   2   1
08   07   06   05   04   03   02   01   00   99

Printed and bound in Great Britain by
Antony Rowe Ltd, Chippenham, Wiltshire

# Contents

# Foreword

John Smith asked me to take on the role of Shadow Minister for Women in 1993. It was a fascinating responsibility. It touched strong emotions amongst women, men and tabloid newspapers. There were deep stereotypes about feminism and feminists raging at the time, and the changes taking place in women's lives were creating a powerful current of historical change that was remaking patterns of work, family life and social and political power worldwide.

I immediately found myself inundated with demands to write and speak at a massive range of events. I had responsibility for an agenda that touched every area of public policy and had very large potential consequences for voting behaviour. Yet it had little place in our formal political system – no question time, few debates and no bills to oppose and thus pattern one's political work in a way that is the normal stuff of opposition politics.

And so I had room and need to try to order my thinking, policy prescriptions and influence. I am of the old-fashioned view that ideas and academic thinking can enlarge political ideas. I was conscious that I had read few of the famous feminist texts. And women's studies had grown up and become established as an academic discipline since my time at university. I was keen to know what they were studying and what they had to teach me, and also keen to order and structure my work.

I was lucky enough to find Professors Sylvia Walby and Joni Lovenduski. I was clear that women's votes were potentially moveable and that could shift political power in Britain. Joni gave me access to analysis and worldwide experience that helped me to contribute to the increase in women's influence and representation throughout the Labour Party and, after the 1997 election, in parliament. Some of this understanding was fed into the party's campaigning and polling sensitivities and helped Labour win more women's votes.

Sylvia gave me access to women academics who made available to me the whole range of knowledge honed by women's studies – from violence and child sex abuse to changes in patterns of work and caring. We analysed the changing patterns of women's lives and the consequent rise in the number of lone parents and the disproportionate number of women pensioners living in poverty. But also we focused on the new energy and strength that women – especially older women – brought to public life.

I am enormously grateful to all the women who gave their time, wrote papers and travelled across the country to contribute their insights at my Friday seminars.

As the seminars progressed, our focus shifted from women as a group suffering inequality and demanding change to an appreciation of the remaking of all aspects of the personal, social and political that women's demand for change was invincibly bringing about. We came to appreciate more and more clearly that those same forces left women of different ages and income levels in vastly different positions which were related to differences of class, but also to differences of time and place in the major remodelling of society that women's demand for change was driving.

Later in our series, we moved on to examine the reasons for boys' increasingly weak performance in education and the challenge for men and their concept of masculinity that these changes were bringing about.

I enjoyed this process of sharing ideas enormously, learned a great deal and it helped me to order my thinking on the relevance of all this change for politics and public policy. I have been conscious for a long time of the deep changes that explain the difference between my grannies', my mother's and my own and my sisters' lives. I have known for a long time that I have had enormously more opportunities than previous generations of women in my family, but that the increased freedom brings with it responsibilities and difficulties. In the course of the seminars, It became very clear that when social movements that denounce injustice move on to create their own positive agenda they become more powerful.

There is more to do to create the new settlement that allows women and men to enjoy all aspects of their ability and humanity. But I am clear that the world is moving in the right direction and that this is a major historical change and it cannot be reversed.

I am enormously grateful to Sylvia Walby and all the contributors to this volume and many more who helped me deepen my understanding of this process of change.

Clare Short
October 1998

# Acknowledgements

This book is the outcome of a series of meetings between academics and successive Labour Shadow Ministers for Women, especially Clare Short. This involved seminars, larger conferences and the development of a think tank on women's issues. These meetings between Shadow Ministers and academics continued with Tessa Jowell, MP when she was Shadow Minister for Women and were only interrupted by the general election in 1997. One meeting on violence led to a working group which produced a policy consultation document, 'Peace at Home', which was the subject of debate at a special conference held at the Institute for Public Policy Research.

This book emerges out of the papers presented at the seminar series or at the larger conferences. Its combination of engagement with the wider issues of our day simultaneously with practical politics and rigorous research owes much to the inspiration derived from Clare Short. she stimulated the role of new thinking and of ideas in new policy relevant to contemporary dilemmas.

The contributors to the volume have extensively and generously commented on each other's work, both in the seminars and in the revised papers and introduction.

# Notes on the Contributors

**Sara Arber** is Professor of Sociology at the University of Surrey. Her books include: *Gender and Later Life* (Sage, 1991, with Jay Ginn); *Women and Working Lives* (Macmillan, 1992, with N. Gilbert); *Families and Households* (Macmillan, 1992, with C. Marsh); and *Connecting Gender and Ageing* (Open University 1995, with J. Ginn).

**Julia Brannen** is Professor in the Sociology of the Family, University of London and Senior Research Officer at Thomas Coram Research Unit, Institute of Education. Recent publications include: *Young People, Health and Family Life* (Open University Press, 1994, with K. Dodd, A. Oakley and P. Storey); *Mixing Methods: Qualitative and Quantitative Research* (Gower, 1992); *Children in Families: Research and Policy* (Falmer, 1996, with M. O'Brien); and *Children. Research and Policy* (Taylor and Francis, 1997, with Basil Bernstein). She has a particular interest in research on the relationship between employment and family life and is a director of a virtual Work-Life Research Centre.

**Jay Ginn** is a Research Fellow in the Sociology Department at Surrey University. Her books include: *Gender and Later Life* (Sage, 1991) and *Connecting Gender and Ageing* (Open University Press, 1995), both with Sara Arber.

**Jeanne Gregory** is Visiting Professor and Head of the Gender Research Centre at Middlesex University. Her book *Sex, Race and the Law: Legislating for Equality* was published by Sage in 1987; since then she has published articles on equal pay, sex and race discrimination, sexual harassment, rape and sexual assault, women in legal systems and women refugees. She has undertaken research for the Equal Opportunities Commission and the European Commission on the functioning of sex equality legislation. She is joint author of *Policing Sexual Assault* and joint editor of *Women, Work and Inequality*, both forthcoming in 1999.

**Jeff Hearn** has been involved in men's groups and anti-sexist activities and in researching and writing on men since 1978. His publications include *'Sex' at 'Work'* (with Wendy Parkin), *The Gender of Oppression, Men in the Public Eye* and *The Violences of Men*, and he has co-edited *The Sexuality of Organization, Taking Child Abuse Seriously, Men, Masculinities and Social Theory, Violence and Gender Relations, Men as Managers, Managers as Men, Consuming Cul-*

*tures, Transforming Politics* and *Children, Child Abuse and Child Protection*. He is Professorial Research Fellow in the Faculty of Economic and Social Studies, University of Manchester, based in the School of Social Policy, and Donner Visiting Professor in Sociology with particular reference to Gender Research, Åbo Akademi University, Finland.

**Liz Kelly** is a senior researcher in the Woman and Child Abuse Research Unit of North London University. She is an expert consultant to the Council of Europe on violence against women. Her books include *Surviving Sexual Violence* (Polity, 1988); and *Women, Violence and Male Power* (Open University, 1996, with M. Hester and J. Radford).

**Ruth Lister** is Professor of Social Policy at the Department of Social Sciences, Loughborough University. She is a former Head of the Child Poverty Action Group and former member of the Commission on Social Justice. Her publications include *Women's Economic Dependency and Social Security*; *Welfare Benefits* (Equal Opportunities Commission, 1992); and *Citizenship: Feminist Perspectives* (Macmillan/New York University Press, 1997).

**Joni Lovenduski** is Professor of Politics at University of Southampton. Her books include *Contemporary Feminist Politics* (Oxford University Press, 1993, with V. Randall); *Gender and Party Politics* (Sage, 1993, with P. Norris); *Different Roles, Different Voices* (1994); *Political Recruitment: Gender, Race and Class in the British Parliament* (Cambridge University Press, 1995, with P. Norris); *Women and European Politics* (Wheatsheaf, 1986, with J. Hills); and *The Politics of the Second Electorate* (Routledge, 1981, with J. Hills).

**Mary Maynard** is Professor in the Department of Social Policy and Social Work at the University of York, where she was formerly Director of the Centre for Women's Studies. Her books include *Sexism, Racism and Oppression* (Blackwell, 1984, with A. Brittan); *Women, Violence and Social Control* (Macmillan, 1987, with J. Hanmer); *Researching Women's Lives from a Feminist Perspective* (Taylor and Francis, 1994, with J. Purvis); *The Dynamics of 'Race' and Gender* (Taylor and Francis, 1994, with H. Afshar); *New Frontiers in Women's Studies* (Taylor and Francis, 1996, with J. Purvis); and *Science and the Construction of Women* (UCL, 1997).

**Lydia Morris** is Professor of Sociology at the University of Essex. Her books include *Dangerous Classes: the Underclass and Social Citizenship* (Routledge, 1994); *The Workings of the Household* (Polity, 1990); *Household Finance Management and the Labour Market* (Avebury, 1989, with S. Ruane); and *Social Divisions: Economic Decline and Social Structural Change*

(UCL, 1995). She has a long standing interest in gender relations, economic restructuring and their policy implications.

**Judith Squires** is Lecturer in Politics at the University of Bristol. Her books include *Gender in Political Theory* (Polity, forthcoming); *Feminisms* (OUP, 1997, with S. Kemp); *Cultural Remix: Theories of Politics and the Popular* (Lawrence and Wishart, 1995, with E. Carter and J. Donald); *Space and Place: Theories of Identity and Location* (Lawrence and Wishart, 1993, with E. Carter and J. Donald); and *Principled Positions: Postmodernism and the Rediscovery of Value* (Lawrence and Wishart, 1993). She was editor of the journal *New Formations* 1991–7, and is currently an associate editor of the *International Feminist Journal of Politics*.

**Sylvia Walby** is Professor of Sociology at the University of Leeds. She was previously Professor and Head of Department of Sociology at Bristol University; and Director of the Gender Institute at the LSE. She has been Chair of the Women's Studies Network UK and President of the European Sociological Association. She is author of *Gender Transformations* (Routledge, 1997), *Theorising Patriarchy* (Blackwell, 1990) and *Patriarchy at Work* (Polity 1986), joint author of *Sex Crime in the News* (Routledge, 1991), *Localities, Class and Gender* (Pion, 1985), *Contemporary British* Society (Polity, 1988, 1994), *Restructuring Place Class and Gender* (Sage, 1990), and *Medicine and Nursing: Professions in a Changing Health Service* (Sage, 1994); editor of *Gender Segregation at Work* (Open University Press, 1988) and co-editor of *Out of the Margins: Women's Studies in the Nineties* (Falmer, 1991) and *European Societies: Fusion or Fission?* (Routledge, 1999)

# 1 Introduction
## Sylvia Walby

### A NEW GENDER SETTLEMENT

Gender relations are being transformed. A new gender settlement, a new social contract between women and men, is being created. These arrangements are potentially more equitable, productive and socially inclusive for both women and men. Government has a crucial role in supporting this new settlement, especially a new Labour government with an ethos of modernising and reducing social exclusion.

This book is about the dilemmas in the new policy agendas for women and government. It presents research findings from leading academics as a contribution to their resolution through informed debate. The dilemmas hinge on how to engage with these changes positively without neglecting those who built their lives around a previous gender settlement; how to modernise policy while respecting the practical diversity of people's lives; and how to engage with proposed new ways of addressing old problems of injustice.

The continuing development of women's employment in particular presents an opportunity to promote a positive restructuring of gender roles in society. Many young women are seizing educational opportunities. They have already noticed that what is important is education, education and education, and they are entering the job market better qualified than ever before. They are rebalancing their commitments to work and family. Older women, brought up in an era with different expectations and opportunities, more often built their lives around caring in the home. It is important that new policies are sensitive to the needs of a diversity of women, the young and the old, those with and without educational qualifications.

There remain, however, some long-standing dimensions of gender inequity which need to be addressed anew, especially that of men's violence against women, which is, at last, now an issue of public debate. This is an area where women's newly developing political voices have forced an old social problem onto the political stage and hence created the context within which adequate new policies could be created.

Government needs to engage with these developments positively. They need to address the concerns of both the younger women who are expecting and prepared to enter a lifetime of employment, while also providing support for those who have difficulty following this new path without assistance, as well as for those for whom employment opportunities are not, or are no longer, relevant, such as those who are retired or severely physically impaired. There are growing age divisions in patterns of gender relations, a new form of diversity which needs to be recognised, so that the possible divisions do not become the basis of new forms of social exclusion.

Yet there is a continuing diversity of forms of social and economic contribution. There are dilemmas of how to support this, without entrenching those practices which look backwards to an era which has gone; how to move with the times without creating hardship for those with skills and resources more appropriate to a previous era; how to lay the foundations for future growth and development, while respecting previous contributions.

These involve changes for men as well as for women. These are new forms of gender relations, new ways of thinking and practising the relations between men and women. It is time to rethink traditional forms of masculinity, so that men can see the opportunities opened up by these changes, rather than focusing on the limitations to their traditional forms of power.

The new gender settlement could deliver both increased equity and efficiency in the economy, as women's skills are used rather than neglected, as women are included on an equal basis in all institutions rather than excluded by discriminatory practices. There is a role for government in support of the equal opportunities and social justice through which social inclusion can be enhanced.

This is a time to respond to challenges of a new world order consequent upon globalisation, with the modernisation not only of the economy but also of the British polity. It is time to facilitate women's inclusion in the workforce as a result of new forms of economic restructuring, and to expand their role in the decision-making forums in our society. There is the possibility of virtuous circle, if government accepts the challenge and updates its policies in relation to gender relations, assisting the transformation, rather than hindering such developments.

It is essential that women are fully involved in the decision-making about the new gender settlement. While there has been much progress with the increased intake of women into the House of Commons, nevertheless, the general under-representation of women in the corridors of power remains. This requires new ways of thinking about political representation and participating in decision-making.

## SOCIAL EXCLUSION AND CITIZENSHIP

A desire to combat social exclusion rightly lies at the heart of much government social policy. The focus on contribution and participation in society through paid work is widely regarded as appropriate for all whose circumstances allow it. The problems come in determining how the polity is to take account of both the need to care and to be cared for. Who is not expected to take paid work? In particular, do women's contributions to caring, for children, for the elderly, for husbands, exempt them from such a duty? There is the dilemma of how to focus on the dignity of labour in a world where labour markets are increasingly flexible and deregulated without causing the impoverishment of those who cannot labour due to old age, sickness or physical or mental impairment; how not to disable socially and economically those who are infirm or impaired; how to balance paid work and family care; how to provide welfare which does not entrench its recipients in poverty.

One of the advantages of the new gender settlement is that improving justice for women can go hand in hand with increasing economic efficiency, instead of there being a trade-off between the two. Growing employment among women, especially young educated women, increases economic growth as well as women's financial rewards.

Of course, some women are in a better position to benefit from these changes than others. Women who, for whatever reason, are not part of the growing economy and core workforce will face intensified social exclusion as a consequence. Thus those women who lack educational or vocational qualifications, who are not fit and able, who care for children or the elderly may face the prospect of social exclusion. Many young lone mothers face the possibility of remaining on the margins of the labour market as a result of both lack of qualifications and their caring. Many older women do not maintain continuous employment; and their pension contributions are thus interrupted or non-existent, so they will also often face poverty. These are simultaneously issues of class and of gender.

There are new divides opening up, between younger and older women, as younger educated women are more likely to be in employment, more likely to get better jobs and careers, while older women who built their lives around quite different expectations of a woman's life, as a carer rather than employee, face an older life in poverty. In practice, of course, this divide may not always be clear-cut, since many women combine part-time work with caring. There are also polarisations among younger women between those who can command a sufficiently high salary to afford comprehensive childcare and take only a minimal career break; and those whose childcare responsibilities prevent full-time employment for a number of years. Age is one of the new divides leading to potential for social exclusion, but it is in addition to, not a replacement of, those of class.

The concept of 'citizenship' is a way of capturing the roundedness of the aspiration for social inclusion. It is a concept which goes beyond simply civil rights, such as those to free speech, political rights, such as that to vote, to include the social and economic right to sufficient income to be able to participate fully in society. When the lens of citizenship is applied to the concerns of women we see slightly different issues from those for men. We see the importance of the civil rights to bodily integrity, to freedom from the fear of violence in the street and the home; the importance of effective political representation and participation, of the diversity of women's views, not just the right to vote; the right to an income sufficient for independence, rather than dependence upon a husband.


## EQUAL OPPORTUNITIES

The effective implementation of equal opportunities policies is one of the prerequisites to securing social inclusion and citizenship for women. Equal opportunities has meaning as a set of established and still developing practices to deliver justice for women in the workplace.

The principle of equal opportunities is now accepted as fair and legitimate across much of the UK. Equal opportunities is seen not only as fair to women who receive justice, but also as improving business efficiency by removing barriers to the utilisation of women's skills and efforts. It is the practical implementation, rather than the principle, of equal opportunities which is now the site of debate. How is this to be done, by whom and by what procedures, institutions and level of bureaucratisation? How could the sex discrimination legislation be improved in the light of experience, to ensure sex equality in pay, promotion and all aspects of employment? Should there be exceptions to equal treatment?

Equal opportunities potentially has a much wider remit than employment and education. The principle is now enshrined in the Treaty of Amsterdam and reaches way beyond the original focus on equal pay. There is a determination in the European Union, especially by the Commission and the Parliament, to 'mainstream' equal opportunities, so that it applies to all areas of policy-making, from regional funds to macroeconomic policy, from education to agriculture.

However, there are potential weaknesses in a conception of equality if it is too simply defined and does not take sufficient account of the diversity of patterns of gender relations and of differences between women. It has been argued that we need to consider special treatment for women, forms of positive or affirmative action, in order to deliver justice, since women have suffered not only historic discrimination, but are now leading lives fundamentally structured by that inequality. So, for instance, in this volume Brannen argues that:

> Until the goal of equality with men in both the labour market and in the home is achieved, there is a strong case for treating women as equal to men but also as different from them (p. 55)

She suggests that while, in the long run, things may change so that men do as much caring as women, in the short run 'policy has to recognise and support the current, highly gendered distribution of care'.

Gregory, also in this volume, argues that we need to transcend the limits of formal equality, in that we need to recognise special cases for exceptions to equal treatment, so as to allow, for instance, women-only facilities, such as taxis and for sports.

In these formulations the issue might appear initially to be whether we should treat women equally or differently from men. However, the question is rather that of defining the norm in relation to which claims for justice are made. Traditionally, this has been the male norm, that of the typical or representative man. Obviously this has been contested by the call to treat women's experiences as the basis of the norm, for instance, to endorse an ethic of care, rather than of work. In practice, however, what is often being sought is the transformation of the old dichotomies, the construction of new norms which create new conceptions of justice respecting the lives of both men and women. Respect for different identities can lead merely to the entrenching of existing patterns, as Squires notes in this volume.

These issues underlie several of the papers which address the relation- ship between caring and employment in the lives of women and men (for instance, see Lister, Ginn and Arber, and Morris). Women have a disadvantaged position in the labour market as a result of their work caring in the home for others, especially for children, elderly relatives and husbands, which leads to a disadvantaged position in relation to benefits, such as pensions. Poorly devised benefit systems can lead to the entrenchment of women in caring roles, and discourage their participation in employment, but this is not a necessary consequence. Lone mothers on benefits face a poverty trap which might entrench their position in the home and out of the labour market when the only employment offered to them is at low wages, unless benefits are designed so as to encourage employment. In the context of a society in which employment plays such a central role, and in which this is increasing, supporting strategies which do not involve employment do women no favours in the long run. The dilemma is real and acute. But there are types of benefits which can overcome this problem, such as higher child benefits, which do not have the effect of discouraging employment. There are various policy options, including some which involve changing the norm itself. For instance, men could equalise their contribution to caring, perhaps breaking the historic entrenchment of gender roles. Or, a benefit system could be remodelled to take account of contributions to care and attempt to sustain diversity. All of these options are thoroughly debated in the essays that follow.

*Sylvia Walby*

## CHANGES IN THE FAMILY–WELFARE–EMPLOYMENT NEXUS

Many of the new dynamics and new dilemmas of women's quest for justice and opportunity stem from the massive changes in the gender regime which have been occurring over recent decades. In particular, there is a change in the critical nexus between employment, welfare and the family. All three of these have undergone massive changes in their gender composition and structuring.

Women are participating in employment as never before in Britain. Women comprised 44 per cent of those economically active in 1998, indeed of those employees in employment they comprised 49.6 per cent in 1996 compared with 34 per cent in 1959, 38 per cent in 1971 and 43 per cent in 1991. This change is a result not only of women's increasing economic activity, but also the decreasing rates of employment among older men as a result of early exit from the labour market and among younger men as a result of higher male youth unemployment. Nearly half of the women in employment are working part-time – 47 per cent in 1995 compared with 34 per cent in 1971 (*Employment Gazette*, 1987, 1995; *Labour Market Trends*, 1996, 1998). Some of the increase in women's employment may be related to the rise in young women's educational levels, which have now overtaken those of young men (DfEE, 1998). Other factors include the introduction of equal opportunities laws and changing household and family structures. However, while the exclusion of women from higher-level jobs is decreasing, extensive occupational segregation remains. While the wages gap has reduced, especially for women working full-time, it still remains, with women who work full-time earning 81 per cent of men's hourly rates, and those working part-time earning only 59 per cent of men's hourly rates (*New Earnings Survey 1997*). While some gender inequalities are decreasing, new inequalities are opening up, especially those between younger and qualified women and women who are older or unqualified. Since it is primarily, though not uniformly, among younger women that the higher rates of education and higher-level jobs are to be found, age inequalities can compound those of class.

With increasing cohabitation and divorce, the typical household is becoming more varied and marriage more fragile. Women are much less likely to bring up children in the context of a life-long marriage – the number of lone parents has increased from 8 per cent in 1971 to 21 per cent in 1996 (*Living in Britain 1996*). This means both greater choice, with women and men leaving partners who cause them misery, as well as constraints, as lone mothers often face living in poverty.

The role of the state as the provider of welfare is undergoing continuing transition as individual private provision is being encouraged rather than reliance upon the state, especially in areas such as pensions and social care for the elderly, a transition that has particular effects on women, who are typically less able to afford contributions to private pensions or insurance funds as a result of their caring activities, and who can face the alternative of dependence on individual male partners.

This is producing a complex reconfiguration, since it is not only the care/work boundary that is being renegotiated, with all its implications for the rebalancing of work and family life, but also the interface of each of these with state welfare provision. This has complex consequences for men as well as for women, with various implications for forms of masculinity, even as high rates of male unemployment challenge traditional conceptions of men's family role. For women the changes are profound, as traditional expectations of women's roles as mother and housewife are fundamentally restructured. For employers there are challenges and opportunities in providing the kinds of employment which mesh with caring responsibilities.

These changes can create new opportunities for women and men to balance their lives to reflect their own priorities, but they can also mean new sets of constraints. The challenge for government is to meet the new expectations and needs of this reconfiguration constructively, and to avoid the temptation of some sections of the popular press, which has tended to scapegoat those vulnerable groups who are the losers in this restructuring: lone mothers, for example, are sometimes targeted as the new undeserving poor.

## TIME: A DIFFERENT WAY OF THINKING ABOUT RESOURCES

Time is as much an issue here as money. Indeed, to consider the distribution of scarce resources in terms of time rather than money provides new insights. Thinking in terms of time provides us with a new dimension on the balancing of care and employment, which can be hidden from view if the focus is money, since only one of these, employment, is routinely accounted for in terms of money. The lens of time enables the competing needs and contributions to be assessed in a more symmetrical way, more in tune with the vocabularies and concepts of the actors involved. Many of the issues and activities around caring are hard to quantify in money terms because they are not freely exchanged on the market.

Employed mothers often speak of the complications and difficulties of the juggling of time, to make sure that their various activities as both carers and workers dovetail. Some have identified the long hours culture of some workplaces as part of the problem, making it especially difficult for women to be both successful workers and mothers. Such long hours also militate against men doing their share of care.

The regulation of time is a topic on the EU agenda, encompassing parental leave, the rights of part-time workers and the Working Time Directive.

Time is also an issue for women's political representation. Traditionally time has been seen as one of the constraints on women's political participation, and it may be considered a necessary resource for citizenship.

## NEW FORMS OF POLITICAL REPRESENTATION?

While women's political presence in Parliament has increased with the new women elected in 1997, they still are a small minority of MPs. Women are no longer simply excluded from formal politics, but neither are they yet fully included. Women's increased presence may encourage new thinking about women's political preferences, though presence in Parliament is only one route to the increased representation of women's views.

There is an issue as to whether, or how far, it is appropriate to speak of women as a group, given the diversity of women's social positions and views. In particular there are age divisions, as older women have shown greater tendency to vote Conservative than older men, while younger women are more likely to vote Labour than younger men. The reasons are complex.

A new gendered political settlement would find routes through which women's views could be more effectively expressed. Women are active at the level of community organisation and politics, in social movements, in informal political activity. It is time that this found expression at the centre of political power as well as at the margins, so that women can move from protest to power. In the context of considerable constitutional change, such as devolution in Scotland and Wales, and a new political agreement in Northern Ireland, and proposals from the Women's Coalition in Northern Ireland for a 'civic forum', there is scope to introduce forms of representation that are more woman-friendly, and timely to rebuild and renew political democracy at different levels.

## THE EUROPEAN AND GLOBAL CONTEXT

These challenges and opportunities in the UK exist within a European and a global context which both lead to further change and constrain options.

Increasing EU integration has been an important factor behind the development of equal opportunities laws and policies in the UK. The EU has taken a series of equal opportunities initiatives, the most important of which have been legally binding, and the UK has been obliged to comply. The original basis of these was Article 119 of the Treaty of Rome, which required that women should receive equal pay with men for doing equivalent work. This was developed by a series of Directives, including those on Pay, Equal Treatment, and Social Security, which clarified the depth and breadth of the concern. The European Court of Justice has proved adept at insisting on the implementation of the law in those cases brought before it, developing legal doctrine which clarifies the power of Community law above domestic law. Following the Treaty of Amsterdam it is likely that there will be further developments since this Treaty enshrines a commitment to a more broadly defined equal opportunities programme, no longer limited to employment-related matters. Perhaps there will be development of EU policies on violence against women, following the Daphne and STOP initiatives and proposals for 1999 to be European Year Against Violence Against Women. Indeed, there is now a commitment to mainstreaming equal opportunities policies into all corners of the EU's newly extended remit.

It has been the power of the EU in the field of regulation of the labour as well as product markets which has been crucial to the ability of the EU to develop equal opportunities policies, in the face of the reluctance and indeed resistance of many member states. Without the EU effectively overriding the British state on these issues it is unlikely that such policies would have developed to the extent that they have in Britain, or indeed in most other member states. The EU is a powerful gendered polity whose policies have been more woman-friendly than those of many member states, especially in employment-related areas, although there have been some limitations, such as the levelling down of social benefits in some areas. Increasing EU integration, with the implication of increased power of the EU over that of the member states, has been an important dynamic in the development of equal opportunities policies for women in the UK. There are, of course, EU policies which have less positive implications for gender relations, and the outcome of some future developments, for instance, a monetary policy which prioritises inflation control over full employment, and an exclusionary policy towards migrants, may have negative implications. However, it is hard to underestimate the significance of the EU for gender relations.

The EU itself is constrained by wider pressures, especially those stemming from globalisation. Indeed, many of the policies of the EU can be seen to stem from an attempt to resist the negative implications of globalisation. The increased competitive pressures flowing from the creation of global financial markets raises questions about the extent to which traditional nation-states can maintain an effective social policy capacity, in particular to support programmes of welfare. The creation by the EU of a large single market with a set of cohesive internal policies is an attempt to create a polity powerful enough to match the scale of competitive global pressures. Whether the EU and the UK are able to resist global competitive pressures, which arguably tend to depress the level of state spending on welfare, is an open question. A route associated with the EU and the New Labour government is that of seeking to increase the skills of the population so as to compete globally on the basis of a high skill, high productivity economy rather than that of cheap labour.

In the context of such a strategy to meet global competition, the eagerness of many young women to gain educational qualifications greater than those of their mothers and their male peers and to use them to good effect in the labour market is a particularly interesting development. Perhaps this is the group that is adapting best to the challenges of globalisation?

Although globalisation can be seen as a problem for the UK, positioning the economy in a less advantageous way, it should not be forgotten that the UK is still part of the rich North rather than the poor South. Despite the growth of institutions of global governance it is still the North which takes the lead in setting the terms of trade around the world, controls the international banks and the lending which sets the terms of the structural adjustment of the economies of the poor and indebted countries of the world. There are responsibilities and opportunities associated with such power. For instance, can human rights conditions be effectively attached to trade, or to loans? The current development of UK government policy along these lines could be a significant contribution to a new global standard for human rights.

These concerns about the new agenda for women, for a new gender settlement, are raised in depth by the contributors to this book.

## THE CHAPTERS

Ruth Lister addresses the question of what welfare provisions women need to become full citizens. The dilemma underlying much policy in this area is whether the typical woman is seen as a worker or a mother, whether the model is that of 'citizen-the-carer' or 'citizen-the-wage-earner'. On the one hand, there is a desire to validate and support women who care by providing some state financial aid, on the other, this can make it harder for mothers and other carers to establish the presumption that they can work on equal terms with men if they wish to. Much policy presumes one or other model, yet many women experience both these models at different stages of their lives, or even at the same time. Should policy prefer or promote one over the other as the route for women to take, and if so which? Or can we create policy which simultaneously deals with both? Can we move beyond the cul-de-sac of the equality/difference debate? There is a variety of ways in which countries have addressed this dilemma and Ruth Lister's chapter explores some of the lessons from comparative policy in this area. These include interventions to regulate working time so as to encourage men to spend more time in caring and household activities rather than paid work; encouraging men to take parental leave; modifying benefit payments so as to encourage women partners of the unemployed to work; improving the status of unpaid care work in building entitlements to benefits; parental leave; among many others, including the controversial modification of the New Deal package to lone parents to encourage and facilitate their employment. She concludes that we can and should find a way of doing both; that is, find policies that respect and support the diversity of women's lives as both workers and carers.

Lydia Morris addresses the transformation of the relationship between the welfare state, the nuclear family and the sexual division of labour in recent years, examining its effects on men as well as on women. The post-war settlement has broken down and the new work–family–welfare nexus is still emerging. Men have been losing employment while women have been gaining it, resulting in high rates of male unemployment in the 1980s, which continue in some regions of the UK. Flexibility has produced precariousness of employment for many men, which, though challenging to their traditionally assumed role in the family, has not undermined it. Nevertheless, family structures have been changing, with increased divorce rates and levels of single parenthood. Social polarisation has been one of the consequences, with work concentrated in two-earner households, while other households have no earner. The changing place of the benefit system in this three-way nexus is explored. Whether this has created an 'underclass', and whether this is related to the increase in lone motherhood, are both addressed. Morris concludes that the radical transformations of society should not be laid at the door of a stigmatised minority, since they have more far-reaching causes. Yet the social inclusion of women is difficult when women's weak position in the labour market means that it is hard for them to be self-supporting, when full-time employment would conflict with their mothering role, and when welfare recipients are stigmatised as members of the 'underclass'.

Julia Brannen addresses the dilemmas underlying policies on childcare. There is a new set of relationships between state, family and labour market which demands new policies. Like Lister, Brannen engages with the issue of whether policies should presume that women are workers or mothers, and concludes that both are required. She calls for equal value to be placed on caring work done by men and women whether performed in an informal role or as paid work. There been an increase in the employment of women, although this affects some women more than others. She argues that government policy is now increasing the importance of employment for British mothers. The restructuring of labour markets and the new policy emphasis on employment for mothers are taking place in the context of changes in family life: changes from a discourse of obligation to one in which family relationships are negotiated; that commitment to children should survive divorce for fathers as well as mothers; that duty is an inadequate basis for parental childcare as compared with love; that children are a matter of individual choice and individual responsibility rather than a societal responsibility.

Brannen notes how in this context increased pressure is put on mothers as carers as well as workers. Lone mothers are the critical case in these changes and face the most difficult challenges and contradictions. However, despite recent policy developments, the childcare needs of lone mothers especially with under school-age children are still insufficiently addressed. Employed mothers use various sources of childcare: informal support networks, especially other women, including relatives; private commercial arrangements; and some help from partners. Sometimes family-friendly employers provide flexible work practices, leave allowances and childcare vouchers. New government proposals on childcare are to be welcomed, notably financial help. But, Brannen concludes, a viable infrastructure of early childhood services is still necessary, 'not simply to support working parents, but as part and parcel of children's rights to enable them to be active and participative citizens in the future.'

Age is one of the social divisions which has been newly recognised. Mary Maynard considers the position of older women in the UK. They are disadvantaged, yet old age can also be a time of fulfilment. The proportion of the population that is aged over 65 has been growing as we live longer and the birth rate falls. Yet Maynard argues that the 'demographic time bomb' argument has been overstated, and the projected increase in welfare expenditure has been over-dramatised. More important is the gendered nature of the age issue, in that the majority of the very old population is female. Furthermore, older women are especially likely to live in poverty. But the older population is not uniformly frail and ill. Such misleading stereotypes can lead to inappropriate advice and policy development for older people. Most older people live in their own homes (owned or rented) and only a small minority are in residential accommodation or sheltered housing. Maynard draws attention to the need for a wide range of policies to be oriented more effectively to the needs of the growing older population. For instance, older women are less likely to own a car or drive than younger women or other older men, and hence are more dependent on public transport. Maynard emphasises the need to understand the positive as well as negative aspects of ageing for women, to recognise the capacity for change and development, as well as declining physical capabilities. For instance, older women can become crucial to voluntary and charity activity, join clubs and develop new friendship networks. Maynard suggests that older women seek independence and autonomy, respect, a sense of purpose and a friendship network; they wish to live less on the margins of society and to be more integrated within it. In order to achieve this they need sufficient income, appropriate housing, transport, and health services.

Jay Ginn and Sara Arber detail the mismatch between pension provision and women's needs, and put forward suggestions as to how this can be improved. Women's greater poverty than men's in older age is primarily a result of a pension system ill-adapted to women's lives. While most men receive income from a private pension, older women are largely dependent on an inadequate and relatively declining basic state pension. Women's low private pension income is largely due to their lower earnings from employment and their complex and disrupted employment patterns, both related to their family roles as carers. Indeed the main exception to women's pension poverty is to be found among those single women who were able to maintain full-time continuous employment. Divorce has a further detrimental impact on women's income in older age, though plans to split private pensions at divorce will go some way to help women who divorce in the future. However, women's traditional pattern of employment only has such a detrimental impact on particular types of pension systems, such as in the UK. In other countries, such as Denmark, where a basic pension entitlement is based on citizenship rather than earnings, women do not suffer from such poverty in older age. The lessons from comparative public policy are instructive: whereas private pensions penalise caring, the state has the capacity to compensate carers and the low paid. Ginn and Arber suggest two reforms which would improve women's income in later life. First, increasing the basic pension above the Income Support level and basing eligibility on residence. This would benefit women because the level is not linked to employment, and would eliminate the need for the cumbersome, demeaning and administratively costly means test to establish eligibility for Income Support. It would also remove the pensions poverty trap, making contributions to a second-tier pension worthwhile. Secondly, they suggest restoring and revitalising SERPS as a second-tier pension. If the pension were to be calculated on the best 20 years of earnings rather than the whole lifetime, then women would be less disadvantaged as a result of taking several years out of the labour market in order to care for others.

Jeanne Gregory's focus is on the development of equal opportunities law in the workplace. These have been very important interventions in women's rights at work, though there are some inadequacies in the mechanisms available to implement the law. Improved implementation depends on the political will to make the law work. Much of the initiative in the development of equal opportunities law has come from the European Union, where the European Commission and the European Court of Justice have worked to upgrade the provision and its implementation. The superiority of European law over domestic law has been an important feature in the upgrading of UK provision. The provision will be further widened and deepened by the new Treaty of Amsterdam and the Commission decision to 'mainstream' equal opportunities throughout EU policy. Limitations of the law can be found in instances where the nature of the labour market makes it hard to implement, such as in atypical, flexible employment, that is short-term or part-time work, though the development of the law to include part-timers will mitigate this.

Gregory considers possibilities for the development of the law, including the wider use of positive action, which is facilitated under the Treaty of Amsterdam. She argues that an important part of the way forward is to ensure that affirmative action is possible in the public policy and political arena so as to make representative bodies representative, and that the insistence on formal equality, while generally important, should be flexible on those occasions where special services for women are needed. The development of mainstreaming of equal opportunities policies provides an important opportunity to extend these policies, though attention needs to be paid to the dangers of the loss of specialist expertise. Effective machinery for implementation of policies is the key to the next stage of development of equal opportunities in the UK.

Liz Kelly analyses policy developments to prevent violence against women, arguing that so far much of this has taken place outside government circles under pressure from feminist groups over the last three decades. The potential for a future co-ordinated government response is thus all the more important. This issue has become a matter of international concern in recent years, including for instance a declaration by a UN conference on human rights that violence against women constitutes a violation of human rights. A variety of forms of violence have been named and made subject to critical scrutiny: not only domestic violence and rape, but also sexual harassment, stalking and genital mutilation, among others. It has been shown that this violence is widespread, with most women experiencing some instance in a lifetime, that the perpetrators are more often known to the women rather than strangers, and that the home is a site of violence. Yet the official data sources still remain insufficient – there is no comprehensive survey of the prevalence of violence against women in Britain, nor are there any Criminal Statistics on domestic violence, despite repeated requests for this by House of Commons Select Committees. Policy developments need to combine short- and long-term strategy. These include changes in the forms of policing, which is very uneven, with best practice including specialist expert Domestic Violence Units; in the policy of the Crown Prosecution Service, whose record of prosecution is widely considered to be inadequate; in court procedure, so as to protect the woman; and the securing of the provision for abused women which has developed in the voluntary sector.

Jeff Hearn takes a broad look at the changes in masculinities in recent years and the implications of this for a wide spectrum of policies. While he argues that there has not in fact been a sudden rupture in the form of gender relations, none the less, there are considerable changes. Further, we need to consider the problem of certain forms of masculinity, rather than assuming that gender issues are a problem for women only. Hearn looks at the new academic studies on masculinity and asks what they offer for a practical analysis in fields ranging from culture, media and representation, to economic and social change. In employment men are more likely than women to be managers, especially at senior levels, and recent changes demand new forms of management, such as the implementation of equal opportunities policies. Greater equality in the workplace is partly dependent on greater equality in the home. Fatherhood itself is undergoing change, not least in the conception of continuing responsibilities for children after divorce, in relation to provision of financial support and caring, with a growing role for government, as in the development of state agencies such as the Child Support Agency. In education today boys are performing less well than girls, perhaps provoking a crisis of boyhood, in that the typical values of boys do not sit well with the needs of educational success. Men's sexuality is rightly a matter for public debate, rather than a simply private issue, whether in relation to the regulation of sex on the internet, to AIDS, or to issues of homophobia. Men's propensity to violence, especially against women, requires firmer regulation by government. Hearn concludes with a call for a government strategy to wean men away from power and oppression and not to treat gender as a women's issue only.

Judith Squires starts from the premise that existing forms of democratic political representation are in crisis, with the majority of people not involved in party politics, a disillusion especially concentrated among the young, the black and the female. In the context of a Labour Party committed to reconnecting politics by making it more inclusive and authentic, Squires asks what lessons can be drawn from feminist political theory to improve the situation, since many of the issues now emerging around social exclusion and political participation have been debated within feminism. There are three ways of attempting this reconnection: the rejection of the narrow representative conception of politics in favour of a participatory move-ment-based politics; calls for inclusion into existing political structures; and attempts to modify the traditional structures themselves to make them more open. One of the dilemmas underlying the inclusion of women in politics is that of the complexity of the apparently simple notion of representation. Squires identifies three divergent perspectives: equality, identity and differ-ence. Equality politics assumes that representation is about the representa-tion of pre-existing interests of women as a group; identity politics that representation requires the presence of women since only they know what women want; while the difference position seeks to dissolve too rigid cate-gories which can reify existing differences and inequalities and which can fall foul of essentialism. For instance, quotas are considered particularly import-ant by those who embrace identity politics, but not by the difference position. Do multi-member constituencies and proportional representation constitute a compromise in which women can do better? The divergences outlined by Judith Squires help to explain why there is not a single feminist strategy for the inclusion of women in political decision-making.

Joni Lovenduski addresses the sexing of political behaviour in Britain. The challenge of including women in British politics is formidable. Despite the 'breakthrough' of women MPs in the 1997 election, women are still poorly represented in Parliament, especially as compared with Nordic countries. The lesson from other countries suggests that increasing women's representation requires a combination of pressure from both women's movements and from women organised in political parties. Women can have different political priorities from men, though obviously the nature of these differences is complex and cross-cut by other differences, including class, age, education, ethnicity and housing. Women and men have voted in different ways, although this has often been hidden or ignored. Older women are more likely to vote Conservative than older men, while younger women are quite different, being more likely to vote Labour than men of their own age. Yet, despite the potential significance of these gender gaps in voting for political parties' strategies, they have been little addressed. Lovenduski gives an account of recent attempts within Labour to move these issues higher up the agenda, including the 'winning words' group, which drew attention to these differences. The difficulties in achieving this are ironic given that Labour has much to benefit from tapping into the women's constituency which is more left-leaning in its policy preferences, even if not in its voting practices. Constitutional changes in Scotland, Wales and Northern Ireland provide the opportunity to bring electoral systems up to date so as to better achieve the representation of population, especially women, in the new elected assemblies.

## CONCLUSION

This book raises the new agendas for women that are needed for government to respond to recent changes in gender relations. It addresses the potential of a new gender settlement which could more adequately meet women's needs and facilitate women's contributions. The contributors address the dilemma of how to provide justice for women (and men) by equal treatment where appropriate while recognising women's special needs and the diversity of women's circumstances. It considers how to ensure that women, young and old, are not socially excluded in a rapidly changing social and economic environment.

# 2 What Welfare Provisions do Women Need to Become Full Citizens?[1]

## Ruth Lister

### INTRODUCTION

'Citizen-the-carer' or 'citizen-the-wage-earner'? – this is the choice that all too often faces us when pressing the case for women's full citizenship in the social sphere. In other words, does the route to women's social citizenship rights lie through recognition of the care work still undertaken largely by women or through equality in the labour market? This question expresses at the policy level two competing theoretical and political strands that have for many years run through feminism – commonly described as difference vs. equality.[2] They represent a contemporary variant of what Carol Pateman has summed up as Wollstonecraft's dilemma, after the tensions that ran through Mary Wollstonecraft's work. On the one hand she writes, women

> have demanded that the ideal of citizenship be extended to them, and the liberal-feminist agenda for a 'gender-neutral' social world is the logical conclusion of one form of this demand. On the other hand, women have also insisted, often simultaneously, as did Mary Wollstonecraft, that *as women*, they have specific capacities, talents, needs and concerns, so that the expression of their citizenship will be differentiated from that of men. Their unpaid work providing welfare could be seen, as Wollstonecraft saw women's tasks as mothers, as women's work *as citizens*, just as their husbands' paid work is central to men's citizenship.
>
> (Pateman, 1989, pp. 196–7, emphasis in original)

Increasingly, though, feminist theory is marked by an attempt to move beyond dichotomies like equality vs. difference and either transcend them or reach some kind of synthesis. In particular, equality vs. difference represents a false dichotomy, which treats equality as synonymous with sameness and obscures the inequality that is its antonym. It implicitly privileges men by assuming a male standard against which women are measured. It also suppresses the differences that exist within the two categories of women and men, generally to the advantage of the more powerful within these two groups. Theoretically, the challenge is to reconstruct both equality and

17

difference as complementary rather than incompatible; we need to break down the male standard in favour of a gender-differentiated standard which acknowledges caring responsibilities as well as diversity. In this way, we can spring the theoretical trap laid by the equality vs. difference dichotomy as a first step to rethinking the policy dilemma posed in the opening paragraph.

This dilemma is crystallised for those feminists who are torn between two strategic approaches: on the one hand, a desire to validate and support through some form of independent income maintenance entitlement, the caring work for which women still take the main responsibility in the private sphere and on the other, to liberate women from this responsibility so that we can achieve economic and political autonomy in the public sphere. An example of the first approach would be a benefit paid to those who stay at home to care for children. The problem is that this runs the danger of undermining the second approach by creating an expectation that mothers *will* stay at home to care for their children, so that it becomes harder for them to compete on equal terms in the labour market and the political system.

If we take as our starting point, the needs of children and others for care, this opens up to question the implicitly male construction of citizenship, underlying much of social policy (as well as political theory), which ignores the implications of these needs (Pateman, 1989; Bacchi, 1991; Knijn and Kremer, 1997). If we then question the current division of responsibility for the provision of care as between women and men and as between individual families and the wider society, we can begin to see a path through the policy dilemma created by the false antithesis between equality and difference.

This chapter, therefore, starts by discussing policies for tackling the traditional sexual division of labour, before looking at wider societal responsibilities for the support of those providing care for adults or children, including the particular case of lone parents. It concludes by drawing out some of the implications for our understanding of citizenship.

## SHIFTING THE SEXUAL DIVISION OF LABOUR

In order to avoid being stuck in the political cul-de-sac into which the equality vs. difference debate can lead us, any discussion of women's citizenship has to start with men's citizenship and the ways in which it is privileged by the sexual division of labour. It is much easier to 'succeed' in a career, to be active in formal politics or be a trade union activist, if there is a 'wife' at home to see to your domestic needs. For all the talk of the 'new man' and the limited contribution he is now making to unpaid care and domestic work, cross-national evidence suggests that he is in fact hard to find and that the traditional skewed pattern of responsibilities (and it is responsibility as well as time which is important) in the domestic sphere has not, in general, been disturbed to any significant extent.

A four-nation study of East and West, for instance, concluded that, variations notwithstanding, the one constant finding was that 'the primary burden of domestic labour falls upon wives' (Stockman et al., 1995, p. 100). A Eurobarometer survey revealed the tenacity of the traditional domestic division of labour as, according to their spouses, two-thirds of men in the EU do no domestic chores, with male domestic absenteeism particularly high in the UK (Kempeneers and Lelièvre, 1991). Although research by Jonathan Gershuny suggests that there is a gradual movement to a more equitable division of domestic work, the emphasis is on the word 'gradual': 'women still do the bulk of all unpaid work' (Gershuny, 1997, p. 151). Moreover, survey evidence suggests that in so far as men are doing more in the home, there is a tendency to cream off the more enjoyable tasks, such as playing with the children and to contribute help, sometimes on an ad hoc basis, without sharing the daily overall *responsibility* for childcare and housework (see, e.g., Brannen and Moss, 1991; Gregson and Lowe, 1994).

The sexual division of labour and responsibility in the domestic 'private' sphere helps to shape the relationship of both women and men to the 'public' sphere of the labour market and the polity. It does so by constructing the access each has to time, which is a resource like money. It has profound implications for the ability of women and men to act as citizens in the public sphere, for instance as paid workers, and gain access to the social rights of citizenship, through the contributory social security scheme, which derive from that. Formal equality for women in the public sphere is undermined by the weight of their responsibilities in the private. By the same token, to the extent that men are serviced by women, and the public sphere is organised on the presumption that they are, men, as a group, gain a collective advantage over women which can affect even those women living without men, such as lesbians or lone mothers, including many African Caribbean mothers.

Changes in the sexual division of labour will require changes in both private behaviour and public policy. I concentrate here on the latter and ask to what extent *can* public policy change men's behaviour and *their* relationship to private and public spheres? Some have answered the question by asserting that caring work should be enforced as a public citizenship obligation just as paid work is. Peter Taylor-Gooby (1991), for instance, argues that it is the state's role to apply sanctions to those who do not undertake their fair share of unpaid care work. But he does not address the problems of both practice and principle involved in policing such an approach. It conjures up visions of DSS special investigators checking how many nappies a father changed in a week!

Scepticism about giving government the power to apply penalties in this area does not mean that it has no role. Indeed, there is much that government can do to encourage a change in men's behaviour. Such an attempt has been made by Scandinavian governments using three main, interlinked strategies: parental leave, working time and public education programmes. Parental leave has certainly had some impact: in Sweden, for instance, by the end of the 1980s nearly half of fathers were taking some leave, albeit for short periods. Nevertheless, although in theory a gender-neutral model, it has in practice proved to be highly gendered, with women remaining the majority of users. This has prompted both the Swedish and Norwegian governments to reserve a month of the leave for fathers. Danish research suggests that financial considerations continue to act as a significant deterrent to male use of parental leave but that important too is a workplace culture of male indispensability which constructs male use of parental leave as inappropriate.

This points to the importance of changes in both attitudes and the organisation of work, which also raises the question of working time or conversely time to care. Again, this is recognised in Sweden where parents of under-seven-year-old children can work six rather than eight hours a day. The European Commission's Directive on working time is of relevance here. The Directive will set a maximum 48-hour week, averaged over four months, for most workers but with a number of specified exceptions. It was opposed by the Conservative government, though if any country needs it, it is the UK where men's paid working hours are above the EU average. In 1995, men in the UK worked an average of 43.6 hours a week compared with an EU average of 40.1 hours. At the other end of the spectrum, Dutch men worked an average 36.1 hours (Hantrais and Letablier, 1997). Similarly, the UK has the highest proportion of its workforce working more than 40 hours a week, at 47 per cent, compared with only 10 per cent in France and 14 per cent in Germany (*The Guardian*, 23 June 1997). An Equal Opportunities Commission study on the issue concluded that the single most effective way of promoting equality might be to regulate the hours of paid work undertaken by men (Marsh, 1991). Although this would not automatically translate into an increase in the hours they devote to unpaid work, it could help, especially if backed up by public education campaigns directed at men and boys.

Just such a campaign has been conducted in Austria under the rubric '*halb halb*'. It is now proposed to enshrine in law an expectation that men and women should take equal responsibility for domestic work (*The Guardian*, 24 February 1998; *Independent on Sunday*, 1 March 1998). While this would not be enforceable, such a legal principle could, at least, help to create new gendered expectations and, in negotiations with employers, strengthen the hand of those male employees who did want to take their domestic responsibilities more seriously.

The government has moved to challenge the traditional 'male breadwinner' model through the Budget proposal to include childless partners of unemployed claimants aged under 25 in the New Deal and to encourage and help the partners of other unemployed claimants to seek work. This is an important step. The policy does, though, need to be implemented sensitively, as a recent study of couples receiving social security suggests that gendered identities, female as well as male, can be invested in traditional breadwinner models (Goode, Callender and Lister, 1998). In some cases, cultural sensitivities would also need to be respected. Having moved on the 'public' front, the next step is for the government to acknowledge a public interest in the 'private' division of responsibility for unpaid care work which represents the other key element of the traditional breadwinner model.

## STATE SUPPORT FOR CARE WORK

Some feminists, such as Lynne Segal (1987) and Diane Richardson (1993), are critical of too great an emphasis on a fairer sexual division of responsibility for the provision of care, for they see it as representing a privatised response which could undermine demands for better public provisions. Clearly, it has to represent only one part of the overall equation, especially in the case of lone-parent families; the other part concerns the division of responsibility between individual families and the wider community, as expressed primarily through state-funded provision. This state-funded provision can be aimed at enabling parents and other carers to combine their caring responsibilities with paid work or at providing financial support for them to provide care themselves at home.

It is the latter which brings us up against Wollstonecraft's dilemma. The problem is how to give due recognition to the importance of care for citizenship without locking women further into a caring role that serves to exclude them from the potential power and economic security which derive from participation in the public sphere of the economy and the polis. Moreover, historical and cross-national evidence suggests that social security entitlements that derive from care work tend to be less generous than those that derive from paid work (Lewis and Åström, 1992). Thus, on the basis of a recent cross-national study of gender equality and welfare states, Diane Sainsbury concludes that 'as long as there is no parity in the benefits accorded by the care-giver model and work-related benefits, a strategy based on the principle of care perpetuates different levels of social provision for women and men' (1997, p. 195). Gender equality is best promoted, she suggests, through benefits that base entitlement on citizenship or residence, such as the non-contributory basic pension schemes in Sweden and the Netherlands or child benefits.

One minimalist path is to provide adequate protection of social insurance records during periods when people are out of the labour market providing care. In some countries, the provision of non-contributory citizenship pensions ensures that all women get a pension in their own right, regardless of employment record, though such pensions tend to be low. New Labour has raised the possibility of such a citizenship pension which would provide a second-tier pension for those who have spent time outside the labour market providing care. It has also indicated that its proposals for a stakeholder pension should address the needs of women with intermittent paid employment records, although this has been disputed by pensions experts such as Alan Walker (see also chapter 6, this volume).

More generally, reform of the social insurance scheme on the lines proposed by the Commission for Social Justice (1994) would help to improve the status of care work in the social security system. The Commission sketched out the contours of a modernised social insurance scheme that would reflect the realities of women's employment patterns and provide better support for those with caring responsibilities. A stronger, more inclusive social insurance scheme would, it argued, represent the best route available at present to promote women's independent social security income.[3] It would include, for instance, protection for those earning below the national insurance lower earnings limit and who therefore do not pay contributions; a part-time unemployment benefit and better recognition of family responsibilities.

The Green Paper on welfare reform's exceedingly brief reference to national insurance talks only of updating the contributory principle through greater emphasis on the 'the link between work and earning benefit entitlement' (DSS, 1998, para. 33). Whether this might point to a more inclusionary system on the lines promoted by the Commission on Social Justice or even more exclusionary entitlement conditions than now, is not clear. Certainly, there is no reference to the gendered issues at stake.

The Commission also supported the idea of a participation income, drawing on Professor A.B. Atkinson's work. The participation income is a possible step on the road to a basic income scheme, in that it provides a basic income for all, but subject to a condition of active citizenship for those of working age able to work. This would include not just paid work or training and availability for it, but also caring work and, in some versions, voluntary work. For basic income enthusiasts, who argue that every individual citizen or resident should receive a tax-free cash payment, without means or contribution test and with no eligibility rules attached, the element of conditionality which remains makes this a poor second best. Nevertheless, arguably, a participation income does more to value caring work than a full-blown basic income in that the latter would be paid regardless of whether or not someone had care responsibilities (representing in some cases a form of wages for housework). It therefore would not place any value on care work as such. The Commission rejected a basic income scheme, but did say that it should not be ruled out in the longer term and that therefore shorter and more medium-term changes should be compatible with a possible longer term move towards it.

Returning to the more specific question of how the state can best provide support for care work in ways that will help promote women's citizenship, I will look in turn at the issues raised by the care of adults and of children.

## THE CARE OF ADULTS

How we best provide for the needs of older and disabled people and of carers is a big issue in its own right. Here, I will simply look briefly at the options for payment for care and their implications for the citizenship of both care-providers and care-recipients, the majority of both of whom are women.

There is a growing academic literature on this subject, including two cross-national surveys (see Glendinning and McLaughlin, 1993; Evers et al., 1994). McLaughlin and Glendinning (1994) identify two main models of paying for care. The first is the social security model as exemplified by the British invalid care allowance. As a non-contributory, non-means-tested benefit, it can be said to represent a citizenship approach. However, its status as an independent citizenship benefit is compromised by restrictive eligibility criteria and the fact that it is paid at only 60 per cent of the equivalent adult contributory benefit rate. Some also criticise it for not rewarding the actual work performed, though research suggests that many recipients see it as such a payment (McLaughlin, 1991).

Whether the second model – that of payment for care undertaken – provides a firmer underpinning of carers' citizenship is debatable. The disadvantages highlighted in the literature include: relatively low rates of pay and lack of employment rights typical of such schemes, with possible implications for those employed in the formal care sector; an increase in the control of carers; and the dangers of increased professionalisation of care work, to the possible detriment of non-professional carers. Clare Ungerson (1995) also warns of the danger of the development of an unregulated 'grey' labour market drawing on cheap and migrant labour, especially where payments are channelled through care-recipients, as increasingly demanded by the disabled people's movement. This highlights one of a number of emergent divisions in the politics of care, as it becomes clear that no one form of payment best meets the varied interests of different groups of carers and of care-recipients.

A danger common to both models is that, by paying for informal care, it could serve to institutionalise further the sexual division of caring labour. As so often is the case, we have to balance short-term and longer-term interests – what Maxine Molyneux (1984) has called practical and strategic gender interests – and few, I think, would argue that we should sacrifice the former to the latter. At the same time, though, it is important that short-term practical demands are framed in such a way as to minimise any negative impact on longer-term strategic interests. Thus, for instance, policy must also focus on how best to support the significant numbers of carers of working age who try to combine paid work with the care they provide. However, that again raises the needs, preferences and rights of care-recipients who are all too often constructed as a burden in such discussions.

The potential clash of interests between carers and disabled people is clearest around the issue of payments for care. Carers' lobbies are pressing for adequate direct payments to carers to safeguard their financial independence. The disabled people's movement has, in contrast, campaigned for payments to be made to them so that they can pay for and thereby control the way in which their care needs are met. (Local authorities are now empowered to make such payments on a limited basis.) Both sets of demands can be justified with reference to the autonomy and citizenship of the members of each group; what is needed is a way of accommodating these demands so that neither group is made dependent on the other.

## CARE OF YOUNG CHILDREN

From the perspective of enabling mothers (and fathers) to combine paid work and family responsibilities, the availability of affordable, good quality childcare for both pre-school and school-age children is clearly crucial (see also chapter 4, this volume). As is well known, the UK comes near the bottom of the EU childcare league, especially for children up to the age of three. In the early 1990s, only 2 per cent of children up to this age were benefiting from publicly funded childcare services, joint lowest with West Germany, Spain and Ireland. At the other end of the spectrum, Denmark provided for 48 per cent of this age group, Sweden for 33 per cent and Belgium for 30 per cent (European Commission Network on Childcare, 1996). The UK position reflects, in part, a liberal residualist philosophy which until very recently has meant that childcare has been treated by government as a private rather than public responsibility.

In contrast, in the Nordic countries, commentators have pointed to a new partnership between families (and, to some extent, women) and the state (although that partnership is now under strain in some cases in the face of cutbacks). Through a range of measures such as parental leave and leave to care for sick children, as well as investment in public childcare (though Norway lags behind here), the Nordic states have made a real attempt to support parents in the fulfilment of their childcare responsibilities.

However, despite the apparent 'woman-friendly' persona of the Nordic model, feminist commentators have expressed some ambivalence about its implications for women's citizenship. On the credit side, the Swedish approach has been described as one which treats women as citizen-workers and then grafts on their claims as mothers through parental leave schemes (which have extended steadily in length). This, Jane Lewis and Gertrud Åström suggest, can be understood as an attempt to synthesise equality and difference claims by 'grafting the right to make a claim on the basis of difference onto a policy based on equal treatment'. Thus, 'the Swedish model guarantees that choosing to care will attract reasonable monetary award only so long as the carer has first undertaken to become a citizen worker' (Lewis and Åström 1992, pp. 60, 80; see also Sainsbury, 1997).

The drawback of the model is that it has inadvertently served to reinforce the sexual division of labour and a highly sexually segregated labour market, in the case of Sweden in a country which lacks effective equal opportunities legislation. Jane Lewis (1992) has, therefore, suggested that France might in some ways provide a better model through a combination of support for working mothers, which is nearly as good as in the Nordic countries, and better developed equal opportunities legislation (as well as generous support for those who care for their children at home).

The lesson would, therefore, appear to be not to abandon the idea of parental leave, which is a way of placing value on care of young children, but to encourage men to take at least some of the leave. In addition, generous family-friendly employment and childcare policies need to be backed up with tougher equal opportunities and sex discrimination measures. As well as promoting the interests of women generally in the labour market, specific measures are required to tackle the barriers which face those groups that are particularly disadvantaged, such as disabled and minority ethnic group women and lone mothers.

There remains the danger, nevertheless, that so long as it is women who are more likely to take advantage of the bulk of parental leave from the labour market, their position within it will be disadvantaged relative to men's. This danger becomes even greater under policies which provide a cash payment for those who stay at home to care for children after the end of any parental leave period. This has been recommended by Michael Young and A.H. Halsey, who see it as an advantage that more women than men would claim it as this would mean 'more jobs for men [which] would have nothing but favourable effects on the position of men in the family' (1995, p. 21; see also Dex and Rowthorn, 1997).

Going even further, Geoff Dench, one of a number of people currently attempting to reassert a more traditional male breadwinning gender order, has made the case for supporting mothers' parenting role by paying their partners a decent family wage: 'For many women in ordinary jobs, full-time work is alienating. The best assistance that the state can provide for them as mothers lies in ensuring decent "family wages" for men, enabling women to receive enough financial support from male partners during the child-rearing years' (Dench, 1997, p. 48; see also Phillips, 1997). This conveniently ignores the growing body of evidence that income is not necessarily distributed equitably within families (Pahl, 1989; Vogler, 1994; Vogler and Pahl, 1994).

Unfortunately, the Chancellor's proposal to replace family credit with a (more generous) working families tax credit paid through the pay-packet could go some way to meeting Dench's objective. In two-parent families, family credit is paid primarily to one-earner couples and in three-quarters of cases, the main earner is the man. (However, there is no clear evidence that it acts as a serious disincentive to mothers to take paid work.) This measure would thus mean a transfer of resources from women to men and a reduction in the income paid directly to women who are caring for children, thereby depriving them of an important source of independent income. It has also been suggested that payment to fathers might discourage mothers' labour market participation, if the result is to reduce the former's net pay.

In response to these criticisms, it has been conceded that one-earner couples can choose whether the credit is paid through the pay-packet or as a cash payment to the partner at home. Although this goes some way towards meeting the concerns that have been voiced, our knowledge about gendered power dynamics in the family raises questions as to how effective the solution of choice will be in practice. In inegalitarian families, where there is a sharp power imbalance, it could be very difficult for the woman to exercise the choice in her favour. Even in other families, research for the Joseph Rowntree Foundation suggests that there may be an initial presumption that the money should go to the father as the 'breadwinner' (Goode, Callender and Lister, 1998). However, if the social security system itself channels payment to the mother, this seems to act as a legitimation of payment to her, so that the logic behind it is then accepted by the father also. It is therefore essential that the publicity about the new credit and the claim form itself present payment to the mother (or non-earning partner) as the default position in one-earner couples.

One way of partially protecting the independent income received by mothers at home would be through a significant increase in child benefit. This could be financed by the abolition of the married couple's tax allowance. The Chancellor made a start in his 1998 Budget when he promised a real increase in the benefit paid for the first child to be funded by a cut in the value of the married couple's allowance. Together with improvements in the means-tested benefit rates for young children, this was presented as providing help for mothers caring for young children at home.

This is consistent with (but distinct from) an alternative approach to supporting childcare which would be to pay an additional benefit to all those raising children in recognition of the costs, including time-costs, incurred in raising children, regardless of parental employment status. This would reduce, although not entirely remove, the disincentive to mothers to take paid employment. However, such a benefit would be expensive and in the current context of welfare state entrenchment and increased government emphasis on 'targeting' and antipathy to cash benefits, a universal benefit of this kind seems something of a pipe dream. Nevertheless, the idea has reappeared in political debate in the form of suggestions for a child benefit premium for families with a pre-school age child.[4]

## LONE PARENTS

At present one group that is provided with a benefit (albeit means-tested) to stay at home to care for children until their youngest child is aged 16 is lone parents. The UK is one of only very few countries that applies such liberal rules and increasingly elsewhere lone mothers have typically come to be constructed as worker-mothers. The evidence of the long-term damage done to the economic interests of women absent from the labour market for long stretches suggests that such a construction is in the longer-term interests of lone mothers themselves. This is not an argument for US-style 'work-welfare' schemes, which require the mothers of infants and very young children to participate in the labour market. It is, though, an argument for saying that once a lone parent's youngest child is settled in primary school, she should be encouraged to think of herself as a worker-mother.

This is the aim of the government's New Deal programme under which lone parents of school age (or younger, if they wish to be included) will receive practical assistance in finding a job. As part of the programme, there will be a much needed significant expansion of out-of-school childcare provision. The accessibility and quality of this provision will be crucial to the New Deal's success. Comparative research underlines the importance of childcare provision and 'family-friendly' employment rights and provisions to lone parents' welfare and successful labour market participation (Bradshaw et al., 1993; Duncan and Edwards; 1997a; Lewis, 1997). Important too will be good training opportunities; otherwise there is a danger that lone mothers will simply get stuck in low-paid jobs supplemented by family credit or its equivalent.

The research evidence suggests that the majority of lone parents would prefer employment to reliance solely on benefits once they feel that their children are old enough, although it has to be recognised that a complex set of decisions is involved for lone parents, not all of whom believe that paid work is compatible with good parenting (Ford, 1996; Duncan and Edwards, 1997b). Nevertheless, for many, paid work can provide sociability as well as a wage and possibly greater self-esteem. Through encouraging their labour market participation, the New Deal should strengthen the long-term economic position and the citizenship status of lone mothers.

Unfortunately, the New Deal's positive message has been compromised by its association by the government with the decision to implement the former Conservative administration's plan to abolish the modest additional help received by lone parents in and out of work and by the government's use of the language of 'welfare dependency' in promoting the New Deal. Although much of the direct financial damage created by the abolition of lone parent benefits will, from 1999, be repaired by the improvement in benefit rates for families with children generally announced in the 1998 Budget, it has still left the impression of devaluing the unpaid care work that lone parents do. A strategy that balanced valuing care and paid work as expressions of citizenship would combine the New Deal with further improvements in social security provision for those with childcare responsibilities.

Controversial too is any suggestion that the New Deal might eventually be made compulsory. As noted above, to require lone parents of older children to register for work would be in line with the practice in most other countries. A requirement to register for at least part-time work was recommended by the Commission on Social Justice on the grounds that we are doing lone mothers no favours by assuming their long-term absence from the labour market. The Commission made clear that imposition of such a requirement would be in the context of the implementation of an ambitious Jobs, Education and Training programme on the Australian model; the provision of good childcare facilities; and subject to various safeguards which, for instance, would protect mothers and fathers during the first year of lone parenthood and the parents of disabled children. We are a long way from meeting the conditions set down by the Commission and from an adequate infrastructure of support for working lone (and other) parents. There should, therefore, be no question of a requirement to register for work at this stage. Should it become an issue in the future, careful thought would need to be given to how old the youngest child should be before it is applied (primary or secondary school age?) and to the safeguards needed to protect the welfare of lone parents and their families. Thus, for instance, as well as the safeguards suggested by the Commission (mentioned above), there might be a case for, at least temporary, exemption of a parent whose child was truanting or excluded from school. And the rules would have to be administered sensitively, requiring a significant culture change in the Benefits Agency.

CONCLUSION

This chapter has attempted to clarify some of the dilemmas raised in think-ing about how welfare provisions can best promote women's citizenship in the social sphere. It has looked, in particular, at some of the options open to us to support those providing care for adults and for children, including lone parents. The underlying argument has been that we should not allow ourselves to be pushed into policies which reflect the philosophies of *either* equality *or* difference. Instead, we need to argue for *both and*, through a range of policies which, on the one hand, give greater value to care work and, on the other, promote women's position in the labour market. Tackling the sexual division of labour and time is central to such an approach, as is recognition of the need for 'time to care' (Knijn and Kremer, 1997) in both social and employment policies. At the same time, parallel changes in the labour market are also required (see chapters 3, 6 and 7, this volume). In this way, women and men can begin to operate as citizen-carer/workers on equal terms.

Underlying this policy approach would be a more 'woman-friendly' con-ception of citizenship responsibilities which acknowledged the value of care to citizenship in place of the implicitly male standard masquerading as the universal against which citizenship has traditionally been measured. Together with a more internationalist perspective and the accommodation of diversity, thereby recognising the citizenship claims of a range of marginalised groups, this represents one key element in the recasting of citizenship on more inclusive lines (Lister, 1997).

NOTES

1. This chapter draws on chapters 4 and 7 of *Citizenship: Feminist Perspectives* (Lister, 1997a).
2. My use of the label 'difference' should not be confused with Judith Squires' use of the term in chapter 10, where her description of 'identity' or 'maternalist' politics is an expression of what I call the 'difference' approach. Her concep-tualisation of 'difference' politics represents, in more extreme form, the accom-modation of diversity for which I argue.
3. For a more detailed discussion of the options for providing women with an independent income through the social security system, see Lister (1997b).
4. See the intervention by Malcolm Wicks, MP in the Minutes of Evidence of the Social Security Committee's *First Report on Taxes and Benefits*, 21 January 1998, HC423–iii, The Stationery Office, p. 47, and his article in *The Guardian*, 'Society Tomorrow', 12 February 1998.

## REFERENCES

Bacchi, C. (1991) 'Pregnancy, the Law and the Meaning of Equality', in E. Meehan and S. Sevenhuijsen (eds.) *Equality, Politics and Gender*, London: Sage.

Bradshaw, J., Kennedy, S., Kilkey, M., Hutton, S., Corden, A., Eardley, T., Holmes, H. and Neale, J. (1996) *The Employment of Lone Parents: A Comparison of Policy in 20 Countries*, London: Family Policy Studies Centre.

Brannen, J. and Moss, P. (1991) *Managing Mothers*, London: Unwin Hyman.

Commission on Social Justice (1994) *Social Justice: Strategies for National Renewal*, London: Vintage.

Dench, G. (1997) 'Nearing Full Circle in the Sexual Revolution', in G. Dench (ed.) *Rewriting the Sexual Contract*, London: Institute for Community Studies.

Dex, S. and Rowthorn, R. (1997) 'The Case for a Ministry of the Family', in G. Dench (ed.) *Rewriting the Sexual Contract*, London: Institute for Community Studies.

Duncan, S. and Edwards, R. (eds.) (1997a) *Single Mothers in an International Context: Mothers or Workers?*, London: UCL Press.

Duncan, S. and Edwards, R. (1997b) 'Lone Mothers and Paid Work – Rational Economic Man or Gendered Moral Rationalities?', *Feminist Economics*, 3(2), pp. 29–61.

DSS (1998) *New Ambitions for Our Country: A New Contract for Welfare*. Cm 3805 London: The Stationery Office.

European Commission Network on Childcare (1996), *A Review of Services for Young Children in the European Union 1990–1995*, Brussels: European Commission, Directorate General V.

Evers, A., Pijl, M. and Ungerson, C. (eds.) *Payments for Care. A Comparative Overview*, Aldershot: Avebury.

Ford, R. (1996) *Childcare in the Balance. How Lone Parents Make Decisions about Work*, London: Policy Studies Institute.

Gershuny, J. (1997) 'Sexual Divisions and the Distribution of Work in the Household', in G. Dench (ed.) *Rewriting the Sexual Contract*, London: Institute for Community Studies.

Glendinning, C. and McLaughlin, E. (1993) *Paying for Care: Lessons from Europe*, London: Social Security Advisory Committee/HMSO.

Goode, J., Callender, C. and Lister, R. (1998) *Purse or Wallet? Gender Inequalities and Income Distribution within Families on Benefits*, London: Policy Studies Institute.

Gregson, N. and Lowe, M. (1994) *Servicing the Middle Classes. Class, Gender and Waged Domestic Labour in Contemporary Britain*, London & New York, Routledge.

Hantrais, L. and Letablier, M. (1997) 'The Gender of Paid and Unpaid Work Time. A European Problem', *Time and Society*, 6 (2/3), pp. 131–49.

Kempeneers, M. and Lelièvre, E. (1991) 'Employment and Family within the Twelve', *Eurobarometer*, 34.

Knijn, T. and Kremer, M. (1998) 'Gender and the Caring Dimension of Welfare States: Toward Inclusive Citizenship', *Social Politics*, 4(3), pp. 328–61.

Lewis, J. (1992) 'Gender and the Development of Welfare Regimes', *Journal of European Social Policy*, 2(3), pp. 159–73.

Lewis, J. (ed.) (1997) *Lone Mothers in European Welfare Regimes. Shifting Policy Logics*, London and Philadelphia: Jessica Kingsley Publishers.

Lewis, J. and Åström, G. (1992) 'Equality, Difference and State Welfare: Labour Market and Family Policies in Sweden', *Feminist Studies*, 18(1), pp. 59–87.

Lister, R. (1997a) *Citizenship: Feminist Perspectives*, Basingstoke: Macmillan/New York: New York University Press.

Lister, R. (1997b) 'Promoting Women's Economic Independence', in G. Dench (ed.) *Rewriting the Sexual Contract*, London: Institute for Community Studies.

Marsh, C. (1991) *Hours of Work of Women and Men in Britain*, London: Equal Opportunities Commission/HMSO.

McLaughlin, E. (1991) *Social Security and Community Care: The Case of the Invalid Care Allowance*, London: Department of Social Security/HMSO.

McLaughlin, E. and Glendinning, C. (1994) 'Paying for Care in Europe: Is There a Feminist Approach?', in L. Hantrais and S. Mangen (eds.) *Family Policy and the Welfare of Women*, Loughborough: Cross-National Research Group.

Molyneux, M. (1984) 'Mobilisation without Emancipation?', *Critical Social Policy*, 10, pp. 59–75.

Pahl, J. (1989) *Money and Marriage*, Basingstoke: Macmillan.

Pateman, C. (1989) *The Disorder of Women*, Cambridge: Polity Press.

Phillips, M. (1997) *The Sex Change State*, London: Social Market Foundation.

Sainsbury, D. (1997) *Gender, Equality and Welfare States*, Cambridge: Cambridge University Press.

Stockman, N., Bonney, N. and Xuewen, S. (1995) *Women's Work in East and West*, London: UCL Press.

Taylor-Gooby, P. (1991) *Social Change, Social Welfare and Social Science*, Hemel Hempstead: Harvester-Wheatsheaf.

Ungerson, C. (1995) 'Gender, Cash and Informal Care: European Perspectives and Dilemmas', *Journal of Social Policy*, 24(1), pp. 31–52.

Vogler, C. (1994) 'Money in the Household', in M. Anderson, F. Bechhofer and J. Gershuny (eds.) *The Social and Political Economy of the Household*, Oxford: Oxford University Press.

Vogler, C. and Pahl, J. (1994) 'Money, Power and Inequality within Marriage', *Sociological Review*, 42(2), pp. 263–88.

Young, M. and Halsey, A.H. (1995) *Family and Community Socialism*, London: Institute for Public Policy Research.

# 3 Work, Gender and Unemployment: a Household Perspective

Lydia Morris

The welfare state, the nuclear family and a traditional sexual division of labour were central building blocks of post-war British society. They constituted what may be thought of as a work–family–welfare nexus in which complementary social structures meshed with individuals' expectations of how life would and should be lived. Under the Beveridge Plan, social security for the working-age population was built around the expectations of secure employment for men, with unemployment no higher than 3 per cent. It also rested on the assumption that 'the ideal social unit is the household of man, wife and children maintained by the earnings of the first alone' (Beveridge, 1942), that those earnings would come from secure, long-term and often lifetime employment, and that this 'breadwinner' role for the man would be supported by the domestic services of his wife.

The argument of this essay is that this work–family–welfare nexus has been gradually unravelling throughout the post-war period, with the most extreme aspects of change becoming apparent over the last 20 years. Very high levels of unemployment for men dominated the 1980s, and while there has been a considerable fall in the figures, this decline is at least partially explained by changes in the way they are calculated.[1] Furthermore, national trends mask stark regional inequalities, with many old industrial areas still showing very high levels of male unemployment. Meanwhile working life has become much less secure for many men, with redundancy an ever-present threat and increased 'flexibility' built around short-term contracts and precarious 'self-employment'. This drive for flexibility is apparent in other ways in women's working lives, most notably through rising levels of part-time employment. In fact, while there *has* been a challenge to traditional work roles for both men and women, with women's employment rising as men's was falling, this has not translated into 'role reversal' within the home. The pattern has rather been one of no-employment households and dual-employment households, and has implications which rebound on both the functioning of welfare and on structures of inequality. Finally, high and increasing levels of divorce and single parenthood have meant that the nuclear family household built upon a lifetime partnership is no longer a taken-for-granted basis of social organisation.

## SOCIAL POLARISATION

Of course, the effects of these changes are experienced differently for different households, and one of the clearest trends to have emerged is the pattern of 'social polarisation' in which work is concentrated in some homes and entirely absent from others. It has been noted in a number of area-specific studies (Pahl, 1984; Harris, 1987; Morris, 1995) that the employment status of spouses tends to coincide, such that when the man is unemployed then so too is his female partner. This is confirmed at national level by statistics throughout the 1980s (see General Household Survey) such that in 1989, for example, 70 per cent of the wives of employed men had jobs in contrast with only 28 per cent of the wives of unemployed men. The figures are no longer available in this form, but in a more detailed local study of Hartlepool (Morris, 1995) it was possible to isolate the *long-term* unemployed. This revealed a much sharper distinction between households, with only 13 per cent of the wives of long-term unemployed men holding jobs as compared with 71 per cent of the wives of men in relatively secure work.

To understand these results we need to look more closely at the trends in employment for women, and particularly for married women. Certainly, one notable feature of post-war society has been a gradual increase in women's workforce participation. Roughly expressed, women made up one quarter of the workforce in 1881, one third in 1966 and currently account for almost one half (see Dex, 1985; Labour Force Survey). Participation has increased most markedly for women between the ages of 34 and 54, which also means amongst married women. There is a link to be made here with changing patterns of child-rearing; women have fewer children per family, return to work sooner after child birth and also return to employment between births.

The role of part-time employment is extremely important in understanding these trends. Although in 1996 there were 10.4 million women in employment, almost equalling the 11.6 million men (Social Trends 27, Table 4.2)[2], 4.5 million of these women were in part-time jobs, as compared with 0.8 million of the men. Male part-time workers were heavily concentrated among very old or very young workers, in sharp contrast with women. It is largely a growth in part-time employment over the last 25 years which accounts for the increase in women's employment generally, with part-time employment absorbing 23 per cent of women employees in 1973 but rising to 30 per cent in 1995 (GHS 1995, Table 4.6). Of course, much of the explanation for why women work full- or part-time relates to the presence of dependent children, with only 22 per cent of the mothers of these children working full-time, as compared with 38 per cent working part-time. The childcare effect should not be overstated, however, as 25 per cent of women in homes without dependent children also work part-time, as compared with 46 per cent working full-time. There are a number of likely factors at play here: other domestic and caring duties, personal preference and/or employer demand, for example.


## THE BENEFIT DISINCENTIVE?

Whatever the explanation, concentrations of women in part time work have been seen as part of the explanation for a marked correspondence between male and female non-employment in couple-based households. The argument here is that the low amount of permitted earnings in benefit-dependent homes represents a disincentive to the wives of unemployed men, particularly if they choose or are confined to part-time employment. Indirect support for this view is found in work by Dilnot and Kell (1989) on Family Expenditure Survey Data; considering the *atypical* case of employed women who have unemployed partners, they found the majority to be working more than 30 hours per week. The focus of concern on the 'benefit disincentive' has, however, deflected more general interest in the differing potential employment profiles both of women with unemployed partners as compared with women whose partners are in work.

Fifty-five per cent of economically inactive women give looking after family or home as the reason for not working, compared with 7 per cent of economically inactive men, and only 4 per cent report a 'discouraged worker' effect which might, of course, include a financial disincentive (Social Trends 27 1997, Table 4.4). Indeed, a number of studies have found only a relatively small proportion of women's non-employment linked explicitly to a 'benefits effect' (see Irwin and Morris, 1993). Even accepting that disincentives may have a latent impact which is not necessarily acknowledged in women's accounts of their work decisions, there are a number of other factors that merit attention.

The principal question to be addressed is whether it is meaningful to compare women married to unemployed men with women married to employed men as if we are comparing like with like. Irwin and Morris (1993) explored this issue using data from the Hartlepool project referred to above. A sensitivity to *differences* between the two groups reveals that married men among the long-term unemployed will have a younger and larger family than their employed counterparts. This partly reflects a national tendency for the low skilled to have larger families and for long-term unemployment to be concentrated among younger workers. The pattern, of course, translates into heavier domestic and childcare responsibilities for the partners of the long-term unemployed. They are more likely to be mothers than the wives of employed men, and more likely to be mothers at a younger age.

Even holding these factors constant, women married to long-term unemployed men were more likely to cite childcare as a reason for not working.

They are also more likely to be in the lower-ranking female occupations than the wives of employed men, and to have had more broken employment histories. One possibility is that when balanced against the low appeal of the poorly paid and unskilled work they are likely to command, then motherhood seems both more important and more appealing. It is in these circumstances that the low earnings allowance for benefit claimants may take on a particular significance, reinforcing women's commitment to their children. This finding may have an even stronger relevance for single mothers who have to contend with the additional demands of sole parenting weighed against unrewarding work.

## 'SCROUNGERPHOBIA'

Another perennial issue linking benefit regulations and work incentives is the assertion that welfare has undermined *men's* will to work. However, alongside this view of the unemployed as habitually dependent lurks the suspicion that they are in fact working. Both views have been expressed by the Department of Employment:

> There is evidence that a significant minority of benefit claimants are not actively looking for work. Some are claiming benefit while working at least part-time in the black economy. Others seem to have grown accustomed to living on benefit and have largely given up looking for work, despite the high level of job vacancies which are increasingly available throughout the country. (Cm 540, 1988, p. 55)

Thus, charges that over-generous welfare has created a dependency culture in Britain sit alongside charges that many of the unemployed have been working all along. These arguments must be set against ample evidence of extreme poverty experienced by the benefit-dependent population (see, for example, Morris, 1996).

There are periodic revivals of these ideas, however, often in the form of campaigns against 'benefit cheats'. Hence, in 1993, the Conservative government's Employment Secretary stated: 'Everyone who is a dole cheat is taking money away from the unemployed and training councils. We cannot allow that to happen...Everyone wants to see law and order restored, and the weeding out of people who do not respect it.'[3] Similarly, in 1995 Frank Field, the Labour spokesperson on Social Security argued: 'A deadly lesson is being taught: the only way to survive is to cheat...Means tests poison the welfare state. They paralyse self-help, discourage self-improvement and tax honesty. They reward claimants for being either inactive or deceitful.'[4]

While ethnographic data on unemployment do reveal that some unemployed claimants take occasional opportunities for paid work, even official estimates of the numbers involved are no more than 10 per cent. Jordan et al. (1992) emphasise the enduring significance of work as a basis for identity and self-respect, noting: 'The men described themselves as active, needing to work to fulfil their personal needs as well as their roles as providers.' However, all writers stress the limited nature of the work available: 'Earnings tend to be occasional lump sums rather than regular weekly incomes and as a result although individuals have earned more than the legal amount in one particular week, over a longer period their earnings have often averaged out at less than this amount' (McLaughlin et al., 1989, p. 82).

Evidence of this kind points to an enduring need for the self-respect attached to work, and also the contradictions of a benefit system which wishes to preserve independence but stifles initiative in a climate in which regular employment for a certain section of the population has long been abandoned as a policy objective. A softer version of the 'work-shy' position is that workers are pricing themselves out of jobs and have an unrealistically high 'reservation wage', i.e. the lowest wage at which they would accept employment. Data on this issue are likely to be unreliable in that the stated wage at which a man will accept work will not necessarily correspond with a 'real' decision, especially given the significance of work as a focus for masculine identity. The problem anyway raises the question of minimum acceptable standards; does the obligation to accept available work extend to any work, whatever the terms and conditions?

One approach to the issue of reservation wages and low pay is the view that if benefits fall low enough, then the unemployed will start to accept jobs they would not previously have considered, and it will become financially viable for employers to create work which at higher wage levels would not have been possible. However, despite falls in the value of benefit in the 1980s (Micklewright, 1986), unemployment continued to rise, and meanwhile the unemployed became more impoverished in relation to the majority of the population. Any attempt to use reductions in welfare support as a means of driving people into employment calls up concern about the sharpening of inequalities, the relative poverty of the benefit population and their growing stigmatisation. This strikes a contrast with a view of the welfare state as the guarantor of social inclusion through 'social citizenship', defined by Marshall (1958) as full membership of the community. Hence, one argument might be that the welfare state has failed in its aim, that the commitment to full employment was never strong enough, and benefit levels were never high enough. An alternative position, however, suggests that the individuals affected are themselves implicated in the process of their own 'social exclusion', and this has been a central position in the underclass debate, explored below.

## THE 'UNDERCLASS'

The concept of the 'underclass' has more generally been used to suggest that there exists in society a group who have rejected the norms and values of mainstream society, and the evidence cited is state dependency, denial of the work ethic, the failure of morality and the rejection of family norms, often also argued to be linked with criminality (Auletta, 1992). A popular usage of the 'underclass' groups these disparate features together into a residual category, located 'outside' a society, which remains otherwise cohesive and free from internal challenge.

These arguments have been most fully developed in an American literature but have been applied in Britain in what may be seen as an exercise in conceptual containment. Rather than revise our understanding of social organisation to accommodate a number of rather complex changes, some explanation is sought which leaves the social world as we understand it more or less intact. The policy of 'Back to Basics' was a symptom of the same unease and search for containment. In particular, attention has focused on high rates of young male unemployment and rising single parenthood, both argued to be linked to aspects of welfare provision, and there has been some suggestion that the two phenomena are interrelated. Doubts have thus been raised about the stability of two key social institutions – paid work and the family.

It is certainly the case that unemployment, even when high *throughout* the male workforce, shows a marked concentration among the young. 1996 figures[5] give rates of 20 per cent for the 16–19 age group and 16 per cent for the 20–24 age group, with no other age group experiencing rates even as high as 10 per cent. If these rates are really a product of disaffection and the rejection of mainstream values we would expect them to remain resistant to change. There is as yet little evidence for or against this argument, but the rate for both groups peaked in 1993 and for the 20–24 age group had fallen four points by 1996 (Social Trends, 1997, Table 4.23). Some have argued, however, that it is high rates of unemployment among the young which explains the rise in single parenthood. Certainly marriage rates are lower among unemployed men than their married counterparts (49 per cent as compared with 71 per cent – GHS 1991, Table 5.27), but this may be a feature of the age profile of the two groups.

The argument has been most fully developed in the US, where Wilson (1987) suggests that high levels of male unemployment, together with high mortality and incarceration rates among young black men, has meant that the pool of 'marriageable' men is far too low for the nuclear family to be a viable option. Conversely, Charles Murray (1984) has argued on the basis of rational choice theory that young women are better off living independently on their welfare cheques than throwing in their lot with the father of their children, hence the argument that welfare has undermined the institution of the nuclear family; these single mothers are then argued to foster a culture of the underclass which reproduces the pattern in the next generation. Furthermore, this culture is thought to take hold because of the absence of a viable male role model offering an alternative way of living. It is this alleged *cultural* reproduction of the underclass which is offered as evidence of a rejection of the mainstream norms and values of society, and Murray has more recently applied the argument to Britain (1990; 1996)

## LONE MOTHERHOOD

The rise in lone motherhood is uncontested; between 1971 and 1995 married couple households fell from 92 per cent of homes with dependent children to 78 per cent, while lone mothers rose from 7 per cent to 20 per cent. The figures can be read in different ways, however, according to the way they are disaggregated. Some have argued (Buckingham, 1996) that single never-married mothers are now the largest group (8 per cent) as compared with divorced (7 per cent) and separated (5 per cent) lone mothers. However, these latter two groupings could be reasonably combined to make 12 per cent separated or divorced as compared to 8 per cent never married. (GHS, 1995, Table 2.7).

Of all lone parents with dependent children 49 per cent rely on benefits and 37 per cent on earned income, as compared with 7 per cent and 88 per cent respectively for couple households. The figures look rather different for homes with only non-dependent children however, with only 10 per cent of the lone parent group dependent on benefits and 71 per cent on earned income, as compared with 3 per cent and 88 per cent respectively for couple households. Clearly responsibility for young children is a major factor in the working patterns of lone mothers, and even more so than for married mothers. Of all women with dependent children 42 per cent of the married group work part-time and 25 per cent full-time, as compared with 24 per cent and 16 per cent respectively for lone parents (GHS, 1995, p. 44). Where the youngest child is over five years old the chances of working are twice as high as when the youngest child is under five.

The employment situation of single mothers is comparable to that of women married to unemployed men, though perhaps more intensely felt. In 1980 the introduction of a Tapered Earnings Disregard for lone parents replaced a low fixed-rate disregard above which earnings were deducted from benefits pound for pound. The expectation that this would increase lone mothers' labour force participation was misplaced (Weale et al., 1984), in that the manipulation of economic incentives had only minimal effects on decisions to take employment. Rather, decisions were based on a complex interaction of preferences; childcare constraints and job opportunities as well as financial rewards. With the introduction of Income Support in 1988 came a policy of special premiums for designated groups with particular needs. One such was single parents, but in 1998 this single parent premium was withdrawn from new or re-applicants, in favour of increased spending on childcare provisions in an attempt to drive single parents into work.

## WHAT MODEL?

There are a number of possible responses to the debate about single parents. One would be to challenge the data. It is certainly the case that rates of *illegitimacy* do not in any direct way reflect the proportion of children growing up without two parents in their life. High numbers of births outside marriage simply reflect a decline in the formal institution of marriage, but tell us nothing about either long-term, marriage-like relationships, or patterns of parenting. Indeed, even household composition provides no *necessary* key to understanding the organisation of family life. It is perfectly feasible, and in the past was financially advantageous, for benefit-dependent couples to live apart but maintain a relationship of daily contact and commitment. This is not to argue that all single mothers are involved in some such arrangement, but rather to point out that this would still be consistent with the statistics which underpin arguments about a growing underclass linked to single parenthood.

While one response to the debate could be to suspect the data, another is to argue that high rates of divorce demonstrate that marriage is no longer necessarily viewed as a life-time commitment. Brown (1990) has suggested that marital, residential and child-rearing patterns are undergoing a revolution which is not confined to low-income groups but is a feature of society as a whole. Rates of divorce have risen steadily since 1961, while rates of first marriage have been falling since 1971, such that the nuclear family household cannot be taken for granted as the cornerstone of social organisation. Just as striking is the rise in the proportion of women who are childless by the age of 35; from 12 per cent of women born in 1944 to 20 per cent of those born in 1954 (Social Trends, 1997, Table 2.21). One possible interpretation of these trends could be a growing dissatisfaction among women with their traditional domestic and mothering roles – and an awareness of the detrimental effect they have on employment prospects.

There is now a generation of young women educated by feminism into an awareness of the disadvantages that traditional family life imposes on women. Those with reasonable career prospects will think carefully before entering into motherhood, while those for whom the future holds only unskilled, low-paid work may find motherhood more appealing. This latter group, however, is made up of women whose potential partners bear a disproportionate risk of unemployment. This may deter either partner from embarking on a marriage, or may disrupt the relationships of those who do – in either case contributing to the rising numbers of single mothers.


## GENDER AND THE UNDERCLASS

I would like at this point to examine the gender subtext of the underclass debate, for although gender differentiation permeates the substance of discussion of the underclass, it is rarely made explicit in analysis. Murray sees the absence of a male role model in the family unit as central to any explanation of the alleged growth of the 'underclass', and seems implicitly to suggest that the underclass is made up of men but reproduced by women. The task of socialisation is thus firmly located in the family unit, and the generation of a subculture of the underclass is argued to emerge because the single mother is unable to perform that duty.

There have been varied responses to this situation, and one is to argue that poverty has, in effect, been feminised (e.g. Bane, 1988). This view maintains that women are being forced to carry the burden of society's poverty, and is supported by the growing proportion of dependent children in single parent households on minimum income. This group is disproportionately and increasingly present in the bottom income quintile, with a concentration twice as high as in the population as a whole (Social Trends, 1997, Table 5.19). Hence, it is suggested that attacks on welfare support may hurt children and better provision should be made for low-income households. More generally, women's responsibility for childcare and household finance in low-income homes mean that the effects of increasing inequalities in society (see Hills, 1995) is managed by them (see Morris, 1995). In fact, recent shifts in government policy indicate an increased concern for child poverty associated with both inadequate benefit levels and low pay, but against special treatment for lone mothers (*International Guardian*, 26 February 1998).

Indeed, there is another view which is also apparent in the concerns of government policy, but more fully developed in the US, which holds that some work requirement is necessary for single mothers, both as a deterrent to welfare dependency and presumably to foster the work ethic in their children (e.g. Mead, 1986). This position introduces a social control dimension to welfare, which seeks to influence behaviour by imposing conditions on welfare support, the most extreme example of which was the workhouse system. Oddly enough, this contemporary manifestation of control seems not to address the real concern expressed in the debate which centres on the alleged withdrawal of young men from the labour force. It ironically offers a solution which, at least in traditional terms, brings women's work role and family obligations into conflict, but does not deal with the problem of male unemployment.

There is, in fact, a more fundamental problem here. To understand it we must return to the issue of social citizenship or social inclusion. Citizenship embodies a set of rights which are held by the individual in relation to the state. One of the obligations required in exchange for these rights has traditionally been the readiness of the able-bodied to work for a living. British welfare provision was originally designed to exempt married women from these obligations. and one of its aims was to protect mothers from the need for employment, and so the basis for social citizenship was gendered, as Ruth Lister's chapter in this volume demonstrates. This is expressed most clearly in the role of work in demonstrating men's personal and social worth, while the traditional expectations of women revolved around home and family. These prescriptions do not entirely hold good for either men or women, but nor has a viable alternative been fully established in terms of work, family and welfare arrangements. The whole set of relationships is being renegotiated.

## THE SEXUAL DIVISION OF LABOUR

In relation to the underclass, single mothers and social inclusion, perhaps there is an argument to say that traditional gender roles have been undermined; that a majority of women are now in paid employment and single mothers should be no exception to this trend. Here we must consider the employment options which are generally available to low skilled women in Britain and which account for the rise in recent years of married women in the labour force. Wages available to most women are not adequate for family maintenance (Brown, 1989), especially where employment opportunities are concentrated in part-time work; work constructed on the assumption of women's domestic role. The corollary of this is that many married women are working for a secondary wage, viable only because there is another wage in the household; not only for a secondary wage, but in secondary employment: low-paid, insecure and designed for cheapness and disposability. For many women, paid employment, together with mothering obligations, still requires some kind of dependency – whether it be on the state or on a husband.

Thus the gender-related issues which arise from the debate about the 'underclass' partly stem from unresolved questions about the sexual division of labour in society. Women's position in the household, and particularly the situation of single mothers, raises a number of problems for conceptions of social inclusion. As welfare dependants they become stigmatised members of the underclass, failing in their role of socialisation. Their weak position in the labour market, which is partly a result of gender segregation, means they are for the most part unable to earn sufficient to be self-supporting, and full-time employment would anyway conflict with their mothering role. It is hard to see what full social inclusion would look like for these women, and without some reassessment of the sexual division of labour in society this will continue to be the case. The underclass debate evades these issues by marginalising the status of single mothers; thus single motherhood is presented as a moral issue, and as a departure from the norms and values of mainstream society. Yet the break-up of the nuclear family household is happening at the centre of society; changes to household structures and the decreasing viability of marriage as a life-time condition are more far-reaching, and more centrally placed in society than the underclass debate has ever suggested. So too is a dependent status for women.

## CONFLICTING OBLIGATIONS

Recent developments in the conceptualisation of social citizenship have placed at least as much emphasis on obligations as on rights, the prime obligation being work as a means to self-reliance, and not ironically to care for the next generation of citizens (cf. Pateman, 1989). This places women in an ambiguous position; either they earn their 'public' citizenship rights by their own paid employment, or they perform their 'private' family obligations and remain dependent. This conflict can only be resolved by either a redistribution of the 'private' obligations of unpaid labour, by some acknowledgement of the 'public' service such labour performs, or by increasing state involvement in the 'private' obligation to care for children, alongside fundamental labour market reform. The current situation, however, leaves individual women in something of a dilemma, especially if the fathers of their children are unwilling or unable to perform *their* traditional role. These women become the new 'undeserving poor'.

Thus, the underclass debate stigmatises women's dependency in the context of a tradition which has constructed women as dependent. This tradition has been challenged but not overcome, and is still maintained by beliefs about appropriate gender roles, beliefs about the significance of motherhood and also by the disadvantaged position of most women in the labour market. For single mothers the dilemma is particularly clear; as benefit dependants they are stigmatised members of the 'underclass', and as such are failing in their distinctively female role of socialising the next generation. It is argued that the children in such households suffer from the absence of a breadwinning role model, and yet the weak position of the majority of sole mothers in the labour market prevents them from easily assuming this role themselves. Even were they to do so this would raise the problem of child-care, and more generally of whether they were meeting their traditional obligations as a mother. One response to this complex of problems has been strongly to reaffirm the strengths of traditional arrangements. More recently we have seen the withdrawal of 'special treatment' for single parents in the benefit system as part of the 'welfare to work' drive, and an ideological assertion of 'family values'. However, any more radical solution to the impasse over women's rights to social inclusion can only be achieved by a fundamental and far reaching review of many taken for granted aspects of social life.

What we are currently witnessing is a breakdown in the family–work–welfare nexus on a number of fronts: employment for men has declined, the nuclear family is under challenge, and the use of welfare to fill the breach is increasingly seen as politically unacceptable. Yet women with children have no easy route to independence, because of their principal role in childcare and their limited labour market opportunities. The public anxieties surrounding these issues have been captured by the rhetoric of the underclass, which by isolating and stigmatising single mothers seems to offer at least a containment of the problem. That problem, however, pervades the whole of society, which is undergoing some renegotiation of the organisation of work, family and welfare. The nature of that change cannot be understood through a focus on a residual group, argued to be inadequately socialised, and without whom it is believed the problems will go away.

## NOTES

1. Young adults on training schemes, for example, are not included in the unemployment count, and there have been numerous other changes since unemployment began to rise in the late seventies (see Morris, 1991).
2. Figures on economic activity show higher rates for men, largely because of their over-representation in self-employment, though women's work in family firms will often be hidden.
3. David Hunt, Employment Secretary, Conservative Party Conference, 1993.
4. Frank Field, 'The poison in the welfare state', *Independent on Sunday*, 14 May 1995, p. 27.
5. ILO definition.

## REFERENCES

Auletta, K. (1982) *The Underclass*, New York, Random House.

Bane, M.J. (1988) 'Politics and Policies of the Feminization of Poverty', in M. Weir, A.S. Orloff, and T. Skocpol (eds.) *The Politics of Social Policy in the United States*, Princeton NJ: Princeton University Press.

Beveridge, W. (1942) *Report on the Social Insurance and Allied Services*, Cmnd 6404, London: HMSO.

Brown, J. (1990) 'The Focus on Single Mothers', in C. Murray, *Losing Ground*, New York: Basic Books.

Buckingham, A. (1996) 'A Statistical Update', in R. Lister (ed.) *Charles Murray and the Underclass: the Developing Debate*, Choice in Welfare Series No. 33, London: Institute of Economic Affairs.

Department of Employment (1988) *Employment in the 1990's*, Cm 540, London: HMSO.

Dex, S. (1985) *The Sexual Division of Work*, Brighton: Wheatsheaf.

Dilnot. A. and Kell (1989) 'Men's Unemployment and Women's Work', A. Dilnot and A. Walker (eds), in *The Economics of Social Security*, Oxford: Oxford University Press, 153–68.

Ermisch, J. (1986) *The Economics of the Family: Applications to Divorce and Remarriage*, Discussion Paper 40, London: CEPR.

*General Household Survey* (Living in Britain), various, London: HMSO.

Harris, C.C. (1987) *Redundancy and Recession in South Wales*, Oxford: Blackwell.

Hills, J. (1995) *Income and Wealth: Report of the JRF Enquiry Group*, York: Joseph Rowntree Foundation.

Irwin, S. and Morris, L.D. (1993) 'Social Security or Economic Insecurity?', in *Journal of Social Policy*, pp. 349–72.

Jordan, B., James, S., Kay, H. and Redley, M. (1992) *Trapped in Poverty*, London: Routledge.

Labour Force Survey (various).

McLaughlin, E., Millar, J. and Cooke, K. (1989) *Work Welfare and Benefits*, Aldershot: Avebury.

Marshall, T.H. (1950) *Citizenship and Social Class*, Cambridge: Cambridge University Press.

Mead, L.M. (1986) *Beyond Entitlement*, New York: Free Press.

Micklewright, J. (1986) *Unemployment and Incentives to Work: Policy Evidence in the 1980's*, Discussion Paper 92, ESRC Programme on Taxation Incentives and the Distribution of Income, London: London School of Economics.

Morris, L.D. (1995) *Social Divisions*, London: UCL Press.

——(1996) 'Income Maintenance and Household Living Standards', in *Journal of Social Policy*, 25, 459–83.

Murray, C. (1984) *Losing Ground*, New York: Basic Books.

——(1990) *The Emerging British Underclass*, Choice in Welfare Series No. 2. London: IEA.

——(1996) 'The Underclass: the Crisis Deepens', in R. Lister (ed.), *Charles Murray and the Underclass: the Developing Debate*, Choice in Welfare Series No. 33, London: Institute of Economic Affairs.

Pahl, R.E. (1984), *Divisions of Labour*, Oxford: Blackwell.

Pateman, C. (1989) *The Disorder of Women*, Cambridge: Polity Press.

*Social Trends* (1997).

Weale, A. et al. (1984) *Lone Mothers, Paid Work and Social Security*, London: Bedford Square Press/NCVO.

Wilson, W.J. (1987) *The Truly Disadvantaged*, Chicago: Chicago University Press.

# 4 Caring for Children
## Julia Brannen

Social policy in the UK is subject to the influence of increasingly globalised economic forces, while the citizens whose lives are regulated by social policy are subject to processes of increased reflexivity including risk calculation and individualisation (Beck, 1994). Government is shedding paternalistic responsibility for providing for its citizens. Instead, it is fashioning an enabling role, which seeks to disperse responsibility for its citizens on to the citizens themselves. Citizens in their turn are forced to take on responsibility for constructing their own pathways through the maze of caring, employment and personal responsibilities and the diverse and expanding range of lifestyle choices which are increasingly available.

In this chapter, I want to consider some of the contradictions and dilemmas of caring for children with which mothers have to contend since their role has undergone considerable change in recent decades. I will also touch on some of the dilemmas for men, especially in their role as fathers and some issues for children. First, I discuss the economic trends in mothers' employment, the ways these play out at the household level and the consequent exacerbation in economic inequality between households that has taken place. Next, I consider different public discourses surrounding family life and care and how these discourses may be changing. I suggest that family life is not only acted upon by economic and global forces, but is also acted upon by cultural forces of how we think and speak about it. I then identify some of ways in which social policy and social policy discourse shape motherhood, concentrating upon lone motherhood as a critical case. My argument is that British mothers are in the process of being reconstructed in the policy arena as workers rather than carers and that if they are to be self-supporting through labour market activity, it needs also to be recognised that they must combine paid work with care. I go on consider some of the ways in which mothers attempt to do this with a focus on the gendered allocation and meaning of work-time across private and public spheres. If mothers and fathers are to be able to perform successfully both caring and employment roles in the future, then it is necessary to address time and work issues for both mothers and fathers, to put in place institutional supports for all groups of parents and children, and to rethink the ways in which costs and benefits are measured across both the formal and the informal economies.

## TRENDS IN MOTHERS' EMPLOYMENT: INTEGRATION, INTENSIFICATION, DIFFERENTIATION AND POLARISATION

The nature of work is changing and in this process more opportunities have been provided for women in the labour market. With the development of technology, traditional forms of semi- and unskilled manual work are disappearing, particularly jobs carried out by men. Labour markets are developing which draw on women's labour not only in the public sector but in many parts of the burgeoning private sector, namely services and finance. In recent secondary analysis of the Labour Force Survey (LFS), which colleagues and I have conducted at Thomas Coram Research Unit, we examined the employment of both mothers and fathers between 1984 and 1994 (Brannen et al., 1997). This analysis suggests some striking trends:

- Mothers' employment has continued to rise. By 1994 59 per cent of mothers were economically active, while in 1984 the proportion was just under one half. The proportion of graduate mothers working full-time – that is bringing in a breadwinner wage or equivalent – rose by more than a half from 28 per cent to 43 per cent. In 1994 nearly one half of graduate mothers (43 per cent) worked full-time compared with only 14 per cent of unqualified mothers.
- Greatest growth has been among mothers of very young children. As Policy Studies Institute research has shown also, mothers are increasingly staying in their jobs following maternity leave; in 1979, 24 per cent of mothers were back at work 9 months after childbirth, but by 1991 the figure had risen to 67 per cent (Callendar et al., 1997).
- Mothers' working hours have increased significantly, reflecting the general intensification of work. Much of the recent growth in mothers' employment is in full-time work; between 1984 and 1994 the average hours of employed mothers rose by 2.3 hours, while the increase for employed fathers, who were already working the longest hours in Europe (Moss, 1996) was quite small.

But only some groups of mothers are benefiting from these increased labour market opportunities; others are not. Those most likely to be in the labour market are: mothers who have qualifications, especially higher qualifications, notably graduate mothers; mothers who are white; those who older and have fewer children; those who have a partner; and those who have a partner in a non-manual job. Conversely, those least likely to be in the labour market are: those without qualifications, those from a minority ethnic group, those with younger and three or more children, those who have a partner who is not employed or in a manual job, and those who have no partner at all. For mothers living with partners, employment rates increased from 50 per cent to 64 per cent between 1984 and 1994 while, for lone mothers, the rate fell from 41 per cent to 39 per cent. But despite this employment growth among some groups, women still have a long way to go in enjoying their share of the more senior occupational positions and in gaining access to particular sectors of the economy.

To some extent women's increased labour market power owes its success to women themselves in their struggle to avail themselves of educational opportunities. It also arises in the context of women's political struggles, notably through the 1970s Women's Movement which focused on women's oppression, and through the 1970s legislation which aimed to end institutional sex discrimination in the workplace (Gregory, chapter 7, this volume). But the growth in women's labour market power is also underpinned by the changing nature of the economy, in particular an increased demand for the kinds of skills which educated women have acquired. This success story has to be counterbalanced by the relative absence of material prospects and educational resources of those mothers outside the labour market. Moreover, the greater integration of many mothers into the labour market brings with it an increasingly polarised household employment pattern. As I have mentioned, employed mothers are more likely than non-employed mothers to have a partner and to have a partner in work. These mothers therefore live in work-rich households. Mothers outside the labour market are more likely to be lone parents. Since their educational capital is low, they have difficulty in gaining a toehold in the labour market. Furthermore, the men with whom many single mothers have borne children are also similarly disadvantaged.

Overall our LFS trend data show clearly that the income gap between work-rich and work-poor households has grown over the 10-year period. The 1994 picture of household employment looks like this: just under half of all families with dependent children have two earners (46 per cent). Two-thirds of these two earners consist of one full-time and one part-time earner, while the remaining third (17 per cent) have two full-time earners. Only a third of families conform to the old breadwinner family. (This decline is mainly due to the increase in full-time work among some mothers and the somewhat less steep rise in no earner households.) One fifth (21 per cent) of households have no earners.

As these huge household inequalities come to be recognised as having political implications, debates are beginning to surface about the measures needed to redress them. For example, supporting the least well-off households through tax reforms (Working Families Tax Credits) involves treating household income collectively. From a gender equality perspective, it is important that policy solutions do not result in reversing hard-won reforms such as women's right to be separately assessed for tax purposes from their male partners. Treating income as collective runs the risk of assuming that income is necessarily distributed equitably within the household. Women's access to and control over household income is an important step in gender equality and is crucial to children's and women's welfare (Pahl, 1989; Brannen and Wilson, 1987).

## CHANGING DISCOURSES OF FAMILY LIFE

Family life is shaped by increasingly globalised economic forces through the growing power of international markets which shape the success of national economies and local labour market opportunities. It is also shaped by different discourses. Some discourses arise through everyday practices and reflect broader social processes of reflexivity and individualisation. In accordance with changes in family life, and the increasing diversity of family forms (single personhood, lone parents and reordered families) both across the population and over the life course, new meanings are created which reflect and act upon changing family forms. Other discourses are sustained institutionally and belong to the public domain, the spheres of politics and social policy. These often tend to hark back nostalgically to an idealised earlier era when all was considered to be well with the family. Even with the emergence of new discourses which reflect how families are, discourses concerning how families ought to be still abound. For example, much of the policy debate about lone motherhood has constructed dependence on benefit as morally indefensible. Lone mothers have been criticised for destabilising family life and have been charged with marginalising fathers (Murray, 1984; 1994). Dennis and Erdos (1992) go so far as to blame the growth of single and lone motherhood on emancipatory feminism of the 1970s which, they consider, goaded mothers into making themselves independent of men. Typically, a highly moralistic tone on the family is often taken by those in power, notably the Back to Basics policies of the 1990s Conservative governments. Under New Labour there appears to be a change of emphasis. In the new discourse, mothers, like all citizens, are entitled to rights, but only if they take on responsibilities, notably in the labour market. So far the tone remains somewhat moralistic and certainly prescriptive (Driver and Martell, 1997).

One of the most significant discourse transformations which reflects the changing reality of family life has been the change from an emphasis on the institutional aspects of marriage to one concerning its contractual nature, that is between two individuals. When contracts are entered into, they must be negotiated, so too if or when they are terminated. This is not a new discourse, but the changes involved are still in train as we can see from the still rising divorce and cohabitation rates, particularly among the younger age groups, and the fall in first marriage (Social Trends, 1996). The negotiability of relations between parents is clearly visible in and around divorce. With the loosening of taken-for-granted family obligations, love between couples today is increasingly confluent and contingent (as Giddens, 1992, describes it). Less and less is a relationship a once and for all romantic commitment. It is acceptable to commit oneself again after divorce to a new partner and leave the old partner behind.

Significant discourse changes are occurring around how we think about fatherhood. They are also occurring around childhood. However, under recent legislation, parents' relations with children have become much less a matter for negotiation. The notion of a 'clean break' from one's children, once acceptable to some groups of divorcing fathers (Maclean, 1994), is no longer accepted in law. We have seen a rewriting of the divorce laws. Divorce was formerly liberal from men's point of view, but now they can no longer be let off the hook of fatherhood (Smart, 1995). After, as well as before, divorce, children are now considered to be the responsibility of both their parents. Here the principle of parental responsibility is paramount. But so too is the principle of the child's right to have contact with two parents. The increased policy discourse focusing on the child, albeit currently couched in terms of children's protection rather than children's rights, represents a further step in the process of reflexivity and individualisation. By this I mean there is a construction of the child as agent shaping his or her own life rather than as an object and recipient of others' care and teaching.

In general terms, family life has been conceptualised as a system of clearly defined obligations. This discourse is itself being transformed. Today's family relationships are typically negotiated (Finch, 1989; Finch and Mason, 1993). Family life is about personal and individualised relationships which we, as individuals, recognise we have a part in shaping. To some extent, we can choose whether we have closer relationships and ties with some family members rather than others. Relationships are no longer set in stone, although this does not mean, as Burgoyne and Clark suggested in the early 1980s, that normative stereotypes are not important (Burgoyne and Clark, 1982). As their work on step-families showed, many step-families sought to reconstitute themselves according to the normative blueprint of the nuclear family. But during family change a lot of onus is put on each family member involved (the onus on children is all too often forgotten) not only to make sense of, and to come to terms with, changes, but also to shape new roles and relationships. With no set script to follow and often minimal support, normative family stereotypes remain potent influences at the level of representation, if not practice. To take the experience of becoming a step-father, currently studied by one of my research students (Burn, personal communication), it is clear that a major identity problem for stepfathers is not simply negotiating a role for themselves but doing so in the context of a great deal of ambiguity about what it means to be a father, never mind being a stepfather.

As feminists have noted, the emphasis placed on love and the voluntary nature of relationships distracts attention from a key issue in family relations namely the caring work that is involved (Graham, 1983). In a Department of Health study currently in progress concerning children's views and experiences of family life, my colleagues and I are finding that children, like parents, play down the significance of the duty and care element of parent–child relations, preferring instead to emphasise the expressive dimensions of parenthood. For example, they say that parents should look after children because they 'love them', rather than because they have a duty to care for them. In this study only those children placed in the public care system, whose parents have signally failed them, subscribe to the idea that parents have a 'duty' to care for their children. This does not, of course, mean that the majority of children living with birth parents do not take their parents' care for granted.

## SOCIAL POLICY DISCOURSE AND MOTHERHOOD

In recent social policy discourses relating to divorce and lone parenthood, both mothers and fathers are being reconstructed as workers and therefore as occupying similar roles. Through policies of Welfare to Work both parents are expected to provide materially for children (Millar, 1997). However, this discourse overlays and supplants taken-for-granted assumptions and old discourses which construct mothers as the best and only persons to care for children, notably when children are young. It ignores the caring role which continues to be played in most cases by mothers in taking the primary responsibility for children. Historically, much UK social policy has been premised on this assumption (Wilson, 1977; Land, 1978; Lister, 1990). But if paid work is to become a prerequisite for lone motherhood, social policy needs to construct motherhood, lone and partnered, as workers and carers, a situation which exists in Scandinavian societies (Leira, 1992) It needs to acknowledge that caring for children limits an individual's autonomy and therefore impedes mothers' desire and ability to participate in the labour market unless proper support is available for them in their parental role and for their children.

Other social policy discourses defining motherhood and fatherhood abound. These are often at odds with the new social policy discourse of mothers as workers. In the recent legislation on children, notably the Children Act 1989, parents' caring obligations to their children are couched in the vague but overarching concept of 'parental responsibility'. But the degendering of parental roles is not sustained by any policy other than to make fathers financially responsible for children. Moreover, in reducing care to personal responsibility, there is an implicit assumption that children are a matter of individual choice rather than an intrinsic part of the adult life course and of societal obligations. Once chosen, parents are required to be totally responsible for children, morally, socially and financially. The duty actually to care for children, whether chosen or not – the everyday work that mothers typically do – is disregarded or rather swamped by the global concept of parental responsibility. We should note here another new and related linguistic emphasis in social policy – the language in which policy is couched is increasingly critical. Through the principle of parental responsibility, children in the public care system are now referred to as 'looked after' by foster carers and 'accommodated' rather than being 'in care', i.e. the care of the state. It is the responsibility that has become important rather than the actual care. Responsibility is shared between social workers (i.e. the state) and the biological parents (typically a lone mother) even though the children may be forcibly taken from their parents. The actual caring work which is done by foster carers suffers a demotion which is also reflected in the change of language from foster 'parent' to foster 'carer' (Rhodes, 1995). So those doing the caring are not charged with what is the key prerequisite: namely, responsibility.

In both social policy discourses – Welfare to Work and policies around parental responsibility – mothers are left with a dilemma, especially when children are very young: whether to do paid work or be a full-time carer: and when children are older, whether and how to combine caring and meet the increasingly demanding labour market. For if mothers' dilemmas are to be confronted, this would mean confronting the need for fathers to participate fully in family life and the need for a proper infrastructure of care services which meets children's needs as well as those of parents. It would entail accepting that the whole of society, not only parents, has a responsibility towards children and towards supporting family life.

Lone mothers with young children constitute the critical case of motherhood since they are effectively solo parents when children are at their most dependent. Between 1971 and 1996 the proportion of households with dependent children headed by a lone parent rose from 7 per cent to 21 per cent (GHS, 1987; Social Trends, 1998). Under half of lone mothers (38 per cent) have never been married (GHS, 1987; Social Trends, 1998). In 1994, 61 per cent were outside the labour market, only 17 per cent in full-time work and 22 per cent in part-time work. Moreover, responsibility for young children is the major factor in lone mothers' dependence on benefit, with significantly higher rates of non-employment among those with children under the age of 5. Only 23 per cent of lone mothers with a child under 5 are employed compared with 62 per cent of lone mothers with a child aged 11–16 (Brannen et al., 1997).

But memories are short. Until the mid-1980s, lone mothers of young children resembled other mothers of young children in Britain: they stayed at home while they had young children. In 1977–9, only 27 per cent of partnered mothers with a child under 5 were in work, and likewise a similar proportion of lone mothers (26 per cent) (GHS, 1985). Moreover, at that time the overall employment rates of mothers of children of all ages differed little and lone mothers were more likely to work full-time than partnered mothers.

As yet the UK, unlike many Northern European countries, has not taken on any significant responsibility for providing for young children's care either in the context of (a) the steady rise in employment in the postwar period among mothers, or (b) growing rates of lone parenthood. With the exception of wartime, the UK has always had a poor record on childcare provision. Traditionally, British mothers have been constructed as full-time carers, that is until their children started school or even later. And even then they entered part-time work with short hours rendering them the subsidiaries of male breadwinners. When the employment rates of mothers of young children began to escalate in the mid-1980s, the Conservative governments of the time and subsequently considered those mothers who opted for employment were making essentially 'private decisions' in which the state should not interfere. This might mean a mother negotiating some support from her employer, but more typically using kin networks and other informal solutions, notably friends and neighbours, and, if they entered part-time employment, drawing upon the services of children's fathers (Marsh and McKay, 1993; Finlayson et al., 1996). 'Family-friendly' policies in the workplace have been increasingly discussed, first by Conservative governments and now by New Labour. Indeed, the Green Paper *A New Contract for Welfare* (1998) states that 'policies to promote family friendly working practices would not traditionally be seen as welfare measures, this Government sees them as being at least as important as changes to the benefit structure' (p. 59). Some employers have introduced such policies, but only big organisations ever seriously contemplate providing childcare for their employees, and few are able to deliver it in practice. There are also problems of low take-up even where such employer programmes do exist (Brannen and Lewis, in press).

Historically, childcare policy in the UK stands in marked contrast to care policy related to dependence in old age. At least until recently, pensions and care in old age were provided by the state on a universalist basis (albeit pensions are provided at a financially low level). But these responsibilities are increasingly being devolved to citizens to sort out for themselves. As I have already noted, in line with this approach, the current government, particularly through its Welfare to Work programme, is challenging taken-for-granted assumptions about the status of mothers as carers. As yet there is no public discourse which takes account of parents' role as both carers and workers. In re-creating a discourse of citizenship New Labour is emphasising economic self-reliance and individual responsibility rather than also highlighting the continuing and growing need to care for younger and older generations, in the context of increased expectations of employability for all (see Morris, chapter 3, this volume). Aimed at ending lone mothers' reliance on the state (benefit), which is seen as an unacceptable cost to taxpayers, current policy focuses upon the public rather than the private rights of citizenship (Morris, chapter 3, this volume). Significantly, responsibility is being devolved to the individual. While the notion of community responsibility is also being invoked, the discourse is largely rhetorical despite the fact that the need to re-create community has been so much vaunted in New Labour's communitarian vision (Driver and Martell, 1997). The promised institutional pluralism, namely the creation of bulwarks between the individual and the state, which were so eroded in the Thatcher period, is yet to be developed. The proposed National Childcare Strategy (DfEE, 1998) will help mothers with childcare costs. However, only limited financial resources will be allocated to providing places, namely for 4-year-olds and for setting up after school clubs, drawing on the cheap labour of unemployed and unqualified young people. This strategy does not fully address the childcare needs of the critical group of lone mothers with children under school age, who are least likely to be in the labour market. Moreover, in focusing on mothers with school age children, it fails to address central problems concerning many mothers' still inequitable status in the labour market. Research has shown that, when mothers take career breaks for childbearing and child rearing, the result is a substantial reduction in women's earning ability and typically entails downward occupational mobility from which few are likely to recover during their working lives (Dex, 1987; Joshi and Newell, 1987; Brannen, 1989). Decisions concerning whether parental leave is to be paid or not, when Britain brings its provisions into line with the European Union, have yet to be made (White Paper, Fairness at Work, DTI, 1998).

If the Welfare to Work policy is to work, it needs to be followed through with policies which address persistent inequalities in labour markets, particularly the pool of low-paid work which the many under-qualified lone mothers are likely to be forced to enter. This is a major issue for fathers of the children of single mothers whose own labour market position is often weak also, making it difficult to provide materially for their children, either as resident or nonresident fathers.

Low-paid work has major consequences also for the *children* of lone parents. These children are likely to be further disadvantaged if they are segregated into low-cost childcare services away from those children who are growing up with two parents in work and whose parents can afford high-cost, high-quality facilities (Brannen and Moss, in press). The economic inclusion of lone parents needs to be supported by social inclusion, the social inclusion of their children, so that they do not start life in a ghettoised childhood.

Social inclusion depends fundamentally upon the recognition and proper remuneration of care work. This means tackling its taken-for-granted association with gender. The entry into the labour market of *partnered* mothers has been accompanied by rather little change in the redistribution of work and responsibility on the domestic front (Gershuny et al., 1994; Horrell, 1994). The issues may be different when parents live in separate households, although research suggests that relationships between parents and children following divorce are likely to reflect the division of care when parents lived together in the same household (Moxnes, 1990). Policy needs to address the fact of fathers' low level of contact and involvement in their children's lives (Richards, 1996), not merely following divorce but, much more importantly, from the outset of parenthood.

At present the assumption that mothers have major responsibility for care remains largely intact. This happens in spite of the fact that parental responsibility is a major theme in other current public policy, notably in education and the law. As research has shown, some groups of lone mothers do not wish to enter the labour market, notably white working-class women (Duncan and Edwards, 1997). This is not surprising. Far from reflecting a 'dependency culture' (it is important to remember that living on benefit means living in poverty), white lone mothers are concerned to take seriously their responsibilities towards their children by 'being there' for them; in not being there, they fear that may add to the already socially stigmatising condition of 'coming from a lone parent family'. By contrast, black lone mothers placed more emphasis upon providing for children through paid work.

Policies which devolve care responsibility to parents and require them to participate fully in the labour market and leave support for children to parents and the vagaries of the market put mothers in an inherently contradictory position. At the heart of this contradiction is the failure to address how to care for those who cannot care fully for themselves. The Green Paper on Welfare (1998) signally emphasises the individualistic concepts of independence, responsibility and empowerment (p. 81). The policy of economic self-reliance has come at a time when we have never had so many citizens outside the labour market. The two bands of people most likely to be outside the labour market are located at either end of the life course spectrum: the young and the old. Moreover, these age bands are getting wider (Deven et al., 1997). The policy of self-reliance is being urged upon a group whose responsibilities for care and paid work increasingly coincide for life course reasons (parenthood) and because of the changing structure of the labour force. This 'coincidence' occurs in people's 'middle years', as they defer parenthood in the context of later and later entry into the labour market. It also occurs in the context of earlier exits from the labour market, because of early retirement, and the lengthening of old age, with increased possibilities for caring for older generations at the same time as caring for dependent children (Brannen and Moss, in press). This coincidence of care and employment falls disproportionately on women's shoulders.

A coherent policy framework and a new public discourse which support both care and paid work are urgently needed and should place equal value on caring work done by men and women, both as an informal role (fatherhood as well as motherhood) and as an occupation in the workforce since paid caring is currently poorly remunerated. These are the necessary conditions in order that men will take on caring roles in both public and private spheres. Only then will the 'either/or' choices that many mothers, lone mothers especially, are forced into – of motherhood versus employment – become a thing of the past. Only then will the unacceptable choice between dependence upon men or dependence upon the state be obviated. Until the goal of equality with men both in the labour market and in the home is achieved, there is a strong case for treating women as equal to men but also as different from them. In the longer term this may change. Increasingly, since women are increasingly well qualified, it is likely that policy will make this change on human capital grounds, as well as on grounds of equity and fairness. But, in the shorter term, policy has to recognise and support the current, still highly gendered distribution of care. A viable infrastructure of early childhood services is also necessary, not simply to support working parents, but as part and parcel of children's rights to enable them to be active and partici-pative citizens in the present and the future.

## PAID WORK AND CARE: MAKING AND RETHINKING TIME

In the absence of policy support and a supportive public discourse, mothers who are both carers and workers, especially the increasing proportion in full-time employment, have created individualised solutions for managing work–family obligations. Increasingly, the management of the work–family interface hinges upon the issue of time. As I have already noted, the working hours of mothers have increased significantly in recent years, especially among mothers with a child under 5 (Brannen et al., 1997). As organisations restructure in their need to create 'leaner' workforces, workers are succumb-ing to the pressures of organisations to 'demonstrate' their commitment. One significant indicator of this is the 'long hours culture'. The time pressure on women workers to be more like men may be experienced internally as well as result from external factors. In the general climate of job insecurity, fear is widespread among those in work, making it difficult for people to resist the long hours culture and full-time working. In a climate of job insecurity, mothers may hesitate to take advantage of family-friendly policies in the workplace, even where they do exist (Hochschild, 1997).

Employed mothers juggle time: time devoted to work and time devoted to care. They are forced to rely on informal support networks, typically other women who provide their services free or for a token fee (in the case of care by relatives). Alternatively, they must purchase other people's time and the increasingly expensive childcare provided by private markets while, for back-up support, some may negotiate help from their partners. If they are fortunate enough to work for a family-friendly employer, typically a large organisation, they may have access to workplace benefits, such as flexible work practices, leave allowances and childcare vouchers (Brannen and Lewis, in press). But even so this does not guarantee that they will be able to make use of these supports.

For the advantaged group of working mothers in 'work-rich' households, negotiating childcare is now a 'planning project' involving the planning of life course time. It is also a reflexive project in which mothers calculate and try to minimise the risks of non-parental care for their children. The media and experts' portrayal of the effects of childcare upon children has continued to focus on the negative rather than the positive consequences, especially with respect to institutional childcare (Mooney and Munton, 1987). This is despite the fact that institutional childcare, provided on a universal basis, has been successfully tried and tested in many European countries.

As Arlie Hochschild (1997) suggests for the US, a country which has a similar childcare situation to the UK, the management strategies of working mothers increasingly reflect those of men. Mothers and fathers are increasingly experiencing pressures in the workplace. These pressures to be more efficient and productive come from the globalised and flexibilised economy. They also arise in the context of the weakening of legislation which used to protect workers from exploitative employers before it was rescinded by the governments of the 1980s and 1990s.

But the pressures to conform to company culture do not necessarily emanate from organisations alone. As Hochschild (1997) has demonstrated, time pressures on working mothers to invest in work may come from family life itself. With more income earned there is more pressure to consume and an ever-expanding array of goods on offer. The heavy reliance of mothers upon informal and market-led childcare means they must create a patchwork of care which involves considerable time organisation and management skills. In addition, children have social and educational careers to be organised and facilitated. All this leads to an increasingly hurried pace of everyday life and an increase in mothers' workload. Hochschild calls this transformation the 'Taylorisation of family life', drawing on a concept developed in the 1920s when assembly-line working was introduced into the workplace. Hochschild provocatively suggests that time at home is becoming more like work used to be – speeded up time, with dozens of tasks to complete in a very limited amount of time. But as employees' fight for survival within organisations becomes fiercer, work takes on more salience in their lives and demands a greater investment of the self – the continuous updating of skills and considerable investment of effort in staying employable. Of course, work has always been a significant source of social contact for women (see, for example, Martin and Roberts, 1984), but it may be even more so today. Even as women's time involvement in home life shrinks, the activities and tasks of home life continue to expand. It is not surprising then that, just as home becomes work, so work takes on the mantle of what home used to be, especially for men. As Hochschild suggests, just as men used to or still do, some working mothers are seeking refuge in the workplace and are discovering work to be a significant source of self-esteem, self-validation and sociability.

Fathers, too, are experiencing qualitative changes in their family lives. They must come to terms with the fact that the breadwinner role is not theirs alone and that they must find a new basis upon which to build their masculinity. But research suggests that men's domestic involvement still has a long way to go. However, women's incursion into the labour market and their increasing educational success forces men to re-evaluate their masculinity. The traditional link between masculine identity and paid work has been eroded, especially for working-class young men who traditionally gave academic achievement and qualifications a low priority. Without these there is little chance of employment in today's world. For such young men lack of work excludes them from the social, if not the biological, status of fatherhood as the high levels of single motherhood demonstrate. In the context of greater time pressure in the workplace, employed fathers must learn the skills of negotiating with their partners not only about domestic work and childcare, but also about who will stay late at the office and how employment commitments are to be met. They must learn also how to relate to their children.

All this requires not only new ways of coping and the necessary resources. For both mothers and fathers, it calls into question the meaning of time, not only its distribution as a quantitative commodity. 'Time to be' is as significant as 'time to do' (Daly, 1996). Time to be is not driven by the clock and accords more with children's rather than adults' experience of time. Childhood, even in a postmodern world, is still a time for dawdling in which time can be strung out as well as cut up into manageable slices. The famous 'quality time' that working parents talk about giving to their children is driven largely by parents' rather than children's timetables and may appear to children to be a poor trade-off. If time is not reconceptualised and revalued, there is a risk that the 'economic project' and workplace time will become over-powerful determinants of both family life and children's childhoods.

## CONCLUSION

Britain may be moving into a new set of relationships between the state, the family and the labour market. As the welfare state is restructured, greater responsibility is placed upon individuals both to care for family members who are not in the labour market, but also for making and keeping themselves employable. This is a major transformation for British mothers who, at least when children were young, have long been expected to take care of children on a full-time basis and then only to join the labour market part-time when children reach school age. Public childcare has never been available in Britain except in wartime.

The current political concern for mothers' employability arises in the context of the high rate of lone mothers in the UK who are dependent upon social security. This group has continued to grow, with consequent burdens upon the public exchequer. However, coterminous with this trend is the escalation in labour market activity of mothers in general, especially those with higher qualifications who also tended to have partners. This latter group has increased demand for childcare which appears to be resulting in the availability of more high-cost care provided via private markets which is purchased by the most economically advantaged groups. Most employed mothers, however, continue to rely upon informal social networks and community-based childminders. Both sets of mothers have to solve the dilemma of managing caring and employment responsibilities: those who are encouraged by government to come off benefit and find work and those who fear to lose their place in the advantaged sections of the job market or cannot afford to do so.

As yet, there is no policy discourse or coherent policy framework which adequately constructs mothers as both carers and workers. An important step in developing such a framework is for policy-makers to consider the transfer of women's labour from the care economy to the formal economy in terms of the costs and benefits to both economies (Himmelweit, 1998). For the entry of mothers into the labour market is not 'cost-free'. Indeed, the economic gains to the formal economy are artificially inflated when women move from caring roles to paid employment (Cloud and Garrett, 1996). This does not mean, however, that mothers who become paid employees cease to do caring and domestic work, even when childcare is available for their children. For lone mothers who join the labour market, caring work is unlikely to diminish very much since, by definition, they have no other parent in the household with whom to share the caring and domestic work. But the degree to which caring and domestic work contributes to the overall economy and to the whole society through the provision of material, emotional, psychological and educational support has to be recognised. As Himmelweit (1998) argues, this is not to suggest that women's labour time should not be transferred between sectors but that national accounting systems and budgetary procedures should calculate the losses to informal sectors of the economy as well as count the gains to the formal economy.

# REFERENCES

Beck, U. (1994) 'The Reinvention of Politics: Towards a Theory of Reflexive Modernism', in U. Beck, A. Giddens and S. Lash, *Reflexive Modernisation, Politics, Tradition and Aesthetics in the Modern Social Order*, Cambridge: Polity Press.

Beck, U. and Beck-Gernsheim, E. (1995) *The Normal Chaos of Love*, Cambridge: Polity Press.

Brannen, J. (1989) 'Childhood and Occupational Mobility: Evidence from a Longitudinal Study', *Work, Employment and Society*, 3, pp. 179–207.

Brannen, J. and Wilson, G. (eds) (1987*) Give and Take in Families: Studies in Resource Distribution*, London: Unwin Hyman.

Brannen, J., Moss, P., Owen, C. and Wale, C. (1997) *Mothers, Fathers and Employment: Parents and the Labour Market in Britain 1984–1994*, London: Department for Education and Employment.

Brannen, J. and Moss, P. (in press) 'The Polarisation and Intensification of Parental Employment: Consequences for Children, Families and the Community', *Community, Work and Family*.

Brannen, J. and Lewis, S. (in press) 'Workplace Programmes and Policies in the UK', in L. Haas, P. Hwang, and G. Russell (eds) *Organisational Change and Gender Equity*, London: Sage.

Burgoyne, J. and Clark, D. (1982) *Making a Go of It: A Study of Step Families in Sheffield*, London: Routledge and Kegan Paul.

Callender, C., Millward, N., Lissenburgh, S. and Forth, J. (1997) *Maternity Rights in Britain, 1996*, Research Report No. 67, London: The Stationery Office.

Cloud, K. and Garrett, N., (1996) 'A Modest Proposal for Inclusion of Women's Household Capital Production in Analysis of Structural Transformation' *Feminist Economics*, 2 (3), pp. 93–120.

Dennis, N. and Erdos, G. (1992) *Families without Fatherhood*, London: Institute for Public Policy Research.

Department for Education and Employment (1998) *Meeting the Challenge of Childcare: A Framework and Consultation Document*, May 1998, London, Department for Education and Employment.

Department for Trade and Industry (1998) *White Paper: Fairness at Work*, London, Department for Trade and Industry.

Dex, S. (1987) *Women's Occupational Mobility: A Lifetime Perspective*, London: Macmillan.

Deven, F., Inglis, S., Moss, P. and Petrie, P. (1998) *An Overview Study on the Reconciliation of Work and Family Life for Men and Women and the Quality of Care Services*, London: Department for Education and Employment.

Duncan, S. and Edwards, R. (1997) 'Lone Mothers and Paid work – Rational Economic Man or Gendered Moral Rationalities?', *Feminist Economics*, 3 (2), pp. 21–61.

Driver, S. and Martell, L. (1997) 'New Labour's Communitarianisms', *Critical Social Policy*, 17 (3), pp. 27–47.

Finch, J. (1989) *Family Obligations and Social Change*, Cambridge: Polity Press.

Finch, J. and Mason, J. (1995) *Negotiating Family Responsibilities*, London: Routledge.

Finlayson, L., Ford, R. and Marsh, A. (1996) 'Paying More for Child Care', *Labour Market Trends*, July, pp. 295–303.

Gershuny, J., Godwin, M. and Jones, S. (1994) 'The Domestic Labour Revolution: a Process of Lagged Adaption', in M. Anderson, F. Bechhofer and J. Gershuny (eds)

*The Social and Political Economy of the Household*, Oxford: Oxford University Press.

GHS (1987) *General Household Survey 1985*, London: HMSO.

Giddens, A. (1992) *The Transformation of Intimacy*, Cambridge: Polity Press.

Himmelweit, S., (1998) 'The Need for Gender Impact Analysis', Proceedings of a seminar 'The Purse or the Wallet?', 12 February 1998, Church House, Westminster, London.

Hochschild, A. (1997) *The Time Bind: When Work Becomes Home and Home Becomes Work*, New York: Henry Holt and Company, Metropolitan Books.

Horrell, S. (1994) 'Household Time Allocation and Women's Labour Force Participation', in M. Anderson, F. Bechhofer and J. Gershuny (eds) *The Social and Political Economy of the Household*, Oxford: Oxford University Press.

Joshi, H. and Newell, M.L. (1987) 'Job Downgrading after Childbirth', in M. Uncles (ed.) London Papers in Regional Science 18: *Longitudinal Data Analysis: Methodological Applications*, London: PION.

Land, H. (1978) 'Who Cares for the Family?' *Journal of Social Policy*, 7 (3), pp. 257–84.

Leira, A. (1992) *Welfare States and Working Mothers: The Scandinavian Experience*, Cambridge: Cambridge University Press.

Lewis, J. (1988) 'Lone-Parent Families: Politics and Economics', *Journal of Social Policy*, 18 (4), pp. 595–600.

Lister, R. (1990) 'Women, Economic Dependency and Citizenship', *Journal of Social Policy*, 19, pp. 445–67.

Maclean, M. (1994) 'The Making of the Child Support Act of 1991: Policy Making at the Intersection of Law and Social Policy', *Journal of Law and Society*, 21 (4), pp. 505–19.

Marsh, A. and McKay, S. (1993) 'Families, Work and the Use of Childcare', *Employment Gazette*, 101 (8), pp. 361–70.

Martin, J. and Roberts, C. (1984) *Women and Employment: A Lifetime Perspective*, London: HMSO.

Miller, J. (1997) 'State, Family and Personal Responsibility: the Changing Balance for Lone Mothers in the UK', in C. Ungerson and M. Kember (eds) *Women and Social Policy*, London: Macmillan.

Mooney, A., and Munton, A., (1997) *Research and Policy in Early Years Services: Time for a New Agenda*, London: Institute of Education.

Moss, P. (1996) 'Parental Employment in the European Union, 1985–1995', *Labour Market Trends*, 104 (12), pp. 517–22.

Moxnes, K. (1990) *Kernesprengning I families? Familie forardring red Samlivsbrudd og dannelse ar nye samliv*, Oslo: Universitetsforlaget.

Murray, C. (1984) *Losing Ground*, New York: Basic Books.

Murray, C. (1990) *The Emerging British Underclass*, London: Institute for Economic Affairs.

Pahl, J. (1989) *Money and Marriage*, London: Macmillan

Pateman, C. (1989) *The Disorder of Women*, Cambridge: Polity Press.

Rhodes, P. (1995) 'Charitable Vocation or Proper Job? The Role of Payment in Foster Care', in J. Brannen and M. O'Brien (eds) *Childhood and Parenthood*, Proceedings of the International Sociological Association Committee for Family Research Conference 1994, London: Institute of Education.

Richards, M. (1996) 'The Socio-legal Support for Divorcing Parents and their Children', in B. Bernstein and J. Brannen (eds) *Children, Research and Policy*, London: Taylor and Francis.

Smart, C. (1995) *The Family and Social Change: Some Problems of Analysis and Intervention*, Research Working Paper 13, Leeds University: Gender, Analysis and Policy Unit, School of Sociology and Social Policy.

Social Trends (1998) *Social Trends*, 28, London: The Stationery Office.

*A Contract for Welfare: New Ambitions for Our Country* (1998) Cm. 3805, London: The Stationery Office

Wilson, E. (1977) *Women and the Welfare State*, London: Tavistock Publications.

# 5 What Do Older Women Want?

Mary Maynard

## INTRODUCTION

This chapter is concerned the needs of older women, the context in which these occur and the social policy agenda for them. It contrasts a social policy perspective which defines older women in negative terms, with one which also recognises their full potential as active citizens and contributors to the households and communities in which they live. The chapter starts by examining some of the basic demographic factors which highlight the gendered nature of later life. There are more older women than men, they are more likely to be widowed and to live alone, and they are more likely to live to an older age when issues of chronic illness, disability and dependency upon state services occur. Yet, paradoxically, when asked what they want, older women seek independence and autonomy, and, especially compared to men of the same age, have a history of being resilient survivors, with an ability to adjust to new circumstances. The chapter concludes that our understanding of the position of older women must be located within a life course perspective; that many of the issues concerning their relative poverty, social isolation, housing circumstances and health are a product of their earlier experiences of the labour and housing markets and marriage and family life. It further suggests that, rather than seeing older women merely as the sources of social policy problems, positive aspects of their lives should be highlighted, as should their potential for making active contributions to both their own and other people's welfare. It is argued that a new policy agenda should start from these positive aspects of older women's lives.

## THE CURRENT CONTEXT TO AGEING

It is well known that, in common with most other Western European countries, the UK has an ageing population. Official statistics indicate that, whereas just under 12 per cent of the population was over 65 years of age in 1961, this had increased to 16 per cent by 1994 and is projected to reach 23 per cent by 2031 (Central Statistical Office, 1996). This contrasts with the proportion of younger people in the population, whose numbers have been falling and are expected to continue to fall. In 1961 those under 16 years of age comprised a quarter of the population. By 1994 this figure had become one fifth and is forecast to drop to under 18 per cent by 2031 (Central Statistical Office, 1996). The reasons for these changes in demographic profile include the falling birth rate and increased longevity. Indeed, the proportion of the over-sixties who are aged 80 years or over has shown a significant increase having grown by a factor of six during the twentieth century.

One highly important aspect of the ageing process relates to its gendered dimension. For the experience of later life is feminised. The older a person gets, the more likely they are to be female; the proportion of older women to older men increases with age and more women than ever reach old age. In 1993 13.1 per cent of the female population compared to 10.6 per cent of the male was between 65 and 79 years of age, putting almost one third more women than men into this age group. For those aged over 80 years, the proportions were 5.4 per cent and 2.4 per cent respectively. This means that there were more than twice as many women as men in this particular age category (Central Statistical Office, 1995). These latter figures are significant for several reasons.

First, despite the ways in which older people tend to be stereotyped and stigmatised as social problems and for their lack of resources, poor health and dependency on state and/or family, it is those in the over-80 age group, that is women, who are most likely to be in chronic or acute need (Arber and Ginn, 1991; Siddell, 1995). Secondly, this indicates the necessity to disaggregate data and material concerning the older age groups, for they cannot be taken as a homogeneous whole with similar characteristics and requirements. There is a huge difference, for instance, in the behaviour and needs of 'young' (usually unproblematically defined as those under 75 years) and 'old' older people. Third, due to the fact that women tend to live longer than men (approximately five years, on average) and tend to marry or have partners who are older than themselves, increasing numbers of them experience widowhood and live on their own. As Arber and Evandrou point out, once men have retired from paid employment, those who survive are unlikely to experience any major change in the composition of their family household until their mid-eighties. In other words, if married, the tendency is for them to continue living with their wives (Arber and Evandrou, 1993b). By comparison, Arber and Evandrou estimate that a tenth of women in their late fifties are widowed, a fifth in their early sixties, over a third in their late sixties, nearly a half in their early seventies and three-fifths in their late seventies. They comment that '[t]here is no age at which the majority of men live alone, and only above age 85 are the majority (54%) widowed. In contrast, the majority of women experience both the transition into widowhood and to living alone in their mid-seventies' (Arber and Evandrou, 1993b, p. 15). Thus, the social policy needs of older women are significantly framed by

the changing nature of Britain's demographic profile. Their living circumstances and experiences of everyday life are also highly influenced by gender.

## WHAT DO OLDER WOMEN WANT?

At first sight, the answer to the question 'what do older women want from
government and social policy?' is relatively simple. All the research which has
asked this kind of question records broadly the same reply. Older women
seek independence and autonomy, respect, a sense of purpose and a friendship network (Bernard, Meade and Tinker, 1993; Jerrome, 1993a and b).
Although many have significant material concerns, their anxieties focus on
the constraints which these impose on their abilities to live useful lives and
their involvement in the community, and not necessarily on the disadvantages *per se*. In short, older women feel that they are often forced to live on
the margins of society. Instead, they wish to be more fully integrated into it.
    Research indicates that when older women refer to independence, they
mean the ability to look after themselves and not be dependent on others for
domestic, physical or emotional care (Arber and Evandrou, 1993b; Baltes,
1996). Older women do not readily give up these former aspects of daily
living and are reluctant recipients of care (Robertson Elliot, 1996). Autonomy relates to 'capacity for self-direction'. It means not having to do as
others say, freedom of choice and lack of interference from outside agencies.
Independence and autonomy are related but not necessarily in a causal way.
It is possible to be physically dependent but to retain a degree of self-
autonomy. Similarly, a person may live an independent life, while being
heavily influenced by some outside party.
    Independence and autonomy are also key indicators of quality of life for
older women, both as perceived by the women themselves and as measured
by practitioners and outside observers (Baltes, 1996; Tinker, 1996). The more
they experience these elements or define themselves in terms of such characteristics, the greater their degrees of self-confidence and self-worth and the
more the nature of their lives is enhanced. Attaining independence and
autonomy, however, is not necessarily as straightforward as might appear.
To begin with, research concerning older people, together with government
policy, too often assumes that dependence and independence are polarised
and opposite states, with the former being seen as a problem, and to be
avoided, and the latter the only status to be valued. Dependence has become
something of a pejorative term, indicating reliance on the state and/or family
and community. However, dependence and independence are not really
dichotomies. Rather, they are part of a spectrum involving both reciprocity
and interdependence, which occurs for everyone, and which is a general
feature of complex industrial societies (Arber and Evandrou, 1993b).

Research indicates that most older people are bound into interdependent and reciprocal relationships, rather than completely dependent ones. Contrary to popular perception, for instance, relatively few older people are completely isolated from family and kinship networks, especially if they have children (Allan, 1996). An ethic of family obligations exists which is both complex, ambiguous and gendered (Finch and Mason, 1993). For older women, in particular, this is expressed in an overwhelming concern not to depend on another, to the extent that acceptance of assistance is likely to involve, 'a complex reckoning of reciprocity between themselves and the potential... provider, with less likelihood of accepting or asking for help if it is perceived as one-sided or cannot be reciprocated in the foreseeable future' (Arber and Evandrou, 1993b, p. 23). Thus, independence is not necessarily under threat if there is a reciprocal or interdependent basis to the support which is provided. Assistance is usually the subject of a degree of negotiation designed to preserve feelings of independence and autonomy for as long as possible. This is tied into older women's feelings of self-worth, personal identity and pride as constituent needs of later life. These needs should be the touchstone of adequacy in addressing the political and social policy agendas.

## THE 'OLD' SOCIAL POLICY AGENDA RELATING TO WOMEN IN LATER LIFE

In the past, policy analysts, policy-makers and politicians have tended to focus upon and emphasise the negative, debilitating and dependent aspects of growing older. Later life has been portrayed as creating inevitable social problems, particularly in relation to the 'demographic time-bomb', concerns about related increasing welfare costs and the likely implosion of the 'intergenerational contract', although some have criticized such a position for being unnecessarily alarmist.[1] (Castle and Townsend, 1996; Disney, 1997; Hills 1997). It is true that older people, generally, are a relatively disadvantaged group in British society and that this is also influenced by factors such as social class and previous occupational status. It is also the case that significant inequalities exist between women and men in the older age groups. Indeed, the 'problems' faced by older women can present a formidable social policy agenda. As Ginn and Arber point out in this volume, 'older women are over twice as likely as men to live in poverty' (p. 75). They are also more likely to have higher levels of disability than men and to experience chronic (i.e. persistent as opposed to acute) illnesses. Older women are also more likely to live in poor housing stock and to have difficulties with such things as adequate heating and maintenance of buildings. As a consequence, research indicates that finance/income, health and housing form an important basis for older women's material disadvantage (Victor, 1994). Also important are access to transport, social mobility more generally and support to enhance the ability to live within the local community. All these elements relate together in ways which can either enhance or debilitate positive effects in the others. Overlying them are ageist views and cultural stereotyping of older people, which are particularly deprecating and demeaning of older women.

One reason for the prevalence of poverty amongst older women is their heavy reliance on the state pension and other benefits for their income. As Ginn and Arber explain in chapter 6, their lower personal income in later life is related to the domestic division of labour and the corresponding limitations put on undertaking paid employment. This has been exacerbated by lower earnings when they have been able to work and compounded by pensions schemes which have been based on assumptions concerning women's dependence on a male breadwinner. Women, generally, are also less likely to be involved in private or occupational pensions schemes. In short, unlike many men, older women have not been able to enjoy the kind of continuity in employment needed to guarantee a degree of financial security in old age. As Groves points out, although savings, investments and inheritance are also important influences on economic status, it is mainly an individual's employment career, together with that of any spouse or partner, which are significant determinants of income in later life. She concludes, '[i]n the past, women's opportunities have been far more restricted compared with men's: many inequalities and double standards remain' (Groves, 1993, p. 44).

Another difficulty faced by those in later life is the commonly held view that ageing involves a steady and largely inevitable deterioration in physical and mental abilities. Professional workers may be particularly prone to this kind of negative view, since they normally meet mainly those who are frail and infirm (Tinker, 1996). As a consequence, older people, and older women in particular, often experience difficulties with the kind of information they are given and the ageist ways in which they are treated when seeking advice on health issues. Siddell (1993) refers to research in which older women objected to their GPs' frequent diagnoses that their condition was a reflection of their age, rather than any other factors. Many older women in this study felt that they were made to feel guilty about visiting a doctor and had extremely low expectations about obtaining relief for their symptoms. The women felt that they were hardly listened to and that their doctors paid scant attention to their version of things, preferring, instead, to offer a prescription rather than engaging in a more lengthy consultation (Siddell, 1993).

There are a number of other problems, however, when considering health issues and older people. Several commentators have pointed out that focusing centrally on morbidity as an indicator of health can be both negative and patronising (Arber and Ginn, 1991; Siddell, 1993). It takes no account of people's subjective feelings, their individual capacities and contributes to the view that later life is a time of decrepitude, dependency and a drain on resources. Further, it fails to recognise that many older people, and indeed older women, are not infirm or in ill-health. The difficulty here is one of dealing simultaneously with two separate issues. On the one hand, there is the need to counter ageist stereotypes. On the other, there is an obligation not to minimise the real health problems which exist for some people and their need for sensitive and co-ordinated health services. For instance, older women are particularly prone to conditions which are not life-threatening but remain highly symptomatic and for which there is usually no cure. Many more women than men have arthritis, for example, and the percentage increases with age, whereas it decreases for men. Siddell comments that this pattern between the sexes reflects a general trend for many chronic illnesses (Siddell, 1995). While it is the case that long-standing illnesses do not necessarily imply disability or immobility, they can lead to degrees of incapacity. Older women are also more likely to suffer fractures. This is due both to osteoporosis and to their higher incidence of falling, linked, it is suggested, to such things as hypothermia, drugs which induce dizziness and overprescribing of tranquillisers (Siddell, 1993). Thus, although the vast majority of people in later life are able to do such tasks as care for themselves, shop and move around outside the home, women are more likely to be incapacitated than men. Those over 65 years are more than twice as likely as men to report impaired mobility, with the very elderly being severely affected. Given the increased possibility that such women will be living on their own, one consequence is that they are likely to require enhanced informal and statutory care.

Another factor which can exacerbate or minimise the financial and physical effects of advancing years is housing. Contrary to some of the stereotypes, only about 5 per cent of those over 65 years live in residential or nursing homes, with the majority of these being in the 75 + year group and, therefore, women. This means, however, that most of the remaining 95 per cent fend for themselves. Approximately 90 per cent of these live in either owner-occupied or publicly or privately rented accommodation. The remaining 5 per cent live in some form of sheltered housing (Tinker, 1996). The tenure patterns of the older population are usually the result of housing choices made in the past when the housing market was rather different to how it is today. The private rented sector, in particular, was more important and, currently, older people are more likely to be in rented accommodation generally and less likely to be home owners when compared to the rest of the population (Victor, 1994). However, low income lies at the root of older people's concerns about housing and this is particularly problematic for women. As Arber and Ginn remark, 'balancing a fear of high heating bills against the discomfort of cold and damp is a dilemma common to tenants and owners' (1991, p. 103).

There are also other difficulties. Widows may experience the dilemma of living in the 'family home', which may contain memories of children and spouses, and the awareness that the building is now too big for one person and both costly and difficult to run and maintain. If home owners, they may find themselves to be 'equity rich' but 'income poor'. This refers to their inability to realise the capital contained in the bricks and mortar of their home, without selling it, and the subsequent reliance of many on the state pension for a weekly income. The presence of steps and stairs in a house may also present an obstacle to independent living. Yet, the policies of the Conservative government in Britain, particularly in the 1980s, in encouraging home ownership have severely restricted the ability of local authorities to build new public housing of any kind. This has especially affected the supply of sheltered housing, which is attractive to many older women because it may offer a degree of social and physical support, safety and security. Instead, the private sector is increasingly taking over provision of retirement apartments and sheltered housing for sale. While this may be attractive to affluent couples, it is often beyond the means of most elderly women.

The financial, health and housing difficulties experienced by women in later life also relate to other aspects of their material circumstances. The first is to do with transport (Tinker, 1996). Older women are less likely to own or to drive a car than older men and are, therefore, more reliant on public transport. However, as state subsidies for public transport have been cut, so the services provided have become less user-friendly, from the point of view of older women. For instance, bus timetables have been reduced and the elimination of bus conductors, train guards and station personnel on many services decreases the perceived efficiency and safety of what is being provided. Yet, many older women depend on public transport for maintaining social networks and for activities such as shopping. This is particularly so if they live on remote housing estates or in areas far removed from out-of-town shopping complexes. Reliance on local retailers often makes purchases much more costly. Even when public transport is more readily available, older people may be discouraged from making use of the facility. Problems of climbing into buses and trains, having to stand in crushed and crowded conditions, and automatically closing doors, which may catch clothes or even limbs, all add to the hazards of travelling. In this context it is interesting to note that Help the Aged is publishing its own White Paper on transport, since the official government document failed to take sufficient account of older people.

Transport difficulties, however, are only one aspect of the more general mobility problems that older women may experience. Independent living is not necessarily easy if there are steps and stairs to countenance at home or a kitchen which is not designed compactly and for efficient use. Access to the local community can also be restricted by buildings which lack ramps or lifts, congested roads and pavements and poor provision of activities which are likely to attract older people and encourage them into social and collective environments. All these things are particularly significant for older women, when so many live on their own. Thus, potential isolation, and possible loneliness, compound the other material disadvantages with which they are faced.

## LIVING THROUGH AGEING

The previous section has identified some of the disadvantages associated with later life and the differences which exist between men and women. However, although a lot of the research and literature concentrates on these negative aspects, more work is beginning to emerge which looks at the process of ageing in a more positive way, focusing more on what older people have to contribute than the extent to which they are a possible drain on resources. While not denying the difficulties which exist for some, this shows that the later years can be both rewarding and enjoyable. Ageing should not be seen as some kind of a condition which requires inevitable treatment by doctors, social workers and other professionals or as some final stage with which an individual has to cope. Rather, women and men live *through* ageing. This involves the possible opening up of new experiences, with the connotation that later life is not some kind of end-state but a time when old pleasures can be enjoyed as well as new ones created. This can be particularly positive for women. As one respondent to research on widowhood exclaimed, as a result of reflecting on life since the death of her husband and the new pursuits followed, so that rather than simply having survived bereavement 'I've surprised myself, I suppose....'[2] While bereavement necessarily involves grief and feelings of loss, widowhood can lead can lead to new freedoms and opportunities, with new roles sometimes becoming available.

Indeed there is considerable evidence attesting to the energy, activities and widespread interests of older people. The latter have a potential for inclusion as active citizens which tends to be under-recognised and under-used. For instance the report, *Getting Around After 60: A Profile of Britain's Older Population,* presents a statistical picture of later life as a time, for some, of increased freedom to travel and involvement in leisure and other pursuits, although the image of 'older people as jet-setting hedonists, pursuing pleasure around the globe is...only applicable to a minority' (Jarvis, Hancock, Askham and Tinker, 1996 p. 20). However, as the report points out, the opposite picture of older people as too poor to have leisure activities is also misleading. Despite the difficulties of defining leisure in this context (one person's form of enjoyment may be another's *bête noir*), it is clear that not all such pursuits need be costly. While participation in both indoor and outdoor pastimes does decline with age (notable exceptions being gardening and bowling), some activities remain at a fairly constant level (Bernard and Meade, 1993b). For older women these are predominantly home-based and domestic, involving watching television, visiting and entertaining friends, reading, needlework and knitting.

Another activity with which older women are involved is voluntary work, although this applies more to those from the middle classes. This may include fundraising, work in charity shops, visiting those in hospital or residential homes and offering practical help in the home. An often neglected aspect of voluntary work is the contribution made to supporting other family members, especially looking after grandchildren and doing relatively simple caring tasks for neighbours (Jarvis et al., 1996). Older women are also proficient in arranging their own leisure activities, with around 30 per cent of them joining clubs. However, only 13 per cent seem to go to those which cater only for older people and these, generally, seem more attractive to those from the working class (Bernard and Meade, 1993b; Scott and Wenger, 1995). Older women, and particularly those from black and minority ethnic groups, are also involved in religious-based activities.

A significant factor in older women's ability to live through ageing is the existence of social and support networks (Jerrome, 1993a and b). Evidence suggests that they have, on average, more friends than men and that the quality of their relationships also differs. While women's female friends are often close confidantes, men tend to rely on their wives to fulfil this function (Scott and Wenger, 1995). Whereas men's work-based friendships may be broken or weakened on retirement, women are more likely to replace lost friendships and to continue to make new friends throughout the life course. As a result, it has been suggested that older women may have a psychological, emotional and social advantage over their male counterparts (Jerrome, 1993b; Scott and Wenger, 1995). Arber and Ginn claim, for example, that,

> although elderly women's opportunities for making and maintaining friendships are constrained by lack of material and health resources relative to elderly men's, their relationship skills acquired in early life are an asset. They are less likely than their husbands to have placed all their emotional 'eggs in one basket' and seem more adaptable to changed circumstances. (1991, p. 169)

Jerrome notes that friendships can help to alleviate the effects of older women's disadvantages in material and health resources (1993a and b). Often embedded in a network of women friends with shared interests, such friendships provide a basis for a variety of joint activities, from shopping and local outings to travel and holidays. This is highly important in a society which values feminine youth and heterosexual coupledom, often making social life difficult for older women who are on their own. As Sontag pointed out in her provocative article two decades ago, there is a social 'double standard' in respect of ageing, whereby men's attractiveness may be deemed to increase with age, particularly in relation to money and power (1978). Older women are rarely regarded as physically attractive or sexually desirable and are, thereby, socially devalued, constructed as inferior and made to feel invisible. Strong and positive friendship groups provide a way of fighting back and a means through which they can re-enter social and community life.

The ability to live independent lives, however, which is what the majority of older women seek, is significantly related to material, social and emotional well-being. In fact, because they are so influential on the other two, material factors are particularly important. Yet, as has already been seen, older women are disadvantaged in ways which are likely to affect independent living. Lack of money, for instance, leads to low standards of living and may make it impossible for them to pay for aids and housing adaptations, thereby forcing them into greater dependence on informal carers or the state. Poor or inappropriate housing accommodation is a further drain on scant resources. The ability to get around may be impaired by inadequate public transport and a reduction in state support services for those with a disability or who are in poor health. All of these things are important in their own right, but they also have repercussions for the extent to which an individual can retain independency or becomes dependent on care-givers. They, therefore, have an impact on older women's self-perceptions, their feelings of dependence/independence and their views about their own autonomy and self-esteem.

The social policy agenda for older women, therefore, needs to address their material needs as a matter of urgency. As a priority, older women require a sufficient level of income, provided by the basic state pension, in order to raise their standard of living above the poverty threshold and to enable them to live with dignity (Castle and Townsend, 1996). They need safe, affordable and appropriate housing (in such forms as sheltered accommodation and schemes of equity release), along with safe, cheap and reliable public or community transport schemes. Another requirement is for equal treatment in health care in order to counter the cycle of disadvantage whereby ageism in professional attitudes limits access to services and reinforces older women's low expectations concerning their health and well-being (Bernard, Meade and Tinker, 1993). Local authority concessionary and subsidised services, such as bus passes, home helps and reduced fees for adult education classes or leisure facilities, can also have an impact on what older women can afford to buy and what they are able to do. While measures such as these will involve costs, failure to act is likely to incur even higher expenditure. When older women are unable to live independent lives, the support they need is at an even greater cost to the public purse and to the community. A more useful strategy is to consider the range of services and opportunities that might enable them to live enhanced lives. This necessitates consulting older women themselves about how to improve what is currently available and what is required to respond to new needs. As Bernard, Meade and Tinker indicate, '[o]lder women know what it is like to be old, but contemporary society does not make it easy for their voices to be heard...[This requires]... acknowledging the rights of older women to a quality of life based on autonomy, security and fulfilment' (1993, p. 190).


CONCLUSION

Despite their growing numbers, older women remain largely invisible or on the margins of most research and policy-making. Further, when their lives are given consideration, lack of knowledge and information can lead to the differences and diversities among them being ignored. For instance, little is known about the lives of older women of Afro-Caribbean or Asian origin or those from other ethnic minority groups. Much of the literature focuses only on the experiences of white women, a tendency which has, regrettably, had to be reproduced in this chapter. There is also little work on older women's sexuality, it being implicitly assumed that they are mostly heterosexual. A concern for older women is also beset with other difficulties. There is a need, for example, to counter ageist and sexist images that older women are 'past it' and an economic burden on society. In fact, many of them are 'skilful survivors' (Bernard, Meade and Tinker, 1993, p. 167). They manage to pursue active and satisfying lives, despite considerable constraints and opposition and require social policies which will support and enhance their ability to do so. More needs to be made of the positive aspects of later life. For instance, local programmes marshalling their skills and abilities to contribute to community life would be attractive, since they combine use of expertise with the provision of support, for those who need it. However, although the very negative stereotyping of older women should be resisted, it is also necessary to acknowledge the very real material disadvantages which they often face and which can impede fulfilment. These disadvantages are best understood by adopting a life course perspective. This situates their contemporary position and status within the context of the sexual division of labour and its influence on their previous domestic and workplace roles and activities. In other words, older women's situation today is partly a reflection of their experiences and treatment in the past, as well as a result of current policies. Thus, in addition to taking account of later life, attention also needs to be paid to the employment patterns and family/household duties of younger women today. This is essential if they are not to be put in a similarly disadvantaged position when they too reach later life.

## NOTES

1. The 'intergenerational contract' involves the working generation paying for the welfare of the older generation on the assumption that the same will be done for them when they reach later life (Walker, 1996). Hills argues that alarm about support ratios tend to ignore changes in school-age populations and taxes paid by older people. Arguing that, even at current levels of spending, expenditure on welfare would increase by only 0.32 per cent per year for the next 50 years, he suggests that such a figure is 'suprisingly undramatic' and that pressures from an ageing population need to be 'kept in perspective' (Hills, 1997 p. 12).
2. Unpublished research by L. Hicks and M. Maynard, Dependence, Interdependence and Autonomy among Recently Bereaved Elderly Widows, University of York, 1994.

## REFERENCES

Allan, G. (1996) *Kinship and Friendship in Modern Britain*, Oxford: Oxford University Press.

Arber, S. and Evandrou, M. (eds) (1993a) *Ageing, Independence and the Life Course*, London: Jessica Kingsley Publishers.

Arber, S. and Evandrou, M. (1993b) 'Mapping the Territory. Ageing, Independence and the Life Course', in S. Arber and M. Evandrou (eds) *Ageing, Independence and the Life Course*, London: Jessica Kingsley Publications.

Arber, S. and Ginn, J. (1991) *Gender and Later Life*, London: Sage.

Baltes, M. (1996) *The Many Faces of Dependency in Old Age*, Cambridge: Cambridge University Press.

Bernard, M. and Meade, K. (eds) (1993a) *Women Come of Age*, London: Edward Arnold.

Bernard, M. and Meade, K. (1993b) 'A Third Age Lifestyle for Older Women?' in M. Bernard and K. Meade (eds) *Women Come of Age*, London: Edward Arnold.

Bernard, M., Meade, K. and Tinker, A. (1993) 'Women Come of Age', in M. Bernard and K. Meade (eds) *Women Come of Age*, London: Edward Arnold.

Castle, B. and Townsend, P. (1996) *We CAN Afford the Welfare State*, London: Security in Retirement for Everyone.

Central Statistical Office (1995) *Social Trends 25*, London: HMSO.

Central Statistical Office (1996) *Social Trends 26*, London: HMSO.

Disney, R. (1997) *Can We Afford to Grow Older?*, London: MIT Press.

Finch, J. and Mason, J. (1993) *Negotiating Family Responsibilities*, London: Routledge.

Groves, D. (1993) 'Work, Poverty and Older Women', in M. Bernard and K. Meade (eds) *Women Come of Age*. London: Edward Arnold.

Hills, J. (1997) *The Future of Welfare. A Guide to the Debate*, York: Joseph Rowntree Foundation.

Jarvis, C., Hancock, R., Askham, J. and Tinker, A. (1996) *Getting Around After 60: A Profile of Britain's Older Population*, London: HMSO.

Jerrome, D. (1993a) *Good Company*, Edinburgh: Edinburgh University Press.

Jerrome, D. (1993b) 'Intimacy and Sexuality among Older Women', In M. Bernard and K. Meade (eds) *Women Come of Age*, London: Edward Arnold.

Robertson Elliot, F. (1996) *Gender, Family and Society*, London: Macmillan.

Scott, A. and Wenger, C. (1995) 'Gender and Social Support Networks in Later Life', in S. Arber and J. Ginn (eds) *Connecting Gender and Ageing*, Buckingham: Open University Press.

Siddell, M. (1993) 'Enhancing the Health of Older Women', in M. Bernard and K. Meade (eds) *Women Come of Age*, London: Edward Arnold.

Siddell, M. (1995) *Health in Old Age*, Buckingham: Open University Press.

Sontag, S. (1978) 'The Double Standard of Ageing', in V. Carver and P. Liddiard (eds) *An Ageing Population*, London: Hodder and Stoughton.

Tinker, A. (1996) *Older People in Modern Society*, London: Longman.

Victor, C. (1994) *Old Age in Modern Society*, London: Chapman Hall.

Vincent, J. (1995) *Inequality and Old Age*, London: UCL Press.

Walker, A. (ed) (1996) *The New Generational Contract*, London: UCL Press.

# 6 Women's Pension Poverty: Prospects and Options for Change

Jay Ginn and Sara Arber

Pensions policy is of particular relevance to women. Women can expect to live five years longer than men, but generally on a much lower income. Older women are over twice as likely as men to live in poverty. Yet policy-makers over the past 20 years have neither addressed the concentration of poverty among older women nor taken seriously the gender impact of their pension reforms, now and in the future.

The immediate cause of women's pension disadvantage in later life lies in their lower earnings and more complex employment patterns, both of which reflect their family roles. However, comparison with other countries shows that the degree of women's pension poverty also depends on the structure of the pension system (Ginn and Arber, 1992; Walker and Maltby, 1997). Thus the concentration of poverty among older women is not inevitable; it results from political choices.

This chapter examines gender inequalities in pension income and in working age individuals' pension arrangements in Britain, noting how women's family roles constrain their ability to build private pension entitlements. We assess trends over time and show how the increasing role of private pension provision has exacerbated women's pension disadvantage. The chapter is organised in four parts. First, we review the extent of British women's pension disadvantage and how this has changed between the mid-1980s and the mid-1990s. Second, we examine how the pension arrangements of current employees have changed over the same period. Third, we consider whether younger women are likely to obtain a relatively higher pension income in later life than today's older women. Finally, we suggest how the adverse impact of women's family roles on their pension income could be minimised, drawing on the experience of other EU countries.

Divorce, cohabitation and widowhood mean that women cannot rely on a husband's financial support throughout life; in fact the majority of older women manage alone financially. Although married women may share their husband's income in later life, economic dependence on an individual man places women's citizenship in question (Lister, 1997) and usually means a lesser share in household resources and decision-making (Brannen and

75

Wilson, 1987; Pahl, 1990). In view of the importance to women of an adequate income of their own, we focus on pension income to which older women have independent access, including their own pensions and any widow's pension.

## GENDER INEQUALITY OF INCOME IN LATER LIFE

Older women's personal income is less than two-thirds of older men's on average. For example, in 1993–4, the median personal income of women aged over 65 was £68 per week, compared with men's £110. Yet older women's income disadvantage is often obscured by the way official statistics are produced and then reported in the media (Ginn, 1993; 1999). Statistics obtained by allocating half the joint income of a married couple to each partner and by reporting the proportion of couples and non-married individuals receiving occupational pensions render married women's low personal incomes invisible. By incorporating an assumption of equal sharing between married partners, such statistics conceal the magnitude of gender inequality of income in later life.

The key indicators of trends in pensioner incomes also need to be examined, as they have been influential in pensions policy-making. The rise in pensioners' real incomes, which have doubled in real terms over the last 50 years (Johnson et al., 1996), is often cited; yet over the same period GDP increased threefold (ONS, 1997). Reporting a rise in the average income of all pensioners disguises the persistence of poverty among older people; in the 1980s, 55 per cent of pensioners lived on the margins of poverty (having less than 140 per cent of Income Support level), compared with 20 per cent of people under pension age (Johnson and Webb, 1990). Quoting the mean income rather than the median gives undue weight to the minority of pensioners with very high incomes, giving no idea of the spread of incomes, nor of widening inequality over time; it also ignores the way in which inequality is structured according to gender, class, age and marital status.

Thus gender-blind and partial statistics have been the source of media stories of rising pensioner affluence, providing spurious justification for cuts in state pensions. The divergent policy implications of different ways of reporting data on pensioners' incomes highlights the political nature of statistics (Ginn and Dugard, 1993; Ginn, 1999).

In order to obtain a more adequate view of gender differences in pensioner incomes in Britain, the distribution of personal income is analysed; this is income to which an individual has direct, independent access, including their own state or private pension and any survivor's pension. We draw on our analysis of data from the General Household Surveys (1985–6 and

1993–4) to examine changes in gender inequality of personal income among those aged over 65 (Ginn and Arber, forthcoming a).

The main sources of older people's income are the state, earnings, interest on savings and private (occupational and personal) pensions. Income from the state includes National Insurance (NI) basic and earnings related pensions, a range of needs-related benefits and Income Support (IS). Among those aged over 65, women comprise three-quarters of those receiving IS. In addition, many married women have a personal income below IS level yet are ineligible for IS due to the amount of their husband's income. Whereas older women rely heavily on the state basic pension, men are more likely to receive income from private pensions; this is a major source of gender inequality of income in later life (Groves, 1987; Ginn and Arber, 1991).

Figure 6.1 shows the gender difference in the percentage receiving income from a private (occupational or personal) pension, including survivors' pensions, in 1985–6 and 1993–4, according to marital status. Older women who were single were most likely to have a private pension, married women the least, reflecting their earlier roles in the domestic economy. Divorced or separated women were less likely than widows to have any private pension income; only 30 per cent did so in 1993–4.

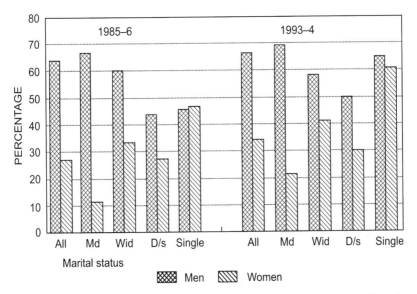

*Figure 6.1*  Percentage of men and women with a private pension, age 65+, by marital status, 1985–6 and 1993–4

*Source*:   General Household Surveys 1985–6 and 1993–4 (authors' analysis).

The gender difference in pension receipt had narrowed over the eight-year period, although the pension disadvantage of married women, relative to men and to other women, remained substantial. The proportion of older women with a private pension increased from 27 to 35 per cent, while that of men was more stable, increasing only slightly from 64 to 67 per cent.

It is important to consider not only the receipt of private pensions but also the amount; small amounts may bring little or no financial gain due to the pensions poverty trap (Walker et al., 1989), in which a small private pension merely disqualifies the recipient from entitlement to means-tested Income Support and associated benefits.

Figure 6.2(a) shows the distribution of weekly income in 1993–4 from state benefits for all older men and women as a series of box and whisker plots. State benefits show a relatively compressed distribution, especially for men.

The second pair of boxplots (Figure 6.2b) shows the distribution of income from private pensions, for those with this source of income. Gender inequality in the amount of income from private pensions was substantial and the dispersion of incomes very wide, especially among men. The impact of private pensions is reflected in Figure 6.2c, which shows the distribution of total personal income.

Gender inequality of incomes had increased between 1985–6 and 1993–4. Older women's median total income as a proportion of men's had fallen from 77 to 62 per cent, largely due to increasingly unequal income from private pensions. Among those with a private pension, women's median income from this source had fallen from 65 to 56 per cent of men's (Ginn and Arber, forthcoming a).

Women's lower income in later life is compounded by gender differences in marital status and living arrangements. Because of women's greater longevity and the propensity of men to marry women younger than themselves, about half (48 per cent) of older women in 1993–4 were widows, whereas only 18 per cent of men were widowed and 72 per cent married. Older women are thus more likely than older men to live alone, with all the diseconomies entailed in solo living (Arber and Ginn, 1991).

Older ever-married women's income from private pensions was much lower than single women's. Among those with a pension, the median weekly amount for married or widowed women was less than £25 and for divorced and separated women £26, well below that of single women, £54, or all men, £46 (see Table 6.1).

The median private pension income received by ever-married older women was comparable with the amount by which the basic state pension has declined in value since 1980, when the pension was decoupled from average earnings. Thus about half of ever-married women have gained no more from their private pension contributions than they have lost through the cut in the basic pension.

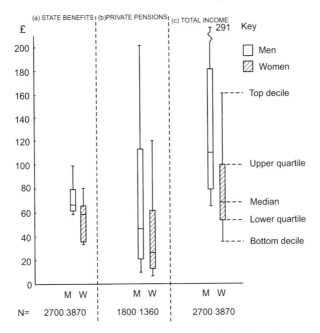

*Figure 6.2* Distribution of personal income from state benefits, private pensions and total, in £ per week, men and women aged 65 +, 1993–4
*Source*: General Household Surveys 1993–4 (authors' analysis).

The way that older women's earlier family roles influence their pension income through limiting their employment participation is illustrated by research using data on employment histories in the Retirement and Retirement Plans Survey 1988 (Ginn and Arber, 1996). Among women aged 55–69,

*Table 6.1* Percentage with a private pension and average amounts (£/wk) for those with a pension, men and women aged 65 +, by marital status of women, 1993–4

|  | % with private pension | | Average amount, for those with pension | | |
|  | % | N | Median | Mean | N |
|---|---|---|---|---|---|
| All | 48 | 6578 | 36.0 | 68.6 | 3160 |
| Men | 67 | 2704 | 46.2 | 84.2 | 1800 |
| Women | 35 | 3874 | 26.0 | 47.9 | 1360 |
| Women: |  |  |  |  |  |
| Married | 22 | 1552 | 23.1 | 40.1 | 338 |
| Widowed | 42 | 1864 | 24.7 | 45.8 | 790 |
| Div/sep | 30 | 149 | 26.4 | 42.2 | 44 |
| Single | 61 | 309 | 53.5 | 71.8 | 188 |

*Source*: General Household Surveys, 1993 and 1994 (authors' analysis).

four-fifths of single women had 'continuous' employment (with at least 30 years employed from age 20 to 55), compared with only 14 per cent of married women, 15 per cent of widowed and 18 per cent of divorced or separated. Women's pension entitlements were closely related to their employment history, especially whether their employment had been mainly full time. Only the tiny minority (7 per cent) of women aged 60 to 69 whose employment pattern approximated to men's (continuous, with at least 90 per cent worked full-time), had a median private pension income comparable to that of men aged 65 to 69. But these were elite women in terms of their educational level and occupational class; significantly, 58 per cent were single. Thus building a good private pension tends to conflict with the domestic roles expected of women in marriage.

The recent trend in which the gender gap in private pension receipt had narrowed but gender inequality of incomes had widened reflects a shift in the balance of state and private pensions. Over the eight-year period between the mid-1980s and mid-1990s, the contribution of private pensions to total income had increased from 17 to 25 per cent for men but only from 7 to 11 per cent for women (Ginn and Arber, forthcoming a). Whereas older men's rising income reflects the maturation of occupational pensions, with younger cohorts retiring on higher pensions, older women have been less able to compensate in this way for the decline in the basic pension.

In the next section, we assess the separate effects of marriage and children on working age women's opportunities to contribute to private pensions and examine trends in pension arrangements following the pension reforms of the 1980s.

## WORKING-AGE WOMEN'S FAMILY ROLES AND MEMBERSHIP OF PRIVATE PENSION SCHEMES

In spite of formal sex equality, the gender division of family labour persists, with women still undertaking the bulk of unpaid domestic and caring work (Henwood et al., 1987; Arber, 1993; Brannen et al, 1994; Murgatroyd and Neuburger, 1997). The disruptive effect of domestic and other caring responsibilities on women's employment histories, combined with gender discrimination in employment, lead to women having different kinds of jobs, lower pay and shorter hours (Joshi, 1984; 1991). Women's earnings remain well below men's, both generally and within families (Arber and Ginn, 1995a; Davies and Joshi, 1998), even for women employed full-time.

Having current responsibility for children constrains women's opportunities in the labour market and hence their chance of belonging to an occupational pension scheme (Ginn and Arber, 1993; 1994; Glover and Arber, 1995). Less obvious is the long-lasting effect of childcare responsibilities on women's employment, bringing irreversible handicaps even after the children have left home, due to occupational downgrading and part-time work after a career break (Dex, 1987). Mid-life women (aged 40–59) who had ever had a child and those with children of any age still living at home were less likely to be employed full-time. Half of childless women were employed full-time, a third of those whose children had all left home, 30 per cent of those with only children over 16 at home, and a quarter of those with any children under 16 at home. The proportions of women employed part-time were in the reverse order; nearly half of those with children under 16 worked part time while only a fifth of childless women did so (Ginn and Arber, 1994).

Among women employees, the effect of child-rearing on pension scheme membership is greater than that of marriage. Women employees aged 20–59 who had never had a child had odds five times greater of belonging to a pension scheme than women who had had any children, after controlling for marital status (Ginn and Arber, 1993). Among mid-life women who were employees, the impact of parental status on occupational pension scheme membership was evident even among those working full-time; 75 per cent of those who were childless belonged to a scheme, compared with much lower proportions among women who had ever had children (see Table 6.2). Membership of an occupational scheme was very low among all women employed part-time. Occupational pension schemes have been less available to those working part-time, those with short employment duration or those working for small private sector employers, all of these being more characteristic of female than male employment (Ginn and Arber, 1993).

These results show that the impact of having children on women's ability to accumulate a private pension is not confined to the period when children live at home, but extends throughout their working life. The earnings cost of

*Table 6.2* Percentage of women aged 40–59 belonging to an occupational pernsion scheme, by hours of work and fertility and parental status

| Fertility and Parental Status | Percentage among women employed full-time | Percentage among women employed part-time | Percentage among all employed women | Percentage among all women aged 40–59 |
|---|---|---|---|---|
| No child ever born | 75 (479) | 26 (192) | 61 (671) | 42 (980) |
| No children now, left home | 59 (887) | 21 (795) | 41 (1682) | 26 (2661) |
| Adult children only | 52 (873) | 16 (1151) | 31 (2024) | 22 (2887) |
| Adult chld and chld < 16 | 44 (250) | 13 (490) | 23 (740) | 16 (1040) |
| Children < 16 only | 55 (295) | 17 (593) | 29 (888) | 20 (1306) |
| All women | 57 (2784) | 17 (3221) | 36 (6005) | 24 (8874) |

Base numbers are shown in brackets.
*Source*: General Household Survey, 1988–90 (authors' analysis).

motherhood for 'Mrs Typical' in Britain has been estimated as £230,000 (in 1994 prices) over her lifetime; she will receive only 45 per cent of her childless sister's lifetime earnings (Joshi, 1996). In addition to bearing the greater share of responsibility for children, women are more likely than men to provide care for elderly frail parents/in-law, with adverse effects on their employment in mid-life (Arber and Ginn, 1995b).

The 1986 Social Security Act widened the range of pension alternatives for employees by making Appropriate Personal Pensions (APPs) available from 1988 for those who wished to opt out of their employer's pension scheme or out of the State Earnings Related Pension Scheme (SERPS). For the self-employed, individual pension policies were already available.

In Table 6.3 the proportions of men and women aged 20–59 contributing to private (occupational or personal) pensions are shown for 1993–4 (Ginn and Arber, forthcoming b). Two-fifths of men and a quarter of women belonged to an occupational pension, while 13 per cent of men and 9 per cent of women contributed to a personal pension (APP). The overall proportion of adults currently making private pension contributions was 64 per cent for men and 38 per cent for women. Thus working age women's private pension coverage still lags far behind men's.

*Table 6.3*  Proportion of men and women aged 20–59 contributing to private (occupational or personal) pensions in 1993–4, by employment status

|  | Men | Women |
|---|---|---|
| *Employees:* |  |  |
| Occupational pension member | 40 | 25 |
| Personal pension* contributor | 13 | 9 |
| No occupational or personal pension | 12 | 27 |
| *Self-employed:* |  |  |
| Personal pension | 9 | 2 |
| No personal pension | 6 | 3 |
| *Not employed:* |  |  |
| Personal pension | 2 | 2 |
| No personal pension | 18 | 32 |
| Column % | 100 | 100 |
| Total contributing to private pension | 64 | 38 |
| Total not contributing to private pension | 36 | 62 |
| Column % | 100 | 100 |
| N = | 11,756 | 12,313 |

* an Appropriate Personal Pension, used to contract out of SERPS, available from 1988 for employees only.
*Source*: General Household Surveys, 1993 and 1994 (authors' analysis).

Among employees, women's occupational pension scheme membership was 42 per cent in 1993–4 but whereas 56 per cent of women full-timers belonged to a scheme, only 23 per cent of part-timers did so. Personal pension plans were held by 16 per cent of women full-timers but only 11 per cent of part-timers. Thus two-thirds of women employed part-time had no private pension coverage in 1993–4.

Many employees with a personal pension had lower contributions into their plan than would have been the case in a typical occupational pension. For 38 per cent of men and 44 per cent of women with personal pensions, contributions were the minimum required to contract out of SERPS, while similar proportions paid extra themselves but had no extra contribution from their employer. Only a fifth of men and 11 per cent of women with personal pension plans had extra contributions paid in by their employer, in contrast to occupational pension schemes, where this is the norm.

Private pension coverage among both men and women has increased since the 1980s, but a substantial gender gap remains. Nor will increased coverage necessarily reduce the concentration of poverty among older women in the future, as we discuss in the next section.

## PROSPECTS FOR YOUNGER WOMEN'S FUTURE PENSION INCOME

The increase in women's employment participation and the effects of sex equality legislation seem to indicate that gender inequality in later life income will largely disappear. However, there are reasons to doubt this, arising from both trends in women's employment and from the changing structure of the British pension system.

Women's economic activity rate has increased steeply since 1970; among those aged 16 and over, it increased from 44 per cent to 53 per cent between 1971 and 1992 (CSO, 1992; 1994, Table 4.5). However, it is crucial to note that the postwar increase in women's employment has been almost entirely due to a rise in part-time employment, mainly of married women (Joshi, 1989; Hakim, 1993). A fifth of employed women work fewer than 8 hours per week, most earning wages too low to allow contributions to either state pensions or non-state pensions. The proportion of employed women working full-time rose slightly between 1984 and 1990, from 55 to 57 per cent, but had declined to 54 per cent by 1994 (calculated from Department of Employment, 1995, Table 7.4).

It is hard to predict future employment patterns of women, in terms of continuity and timing of employed years, yet employment patterns of those currently around pension age show no evidence of a trend towards women conforming to the traditional male pattern of full-time continuous employment. Our research on men and women aged 55 to 69 compared the employment patterns of three 5-year age cohorts; although the youngest group of women (aged 55–59) were more likely than older women (aged 59–69) to return to employment for a substantial period after a career break, there was no difference among the three age groups in the proportion with continuous employment (at least 30 years employed from age 20 to 55) (Ginn and Arber, 1996).

For the majority of working-age British women, the lack of good quality childcare, the cost of childcare, the pressure of domestic work, difficulty in regaining a permanent full-time job after a career break and the recurrence of family caring responsibilities in mid-life are all likely to result in the persistence of fragmented employment, with periods of part-time low-paid work. There are signs of a polarisation among women, with highly qualified, mainly professional women taking shorter career breaks for childbearing; however, these are an elite minority, perhaps analogous to the small group of well-off, single, childless women among the current older population.

The effect of career breaks, part-time employment and low pay can be minimised in state pensions. Women's opportunity to build independent state pensions was significantly improved by the Labour government's Social Security Act of 1975. Home Responsibilities Protection (HRP), which allows up to 20 years of caring for children and others to be ignored in determining entitlement to the basic pension, will allow more women to receive a full basic pension in their own right. The original SERPS, because it was based on the best 20 years' earnings, also minimised the adverse effect of family caring on the amount of pension earned. Married women could expect to receive all their husband's SERPS pension if widowed.

This major advance for women was reversed by cuts in British state pensions and the expansion of private pensions since 1980 under a Conservative government. These reforms, as well as the maturation of occupational pension schemes, contributed to increased inequality of pensioner incomes (Hancock and Weir 1994; Johnson et al., 1996) and will affect working-age women even more harshly.

Indexing the basic state pension to prices instead of national average earnings has eroded its value since 1980 from 20 per cent of average male earnings to 14 per cent by 1993 (Commission on Social Justice, 1994) and the decline in relative value is projected to continue. Since older women are more heavily dependent on the state pension than older men, its erosion has a greater impact on them. The 1986 cuts in SERPS, in which the basis of calculation of benefits was changed from the best 20 years earnings to average earnings over the whole working life, and the accrual rate of SERPS for those retiring in the next century was reduced, also disproportionately affected women. Moreover, the SERPS widows' pension will be cut to half from the year 2000.

Obtaining a full state basic pension and a good SERPS pension will be even harder for women born after 1950. For them, raising the state pension age will further reduce the amount of both basic and SERPS pensions by lengthening the required contribution period (Hutton et al., 1995; Ginn and Arber, 1995). This reform has already influenced managers of most occupational pension schemes to equalise the normal pensionable age at 65 rather than 60, worsening women members' benefits. Although raising the pension age for women may appear to promote gender equality, it will only benefit women in the unlikely event that they are able to obtain full-time employment from age 60 to 65.

The cuts in state pensions were accompanied by financial incentives to switch from SERPS to personal pensions, which are likely to provide poorer value than SERPS for most women and for the low-paid (Davies and Ward 1992; Waine 1995). Although portable between jobs, personal pensions' charging structure penalises the low-paid and those with breaks in employment, reducing the pension by up to 30 per cent (Ward, 1996). Personal pensions generally lack an employer's contribution and there is no guarantee of the level of pension at retirement, since this depends on the performance of the investments and the state of the annuity market at the time. The cost of an annuity at retirement is higher for women than men due to use of sex-based actuarial tables which take account of women's longer life expectancy. The failure of personal pensions to meet the needs of women, especially the lack of coverage of gaps in employment, means that, given the prevailing pattern of women's lives, personal pensions are less likely to provide an adequate second-tier pension than SERPS or an occupational pension (Davies and Ward, 1992).

The rationale for the introduction of personal pensions was to allow employees without access to an occupational pension an opportunity to build a better pension than provided by (a much reduced) SERPS. Among employees who were unable to join an occupational pension scheme, nearly a third were contributing to a personal pension plan in 1993–4, 48 per cent of men and 34 per cent of women (Ginn and Arber, forthcoming b). However, it has been estimated that anyone with annual earnings under £10,000 could receive a worse return from a personal pension than from remaining in SERPS (Waine, 1995), a condition far more likely for women than men. Even in 1998, experts were advising those earning less than £10,000 per annum not to opt out of SERPS into a personal pension because of the disproportionate loss in charges (Budden, 1998). Among those who lacked access to an occupational pension and who were contributing to a personal pension in 1993–4, nearly half were paid under £200 per week and therefore unlikely to receive a better return on their investment than from SERPS, with 70 per cent of the women in this position compared with 28 per cent of the men (Ginn and Arber, forthcoming b).

An occupational pension scheme is generally more advantageous than a personal pension because it involves a substantial employer contribution and promises a defined amount of pension. But occupational pensions are designed in such a way as to disadvantage early leavers and this is especially common among women taking career breaks (Ginn and Arber, 1991; 1993). As noted above, only a minority of women, those with continuous full-time employment, can expect an occupational pension comparable with the average received by men.

Those with a small additional pension may fall foul of the pensions poverty trap in later life, merely disqualifying themselves from Income Support and associated benefits (Walker et al., 1989). For example, a single pensioner in rented accommodation and receiving only a full basic pension would need additional income of £55 in order to be £6 per week better off (Collins, 1993). If the gap between the basic pension and the level of means-tested benefits increases in future, more older people, especially women, will be caught in this poverty trap.

The impact of divorce on women's pensions is emerging as an urgent issue (Joshi and Davies, 1991). Since it is the demands of childcare, more than being female or married, which handicap women in the labour market (Joshi, 1991), the rise in divorce and in motherhood among single or cohabiting women is likely to leave a growing proportion of older women in the future with neither an adequate pension income of their own, nor pension benefits derived from a husband. Although the Pensions Act 1995 allowed divorce courts to earmark part of an occupational or personal pension for the other spouse, until the pension scheme member decides to draw the pension, usually at age 65, the other spouse cannot receive their share. Pension splitting at divorce, which would transfer funds between spouses, is planned for the future. However, a drawback of both an earmarked pension or funds transferred at divorce is that the amount of pension is likely to reflect the years of marriage rather than the years in which a woman's employment and ability to accumulate pension entitlements is constrained by caring for the children of the marriage. Nor is there provision for sharing private pension entitlements between cohabiting partners who separate, even though the pension loss will be no less than for a divorced spouse.

In spite of this bleak outlook for British women's pensions, comparisons with other countries in the European Union show that the relative poverty experienced by older British women is largely avoidable. In the final section, policies which could minimise the impact of caring responsibilities on pension income are considered.

## ALTERNATIVE PENSION POLICIES

As shown in the preceding sections, women's family roles, by handicapping them in the labour market, reduce their ability to obtain private pension entitlements, so that they rely more heavily than men on state pensions. The Conservative government's policy of curbing state pensions has widened the gender gap in later life income, effectively penalising women's unpaid caring work. What could a Labour government do to ensure a fairer deal for women?

There are two main ways in which the links between family roles, employment participation and pension income could be broken. First, women's employment patterns are not freely chosen: lack of public childcare facilities in Britain means that motherhood has a far greater impact on women's employment in Britain than elsewhere in the EU (Joshi and Davies, 1992; Brannen et al., 1994). Improved access to childcare would enable women to minimise their career break, if they wished to do so, and would also remove the major constraint on younger women's full-time employment. Similarly, policies to ensure adequate statutory services for frail older people living in the community would free mid-life women from the need to reduce their hours of employment to provide informal care for relatives (Arber and Ginn, 1995b).

In the long term, a more equal contribution by men to domestic work and to caring for children and others would contribute to gender equality in the labour market and to women's ability to obtain private pensions. However, relieving women of their present unfair share of family caring work, while beneficial in itself, would not on its own be sufficient to end women's pension disadvantage; the gender gap in hourly pay would also have to be closed. Moreover, equal sharing of domestic work between men and women would not address the effects of class, ethnicity, chronic illness and long-term unemployment on lifetime earnings and hence on pension income.

A second approach, compatible with the first, would be to change the structure of the British pension system. The pension systems of two other EU countries – Germany and Denmark – illustrate alternative ways of ensuring that caring roles of women do not deprive them of pension entitlements (Ginn and Arber, 1992). In these countries, as in most of the EU, the state plays a much larger role than in Britain, allowing social policy objectives to be met.

## Germany

The German pension system has traditionally assumed women's dependence on a male breadwinner, providing for women mainly as wives or widows and reflecting a strong family orientation. Thus women's opportunity to obtain a good pension income through their own employment has been very limited. Nevertheless, in certain respects, German women are less disadvantaged than their British sisters.

The main component of the pension system is the state earnings-related pension scheme covering most employees. The contribution rate is 19 per cent of gross earnings, split equally between employer and employee, and the pension replaces a maximum of 70 per cent of previous net earnings, for a person on average wages and with 45 insured years (Clasen, 1997). Few married women have in the past been able to obtain an adequate pension of their own. Part-time employees are included in social insurance only if they both work over 15 hours per week and their earnings exceed a specified minimum, equivalent to £36 a week in 1994 (Marullo, 1995). Those who work part-time for many years are generally unable to acquire a pension of their own above the level of means-tested social assistance, even though this is a lower earnings threshold for social insurance than in Britain. However, fewer older women rely on means-tested benefits than in Britain; only 2.4 per cent of women over 65 claimed social assistance in 1992, mainly because of the relatively high level of the survivor's pension, which is 60 per cent of the deceased husband's pension (Clasen, 1997).

The private occupational pensions sector is selective in coverage, benefitting mainly well-paid salaried staff. Members of these non-contributory schemes can expect a pension replacing 60–70 per cent of final salary for a full career (Sedgwick Noble Lowndes, 1996). As in Britain, women have less access to these generous pensions, due to occupational segregation and to the exclusion of part-timers (Schmahl, 1991).

A recent reform to the social insurance scheme has recognised women's dual roles as workers and carers, and their need to build their own pension. From 1992, a parent taking a career break or switching to part-time work in order to care for a child is credited with social insurance contributions at the rate of 75 per cent of national average earnings, for up to three years per child (Ruland, 1991); time spent caring for other relatives is also credited (Clasen, 1997). Thus the pension effect of women's family caring roles is minimised. For divorcing couples, their entitlements to benefits from the social insurance scheme are split, improving women's chance of building an adequate pension at retirement.

To summarise, those with long periods out of employment or employed part-time receive a low pension income of their own in Germany but survivor benefits in the state pension scheme are higher than in Britain. The new social insurance credits will enable carers to take a career break or work part-time for several years with minimal loss of state pension entitlements.

### Denmark

The Danish pension system, in contrast, provides an income in later life which is only weakly related to employment or earnings. There are three main components of the system. The first, a flat rate Social Pension, is payable to all citizens with 40 years residence at age 67. Funded from general taxation, the pension is independent of employment record. The basic weekly amount, equivalent to £101 in 1996, is payable to each individual irrespective of marital status but the amount is reduced for those with earnings above a certain level. Non-married people received (in 1996) a supplement equivalent to £40 per week. Further supplements, £60 per week for non-married and £44 for each partner of a couple, are income-tested; the resulting guaranteed minimum weekly income in 1996 was £201 for a non-married person and £145 for each married person (Kvist, 1997).

The second element is a compulsory, funded, defined contribution scheme known as ATP, which provided a maximum pension equivalent to £33 in 1996 (Kvist, 1997). The pension amount depends on years employed and contributions paid: full entitlements are gained if weekly hours employed exceed 27, two-thirds for 18–26 hours and one third for 9–17 hours (ATP-huset, 1994). Two-thirds of the contribution is paid by the employer. The scheme covers all employees aged 16–66 working over 9 hours per week and from 1996 most social security claimants as well, the state paying two-thirds of the contributions for claimants (ATP-huset, 1994). This helps those with periods out of the labour market to maintain a full ATP contribution record. Although periods of part-time employment below 27 hours will reduce the pension, the banding of contributions ensures a more redistributive structure than in an earnings-related pension scheme.

The third element is private occupational and individual pension schemes. Until 1993, occupational schemes were confined mainly to salaried employees, comprising less than half the workforce, but coverage has expanded, mainly in the form of defined contribution schemes, with employers paying two-thirds of the contributions (Sedgwick Noble Lowndes, 1996). Due to their concentration in the public sector, a higher proportion of women than men belong to an occupational pension scheme, 71 per cent compared with 66 per cent in 1996, although women's part-time and interrupted employment is likely to lead to their pension amounts being lower than men's, as in Britain (Kvist, 1997). The growth of private pensions will magnify inequalities of class as well as gender among pensioners in the future.

The average disposable income of Danish pensioners, after housing costs, is 77 per cent of that of all adults (Platz and Petersen, 1993). Thus Danish pensioners receive a relatively high income, promoting social inclusion. In sum, the Danish state pension schemes are inclusive of women, ensuring that family caring does not prevent them receiving an adequate income (by British standards) in later life. The universal Social Pension has so far outweighed the effects of the private sector, resulting in a high degree of gender equality of pension income and the lowest pensioner poverty rate in the EU (Walker et al., 1993; Walker and Maltby, 1997).

## Britain

The Conservative government, in cutting state pensions and promoting the private sector of provision, argued that public spending was too high, placing an unacceptable burden on business and on the taxpayer. Such arguments, often backed by alarmist claims of an impending demographic crisis, became the new orthodoxy. For example, a World Bank report predicts 'a looming old age crisis that threatens not only the old but also their children and grandchildren, who must shoulder, directly or indirectly, much of the increasingly heavy burden of providing for the aged' (World Bank, 1994, p. iii). Writers claimed that, in an ageing society, private funded pensions would be fairer to the next generation (Johnson et al., 1989; Kotlikoff, 1992; Kotlikoff and Sachs, 1997). Others have pointed out that this is an illusion: a decline in the ratio of contributors to pensioners adversely affects the viability of funded pensions (in which contributions are invested and the accumulated fund used to pay pensions at retirement), as well as state Pay-As-You-Go (PAYG) pensions (in which contributions by employed people are used directly to pay pensions to the older population) (Mabbett, 1997; Toporowski, 1997). However, state PAYG pensions have more capacity than private funded pensions to adjust to population ageing in a socially equitable way.

Most welfare analysts agree that there is no ageing crisis facing Britain (Hills, 1993; Disney, 1997) and some argue that improved state pensions are affordable if resources are redistributed (Townsend and Walker, 1995). For example, tax reliefs and financial incentives for private pensions represent a poor use of public resources. They provide a substantial subsidy for the better-off, mainly men, one which escalated during the Conservative administration. Tax relief for private pensions grew from £1,200 million in 1979 to £8,200 million in 1991 (Wilkinson, 1993), while the total *net* cost to the NI fund of incentives to transfer from SERPS to personal pensions was estimated as £6,000 million (1988 prices) over the period from 1988–93 (National Audit Office, 1990) and has grown further since then. This public subsidy to private pensions – a process of 'reverse targeting' (Sinfield, 1993, p. 39) – siphons off resources which could have been used to maintain the value of state pensions for older people.

Compared with other OECD countries, 'the UK pension system is currently one of the "cheapest"', costing less than 7 per cent of GDP (Hutton et al., 1995, p.15). The low level of public spending on cash transfers for older people has resulted in British older people being less well-off (relative to average incomes for the whole population) than in 10 other major OECD countries (Whiteford and Kennedy, 1995).

The Labour Party, while in opposition, criticised the Conservatives' pension reforms. In the early 1990s, its *Policy Review for the 1990s* promised that a Labour government would reverse most of the cuts if elected in 1992. The basic pension would be immediately raised and indexed to earnings, while the State Earnings Related Pension (SERPS) would be restored, basing the pension on the best 20 years' earnings and allowing the self-employed to join. These improvements would be financed through removing the ceiling on employee NI contributions, a new 50 per cent tax band and restriction of tax relief on pension contributions to the basic rate (Blake, 1992). However, these commitments have since been withdrawn.

The Labour government elected in 1997 has instead proposed new private funded 'Stakeholder Pensions' (SPs). SPs have been presented as a suitable second-tier pension for the lower paid, especially women. However, SPs, as privately run funded money purchase schemes, share most of the drawbacks of personal pensions. Like personal pensions, they will place the investment risk on the contributor and charge administration fees. For those with no/ low pay for substantial periods, 'It is difficult to see how such a design can... meet the stated objectives' (Ward, 1998, p.16). Money purchase schemes perform best for those paying high contributions early in the working life, whereas this is the time when women's childrearing responsibilities limit their employment and reduce the pension contributions they can make. It has been estimated that for a person on a £12,300 salary, a break in employment of only four years from age 28 to 32 would reduce their pension fund at retirement by £80,000 (BBC, 1996). Pensions experts have questioned whether SPs have any advantages over the State Earnings Related Pension Scheme (SERPS), which has no problem in catering for those with frequent job moves, career breaks and part-time jobs (for example, Ward, 1998).

The following reforms would do much to improve women's income in later life.

### Increasing the Basic Pension and Basing Eligibility on Residence

Over the next few decades, the effect of Home Responsibilities Protection (HRP) will be increasingly evident, extending eligibility for a basic state pension to most women who had periods of non-employment while providing family care. For example, by 2010 nearly all women will be entitled to some basic state pension in their own right (GAD, 1990), although by 2020, between half and a third of women will still fail to qualify for the *full* amount (Hansard, 1994). Extending *full* entitlement to all with long residence would benefit women especially because of its independence of employment record or marital status. Such a universal (or citizen's) pension would be easily understandable and cheap to administer.

The level of the basic pension would need to be raised to well above Income Support (IS) level in order to avoid the disincentivising effects of the pensions poverty trap. For the working age population, this would make it worthwhile to save and contribute towards additional pensions. For older people, such an increase would largely eliminate the cumbersome, demeaning and administratively costly means test required to establish eligibility for IS.

Linking the basic pension level to living standards, through a suitable formula such as earnings-indexing, is important not only to prevent social exclusion of older people. A long-term commitment to such indexing would also send a clear message to younger people that their NI contributions would bring them a basic state pension worth having. It would ensure that the whole population had a stake in the continuation of the basic pension, thus strengthening the intergenerational contract underlying state pensions.

The cost of these improvements would be offset by savings in Income Support and Housing Benefit. Savings could also be made by reducing the tax reliefs and rebates on contributions to private pensions. From 2010, the gradual raising of women's state pension age will bring additional savings (Hutton et al., 1995).

*Second-Tier Pension*

SERPS, as originally formulated, was well designed to deal with women's dual roles as family carers and employees. Discounting all but the best 20 years of earnings ensured that years of no/low earnings due to caring for family members would not reduce the average earnings on which the pension is calculated. The alternative of applying Home Responsibilities Protection (HRP) to SERPS after the year 1998, as promised in the 1995 Pensions Act, would be less satisfactory. However, a SERPS with no assistance at all for carers would run counter to developments elsewhere in the EU.

Applying the 20 best years formula in SERPS is even more appropriate now than in 1975, with the increasing flexibility of the labour market in terms of insecure, temporary jobs and part-time working. Many countries have a state pension formula based on less than whole of working life, so that periods of education, family caring, illness, unemployment or part-time employment do not unduly reduce the pension. If SERPS were restored, it would be inclusive of most people. There would be no need for the nebulous new 'citizenship pension' proposed by the Labour Party. No details had been published at the time of writing.

Although SERPS has acquired the image of a residual pension, due to the savage cuts made by the Conservative administration and to their suggestion that taking out a personal pension is more 'responsible' than contributing to the state second-tier pension scheme, the original SERPS was well designed and cheap to administer. If a fraction of the marketing effort put into selling personal pensions were applied to a revitalised SERPS, we believe it would be the preferred option for the majority of those lacking access to a good occupational pension.

CONCLUSION

Older women's low income stems from the derisory level of the basic state pension combined with their lack of a good second-tier pension. Past family roles, by constraining women's earlier employment, have placed them at a disadvantage in accumulating occupational and personal pensions. The policy since 1980 of reducing the value of state pensions has reinforced women's income disadvantage in later life.

The proportion of women belonging to an occupational pension scheme is rising only very slowly and the gender gap in amount of private pension income is widening. Personal pensions are unlikely to benefit most women, since they generally lack an employer's contribution and only provide good value to those with stable employment and continuously high earnings. The Labour government's proposed Stakeholder Pensions share many of the weaknesses of personal pensions; unlike a restored SERPS, they do not offer a means of ensuring that periods of family caring count towards the pension.

There are two ways in which the gender gap in pension income could be narrowed. First, if working-age women were able to adopt men's traditional employment patterns, working full-time and continuously, they would accumulate better pensions. This would require women to abandon their conventional role of childrearing, by remaining childless, by finding a partner to adopt the caring role or by paying for full-time childcare. However, unless there is a revolution in publicly subsidised childcare in Britain, only the most highly paid women will be able to avoid the necessity to reduce their employment when they become mothers. Moreover, many women wish to stay at home to care for their children, especially in the first few years. Even childless women may have to provide informal care for one or both of their parents, with consequences for their employment in mid-life; cuts in domiciliary services for older people are likely to increase the proportion of adult children who provide parentcare in the future.

There is no sign that women are rejecting these caring roles, although combining them with employment often results in a heavy total workload (Arber and Ginn, 1995b) and, for professional women working full-time, the likelihood of raised levels of stress (Ginn and Sandell, 1997). In spite of women's growing participation in the labour force, most of the increase has been in part-time work, whereas only a record of continuous full-time employment leads to a good occupational pension.

The second way in which women's pension disadvantage can be reduced is by redistributive state pensions, in which periods of caring (full or part-time) count towards the pension entitlement. State pensions can ensure that the enormous pension costs of caring are fairly shared between those who undertake this task and those who do not. Private pensions, on the other hand, allow the costs to lie where they fall: mainly on women in later life. The immediate beneficiaries of Stakeholder Pensions, if they are introduced, will be the financial and insurance companies; the massive influx of new funds would help them to expand their business into the EU. Although private pensions have a role for those who are able to make additional pension provision, we believe state pensions which provide a decent standard of living in retirement are essential as the foundation of the pension system and that the transfer of resources from state to private pensions which has occurred since 1979 should be reversed.

The argument that Britain cannot afford better state pensions has been comprehensively challenged; but the reforms advocated here would also require an ideological shift away from Anglo-US individualism, in which people are exhorted to provide for themselves in retirement. A more humane and long-term view is needed, in which the tasks of reproducing and socialising the next generation of wealth creators and pension contributors, and of providing informal care for frail older people, are recognised as essential for the survival of society and valued accordingly.

It is ironic that over much of the world people regard children as the chief means of providing for their old age, whereas for women in most industrialised countries parenthood is a predictor of poverty in later life. Rhetoric about the importance of the family is plentiful. It needs to be matched by policies on childcare, employment and pensions which support women (and men) in their family caring roles.

## ACKNOWLEDGEMENTS

The chapter is based on a two-year research project funded by the Leverhulme Trust.

## REFERENCES

Arber, S. (1993) 'Inequalites Within the Household', D. Morgan and L. Stanley (eds) *Debates in Sociology*, Manchester: Manchester University Press.

Arber, S. and Ginn, J. (1991) *Gender and Later Life: a Sociological Analysis of Resources and Constraints*, London: Sage.

Arber, S. and Ginn, J. (1995a) 'The Mirage of Gender Equality: Occupational Success in the Labour Market and Within Marriage', *British Journal of Sociology*, 46(1), pp. 21–43.

Arber, S. and Ginn, J. (1995b) 'Gender Differences in the Relationship between Paid Employment and Informal Care', *Work Employment and Society*, 9(3), pp. 445–71.

ATP-huset (1994) *The Wage Earner's Guide to ATP*, Hilleroed: ATP-huset.

BBC (1996) *Ceefax*, 27 October.

Blake, D. (1992) *Issues in Pension Funding*, London: Routledge.

Brannen, J. and Wilson, G. (1987) (eds) *Give and Take in Families*, London: Allen and Unwin.

Brannen, J, Meszaros, G., Moss, P. and Poland, G. (1994) *Employment and Family Life. A Review of Research in the UK*, London: Department of Employment.

Budden, R. (1998) 'Unlocking Charges', *Money Management*, February, pp. 73–81.

Clasen, J. (1997) 'Social Insurance in Germany – Dismantling or Reconstruction?' in J. Clasen (ed.) *Social Insurance in Europe*. Bristol: The Policy Press.

Collins, J. (1993) 'Occupational Pensions for the Less Well-off: Who Benefits?', *Watson's Quarterly*, 28, pp. 4–7.

CSO (1992) *Social Trends 22*, London: HMSO.

CSO (1994) *Social Trends 24*, London: HMSO.

Commission on Social Justice (1994) *Social Justice: Strategies for National Renewal*, London: Institute for Public Policy Research.

Davies, H. and Joshi, H. (1998) 'Gender and Income Inequality in the UK 1968–1990: the Feminization of Earnings or of Poverty?' *Journal of the Royal Statistical Society*, 161(1), pp. 33–61.

Davies, H. and Ward, S. (1992) *Women and Personal Pensions*, London: EOC/HMSO.

Department of Employment (1995) *Employment Gazette*, January, London: HMSO.

Dex, S. (1987) *Women's Occupational Mobility: a Lifetime Perspective*, Basingstoke: Macmillan.

Disney, R. (1997) *Can We Afford to Grow Older?* London: MIT Press.

Ginn, J. (1993) 'Vanishing Trick: How to Make Married Women Disappear from Pension Statistics', *Radical Statistics*, No. 54, pp. 37–43.

Ginn, J. (1999) 'Playing Politics with Pension Statistics: Legitimating Privatisation'. In D. Dorling and S. Simpson (eds) *Statistics in Society*, London: Arnold.

Ginn, J. and Arber, S. (1991) 'Gender, Class and Income Inequalities in Later Life', *British Journal of Sociology*, 42(3), pp. 369–96.

Ginn, J. and Arber, S. (1992) 'Towards Women's Independence: Pension Systems in Three Contrasting European Welfare States', *Journal of European Social Policy*, pp. 2(4)), pp. 255–77.

Ginn, J. and Arber, S. (1993) 'Pension Penalties: the Gendered Division of Occupational Welfare', *Work, Employment and Society*, 7(1), pp. 47–70.

Ginn, J. and Arber, S. (1994) 'Midlife Women's Employment and Pension Entitlement in Relation to Coresident Adult Children', *Journal of Marriage and the Family*, November, pp. 813–19.

Ginn, J. and Arber, S. (1995) 'Moving the Goalposts: the Impact on British Women of Raising their State pension Age to 65'. *Social Policy Review No. 7*, London: Social Policy Association.

Ginn, J. and Arber, S. (1996) 'Patterns of Employment, Pensions and Gender: the Effect of Work History on Older Women's Non-state Pensions', *Work Employment and Society*, 10(3), pp. 469–90.

Ginn, J. and Arber, S. (forthcoming a) 'Changing Patterns of Pension Inequality: the Impact of Privatisation', *Ageing and Society*.

Ginn, J. and Arber, S. (forthcoming b) 'Who Took the Bait? Personal Pension Take-up in the 1990s', *Journal of Social Policy*.

Ginn, J. and Dugard, P. (1993) 'Statistics: a Gendered Agenda', *Radical Statistics*, 58, pp. 2–14.

Ginn, J. and Sandell, J. (1997) 'Balancing Home and Employment: Stress Experienced by Social Services Staff', *Work Employment and Society*, 11(3), pp. 413–34.

Glover, J. and Arber, S. (1995) 'Polarisation in Mothers' Employment', *Gender, Work and Organization*, 2(4), pp. 165–79.

Government Actuary Department (1990) *National Insurance Fund Long Term Financial Estimates*, London: HMSO.

Groves, D. (1987) 'Occupational Pension Provision and Women's Poverty in Old Age'. In C. Glendinning and J. Millar (eds), *Women and Poverty in Britain*, Brighton: Wheatsheaf.

Hakim, C. (1993) 'The Myth of Rising Female Employment', *Work Employment and Society*, 7, pp. 97–120.

Hancock, R. and Weir, P. (1994) *More Ways than Means: a Guide to Pensioners' Incomes in the 1980s*, London: Age Concern Institute of Gerontology.

Hansard (1994) 21 June, col. 146.

Henwood, M., Rimmer, L. and Wicks, M. (1987) *Inside the Family*, London: Family Policy Study Centre.

Hills, J. (1993) *The Future of Welfare. A Guide to the Debate*, York: Joseph Rowntree Foundation.

Hutton, S., Kennedy, S. and Whiteford, P. (1995) *Equalisation of State Pension Ages: the Gender Impact*, Manchester: EOC.

Johnson, P., Disney, R. and Stears, G. (1996) *Pensions: 2000 and Beyond*, Volume 2, London: Retirement Income Inquiry.

Johnson, P. and Webb, S. (1990) *Poverty in Official Statistics*, London: IFS.

Johnson, P., Conrad, C. and Thomson, D. (1989) *Workers versus Pensioners: Intergenerational Conflict in an Ageing World*, Manchester: Manchester University Press.

Joshi, H. (1984) *Women's Participation in Paid Work: Further Analysis of the Women and Employment Survey*, Research Paper no. 45, Department of Employment, London: HMSO.

Joshi, H. (1989) 'The Changing Form of Women's Economic Dependency'. In H. Joshi (ed.), *The Changing Population of Britain*, Oxford: Blackwell.

Joshi, H. (1991) 'Sex and Motherhood as Handicaps in the Labour Market'. In M. McLean and D. Groves (eds) *Women's Issues in Social Policy*, London: Routledge.

Joshi, H. (1996) *The Tale of Mrs. Typical*, London: FPSC.

Joshi, H. and Davies, H. (1991) *The Pension Consequences of Divorce*, Discussion Paper No. 550, London: CEPR.

Joshi, H. and Davies, H. (1992) 'Daycare in Europe and Mothers' Forgone Earnings', *International Labour Review*, 131(6), pp. 561–79.

Kotlikoff, L. (1992) *Generational Accounting: Knowing who Pays and When for What We Spend*, New York: Free Press.

Kotlikoff, L. and Sachs, J. (1997) 'Privatising Social Security: Its High Time to Privatise', *Brookings Review*, 15(3), pp. 16–19.

Kvist, J. (1997) 'Retrenchment or Restructuring? The Emergence of a Multitiered Welfare State in Denmark'. In J. Clasen (ed.) *Social Insurance in Europe*, Bristol: The Policy Press.

Lister, R. (1997) 'Tracing the Contours of Women's Citizenship'. In C. Ungerson and M. Kember (eds), *Women and Social Policy. A Reader*, 2nd edition Basingstoke: Macmillan.

Marullo, S. (ed.) (1995) *Comparison of Regulations on Part Time and Temporary Employment in Europe*, London: Employment Department.

Murgatroyd, L. and Neuburger, H. (1997) 'A Household Satellite Account for the UK', *Economic Trends*, No. 527, pp. 63–71.

National Audit Office (1990) *The Elderly: Information Requirements for Supporting the Implications of Personal Pensions for the National Insurance Fund*, HC 55, London: HMSO.

ONS (1997a) *Economic Trends 1997 Annual Supplement*, Table 1.1, London: The Stationery Office.

ONS (1997b) *Social Trends 27*, London: The Stationery Office.

Pahl, J. (1990) *Money and Marriage*, Basingstoke: Macmillan.

Platz, M. and Petersen, N. (1992) *Social and Economic Policies and Older People*, Danish National Report for the EC Observatory on Ageing and Older People, Copenhagen: National Institute for Social Research.

Ruland, F. (1991) *Survivors' Benefits of the Pension Scheme in Germany: Current Issues and Future Perspectives*, Geneva; International Social Security Association.

Schmahl, W. (1991) 'On the Future Development of Retirement in Europe, Especially of Supplementary Pension Schemes. An Introductory Overview'. In W. Schmahl (ed.), *The Future of Basic and Supplementary Pension Schemes in the European Community – 1992 and Beyond*, Baden-Baden: Nomos Verlagsgesellschaft.

Sedgwick Noble Lowndes (1996) *The Guide to Employee Benefits and Labour Law in Europe 1996/7*, Croydon: Sedgwick Noble Lowndes.

Sinfield, A. (1993) 'Reverse Targetting and Upside-down Benefits – How Perverse Policies Perpetuate Poverty'. In A. Sinfield (ed.), *Poverty, Inequality and Justice*, Edinburgh: Edinburgh University Press.

Townsend, P. and Walker, A. (1995) *New Directions for Pensions. How to Revitalise National Insurance*, Nottingham: European Labour forum.

Waine, B. (1995) 'A Disaster Foretold? The Case of the Personal Pension', *Social Policy and Administration*, 29(4), pp. 317–34.

Walker, A., Alber, J. and Guillemard, A-M. (1993) *Older People in the EU: Social and Economic Policies*, Brussels: CEC.

Walker, A. and Maltby, T. (1997) *Ageing Europe*, Buckingham: Open University Press.

Walker, R., Hardman, G. and Hutton, S. (1989) 'The Occupational Pensions Trap: Towards a Preliminary Specification', *Journal of Social Policy*, 184, pp. 575–93.

Ward, P. (1996) *The Great British Pensions Robbery*, Preston: Waterfall Books.

Ward, S. (1998) 'Castles in the Sky', *Professional Pensions*, 15 January: 16.

Whiteford, P. and Kennedy, S. (1995) *Incomes and Living Standards of Older People* York: Social Policy Reseach Unit.

Wilkinson, M. (1993) 'British Tax Policy 1979–90: Equity and Efficiency', *Policy and Politics*, 213, pp. 207–17.

World Bank (1994) *Averting the Old Age Crisis: Policies to Protect the Old and Promote Growth*, Oxford: Oxford University Press.

# 7 Revisiting the Sex Equality Laws

## Jeanne Gregory

The single most important factor determining the success or failure of civil rights legislation is political commitment on the part of governments. Statements of principle or good intent enshrined in statute but denied the necessary machinery for enforcement or undermined by conflicting government policies will be ineffective. Expectations may be raised, but genuine equality will remain elusive. These are the lessons to be learned from an assessment of the impact of UK equality laws during the past three decades. During the 1970s legislative activity in this area was at its height as Labour governments introduced the Equal Pay Act 1970, the Sex Discrimination Act 1975, the Race Relations Act 1976 and the Fair Employment (Northern Ireland) Act 1976. These initiatives were precipitated by a variety of political pressures, including intense political lobbying by women's groups and civil rights activists, but they also reflected a hands-on style of government and hence a willingness to legislate in an attempt to secure equality of opportunity in all areas of public life. By the end of the decade, the political climate had changed and with the election of a Conservative government in May 1979, neo-liberal policies proclaiming the virtues of the 'free market' were in the ascendant and have dominated the political landscape ever since. Such an environment has made it difficult to test the full potential of equality laws, designed precisely to intervene in the market in order to protect vulnerable groups from exploitation. Nevertheless, none of the legislation has been repealed and much of it has been strengthened in important respects. Taking sex equality laws as the central focus, this chapter examines this contradiction and traces the key developments in anti-discrimination law during the 1980s and 1990s. It then uses this analysis as the basis for assessing the current state of the law and considering the case for legislative consolidation and reform.

## EUROPEAN LAW TO THE RESCUE

During the past 20 years, UK membership of the European Community (EC) has been the decisive factor in ensuring that the sex equality laws passed in the 1970s were not only retained on the statute book but were widened in scope. Article 119 of the Treaty of Rome, signed by the UK

Labour government in 1973, established the principle of equal pay for equal work and this principle was reinforced in three equality Directives passed between 1975 and 1978.[1] Although the probability (and then the reality) of membership of the European Community was one of the factors influencing the UK government's decision to pass laws on equal pay and sex discrimination, it could not have anticipated just how far the equality principle was to be elaborated in the three Directives and in subsequent rulings of the European Court of Justice (ECJ). Over time, these two developments effectively transformed European sex equality law from an aid to fair competition in the labour market to a fundamental human right (Docksey, 1991; Hoskyns, 1996). As a consequence, European law provided a greater degree of protection from sex discrimination in the labour market than the domestic legislation of any single member state. As European law takes priority over national law where the two are in conflict, legislative changes were needed across the Community.

The Conservative government in the UK resisted informal overtures from the European Commission to make the required changes and only after successful infringement proceedings before the ECJ grudgingly altered domestic law to comply with the rulings of the Court.[2] The concept of equal pay was widened to include equal pay for work of equal value (Equal Pay (Amendment) Regulations 1983) and a number of minor changes to the sex discrimination legislation were made (Sex Discrimination Act 1986). This was a minimalist response, a series of minute adjustments, conceding only what was regarded as essential to bring UK law into line with European law (Gregory, 1987). At the same time, the government embarked on a programme of labour market deregulation which substantially increased the proportion of the workforce in casual employment, working part-time or 'flexible' hours, on short-term or temporary contracts, without the benefits of employment protection or trade union membership. These developments impacted particularly severely on the areas of work where women are employed. Without security of employment, women are less likely to know their rights to equal treatment or be in a position to act on this knowledge. In the case of equal pay, the shift from national collective agreements to localised pay negotiation and the proliferation of individualised payment systems made it increasingly difficult for women to access the information which would provide the basis for a claim.

Against this background, experts in sex equality law turned increasingly to European law, using litigation strategically both to compensate for the shortcomings of domestic law and to limit the damage caused by neo-liberal economic policies.[3]

Although the Sex Discrimination Act (SDA) 1975 was in many ways a sophisticated piece of legislation, it pre-dated the EC Equal Treatment Directive and owed its origins to a different set of legal and political traditions. Drawing on the experiences of the Race Relations Acts (passed in 1965 and 1968) and on developments in the United States, the SDA was innovative in its definition of discrimination to cover indirect (unintentional, structural) discrimination as well as direct discrimination. It also gave wide-ranging enforcement powers to a new quango, the Equal Opportunities Commission, although some of these powers were subsequently curtailed by the UK courts (see below). Its provisions on positive action were much more tentative. Rejecting the American-style 'affirmative action', which in its heyday required preferential treatment to be given to black people and women in order to rectify historical and structural disadvantage, the SDA instead embraced 'positive action'. As enshrined in the SDA, this permitted, but did not require, single-sex training to be provided for areas of employment where women were under-represented; positive discrimination at the point of recruitment was not permitted, except in very narrowly defined circumstances.

One of the most serious weaknesses of the SDA was revealed in the admission by Roy Jenkins, the Labour Home Secretary who introduced the legislation in the House of Commons, that it was not intended as a 'money-spending Bill' (Parliamentary Debates, House of Commons, Vol. 889, col. 516). Consequently, the legislation contained a number of exemptions from its provisions, particularly where government expenditure might be involved, and these exemptions have proved to be a fruitful source of litigation under European law.

**Challenging UK Law**

Unlike the SDA, exemptions from the provisions of the EC Equal Treatment Directive were kept to a minimum; governments were expected to provide a lead, rather than to construct their own escape routes from the principle of equality. In the early years, the historical legacy of sexist legislation caused difficulties in several member states. In the UK, the existence of different retirement ages for men and women was one such legacy. Section 6(4) of the SDA exempted any provision relating to 'death or retirement' from its scope and this was challenged by Ms Marshall when she was forcibly retired at 62 although male employees were permitted to continue working until 65. The European Court confirmed that EC law allows member states to set different pension ages, but does not permit unequal treatment to flow from these differences.[4] A second ECJ decision arising from this case established that remedies available to successful complainants must be adequate recompense for the harm suffered and include interest on the award, dating back to the date of the discrimination (*Marshall* v *Southampton and South-West Hampshire Area Health Authority* (No. 2) [1993] IRLR 445 ECJ).

It would be difficult to overestimate the significance of this second decision. It led to the removal of the ceiling on compensation awards in sex and race discrimination cases and in cases of religious discrimination in Northern Ireland, thereby forcing employers to reconsider the costs of discriminating. One group of women to experience immediate benefit from this development were ex-service women challenging another exemption from the SDA, relating to the armed forces. In 1991 the Ministry of Defence (MOD) conceded that its policy of dismissing service women when they became pregnant contravened the Equal Treatment Directive. Some 4,000 claims for compensation were then submitted to the MOD which admitted that by October 1994 the pay-out had reached £30 million. Two years after the removal of the compensation ceiling, average awards in sex discrimination cases had risen by 31 per cent (or by 332 per cent if the MOD cases are included) and in race discrimination cases by 63 per cent. Awards for injury to feelings in harassment cases increased substantially (Equal Opportunities Review (EOR) 1994, Nos 57 and 58 and 1996, No. 67).

The issue of pregnancy dismissal has had a chequered history. It began with the now infamous decision in 1979, to the effect that since a man cannot become pregnant, it was not possible to claim that a pregnant women had been treated less favourably. By 1985 the case law had progressed as far as allowing comparison between a pregnant woman and a hypothetical man who required time off work for medical reasons. In the early 1990s, the ECJ intervened to make it clear that pregnancy discrimination is inherently gender-specific discrimination and that a sick man comparison is only needed in the case of illness arising after the period of maternity leave. This approach was confirmed in a later case when the European Court held that it was contrary to the Equal Treatment Directive to dismiss a pregnant woman, even if she had initially been recruited to cover another employee's maternity leave.[5]

European law has been equally useful in shoring up some potential gaps in the Equal Pay Act. The new equal value regulations were drafted in such a way that employers had plenty of scope to justify inequalities in pay on grounds other than sex. Some industrial tribunals were allowing this provision, 'the material factor defence', to become a very wide escape route, until the ECJ raised the standard of employers' defences. In a case referred to the Court by Germany, the ECJ held that in order for employers to justify inequalities in pay and conditions, they had to demonstrate that the measures corresponded to a real need on the part of the undertaking and were both appropriate and necessary to achieving those objectives (*Bilka-Kaufhaus GmbH* v *Weber von Hartz* [1986] IRLR 317 ECJ). Also, in a UK case brought by speech therapists, the European Court held that the existence of separate collective bargaining structures could not be used to justify unequal pay, as this would perpetuate inequalities rooted in history; nor could employers use skill shortages as a defence without providing detailed evidence that would account for all of the pay difference (*Enderby* v *Frenchay Health Authority and Secretary of State for Health* [1993] IRLR 591 ECJ).

## Limiting the Damage Caused by Deregulation

All the case law developments discussed so far were important in widening the boundaries of discrimination law. During the same period, there were also a number of cases designed to limit the worst excesses of government policies directed at 'lifting the burden' on businesses and introducing the disciplines of the market into the private sector.[6] The case of *Ratcliffe* v *North Yorkshire County Council* ([1995] IRLR 439 HL) was a clear example of two opposing ideologies locked in mortal combat: on one side the goal of maximising competitive pressures and driving down wage costs; on the other the principle of equal pay and the protection of vulnerable groups of workers from exploitation. The case centred on the question of whether the requirements of compulsory competitive tendering (CCT) could serve as a defence for unequal pay. CCT for local authorities was introduced in the UK during the 1980s, requiring them to tender a range of services previously provided 'in house' and unopposed by the private sector. A research project commissioned by the Equal Opportunities Commission (EOC) revealed that the introduction of CCT had impacted particularly severely on women, who had lost out in terms of hours, pay and security of employment even more than men (Escott and Whitfield, 1995).

The *Ratcliffe* case involved a local authority that wanted to retain the provision of school dinners as an 'in house' service. In order to compete with the bids from outside contractors as required by the CCT legislation, it made the catering assistants redundant and re-employed them at lower hourly rates, thereby reneging on its own job evaluation scheme. The House of Lords upheld a claim by the catering assistants for equal pay with male workers still receiving the rates of pay awarded under the job evaluation scheme. This may seem like a pyrrhic victory, with the local authority bid always being undercut by that of outside contractors, but another piece of EC legislation, the Acquired Rights Directive (77/187) was intended to ensure that workers transferring from one employer to another would have their existing terms and conditions protected. In practice, this area of law has become a minefield of complexity, but it has made employers proceed more cautiously, in case an obligation under European law does arise. The operation of CCT is currently under review, with the Labour government elected in 1997 recognising that the quality of service offered is at least as important as the price at which it is offered. This 'best value' approach, in combination with a minimum wage set at or near the recently negotiated local authority rate of £4 an hour, would make it more difficult for outside contractors to undercut in-house bids.

Another strategy designed to overcome the fragmentation of the labour market involves claiming equal pay with men not 'in the same employment'

(Equal Pay Act 1970, section 1(2)) but 'in the same establishment or service', a form of words used in an early ECJ judgment (*Defrenne v Sabena* (No. 2) [1976] ECR 445). This strategy has been successfully used in the field of education, where separate Regional Councils for Education and Training were all providing the same service and receiving funding from the Department of Education and Employment; also in the health field, where the creation of separate hospital trusts and the shift towards local determination of pay and conditions threatened to undermine the hard-won gains in *Enderby*.[7] Without such an approach, an increasing proportion of women would find their choice of male workers to use as comparators when lodging equal value claims shrink to vanishing point.

The growth of individualised pay awards and the declining importance of collective bargaining means that an increasing number of women and men employed on like work or work of equal value are not in practice receiving equal pay. Appraisal systems can discriminate against women workers in a number of ways if the schemes allow managers to apply subjective criteria in assessing individual competencies (Bevan and Thompson, 1992; IRS/EOC 1992; Gregory 1996). The potential conflict between equality and merit awards was acknowledged by the ECJ in a Danish case, in which the Court held that where a pay structure lacks transparency, the burden of proof rests with the employer to demonstrate that the pay criteria are not discriminatory (*Handels- og Kontorfunktionaerernes Forbund i Danmark v Dansk Arbejdsgiverforening*, acting for Danfoss [1989] IRLR 532 ECJ). This case should in theory provide some protection against poorly constructed payment systems implemented by managers untrained in sex equality principles, but cannot of itself reverse a trend which compounds the difficulties women face in mounting an equal pay claim.

In recognition of the growth in 'flexible' and 'atypical' forms of employment, draft proposals for Directives to ensure a minimum standard of employment protection for workers in these categories have been considered by the EC Council of Ministers at regular intervals since 1990, but on each occasion they were vetoed by the UK Conservative government. The ECJ has partly filled this vacuum, at least in relation to part-time workers. As the vast majority of part-time workers are women, any measures discriminating against part-time workers will affect women disproportionately. In a series of cases referred to the European Court by the German courts, the ECJ has held that part-time workers should have rights proportionate to those of full-time workers, unless the employer can justify their exclusion.[8]

**The Uses and Abuses of Indirect Discrimination Law**

Using sex equality laws as a strategy for improving the position of part-time workers is only possible because the majority of them are women. The same strategy, which involves challenging laws or practices on the grounds that they impact more severely on women than men and so constitute indirect discrimination, has been used on other occasions with varying degrees of success. It has been used in two judicial review cases against the Secretary of State for Employment. In the first of these, the EOC challenged the legality of the Employment Protection (Consolidation) Act 1978, which set a two-year qualifying period for claiming unfair dismissal or redundancy payments for employees who worked 16 hours or more per week and a five-year qualifying period for those working between 8 and 16 hours. In the second, two women challenged the two-year qualifying period for claiming unfair dismissal.

In both cases, the plaintiffs argued that it was more difficult for women to comply with the two-year rule than men, so that the legislation was incompatible with EC law. In both cases, the government sought to justify the discrimination on the grounds that there would be fewer jobs available if the rules were changed but in neither case did it present a shred of evidence in support of this assertion. In the first case, the House of Lords found against the government and the hours threshold in respect of employment rights has been removed (EOR 1995, No. 60). The second case has been referred to the European Court of Justice (see EOR 1997, No. 73; and Allen and Moon, forthcoming).

The concept of indirect discrimination was also used to challenge the abolition of wages councils, which left the UK without any form of minimum wage protection, in contrast to other member states. The challenge took the form of an appeal to the European Commission to take action against the UK government for its failure to comply with European law on equal pay. In 1993, substantial documentation was sent to the Commission by the Trades Union Congress (TUC) and the EOC, providing detailed evidence of the adverse impact that the abolition of wages councils would have on low paid women workers and drawing attention to the lengthy and costly procedures involved in equal pay litigation, which effectively constituted a denial of justice (TUC, 1993; and EOC, 1993). The European Commission sat on these documents for some time, perhaps wishing to avoid a further deterioration in relations with the Conservative government at a time of ongoing conflict in a number of areas.[9] There was also the possibility that a change of government would enable the issues raised by the TUC and the EOC to be resolved at home.

## EQUAL OPPORTUNITIES: THE NEED FOR A WHOLEHEARTED APPROACH

The election of a Labour government in May 1997, committed to signing the Social Chapter of the Maastricht Treaty and to introducing a national minimum wage, did indeed represent an important first step on the road towards resolving equality issues at home, instead of relying on European institutions to drag the UK out of the quagmire at frequent intervals. However, much remains to be done, as the piecemeal approach of the last 20 years has left a legacy of unwieldy and complicated laws which provide an uneven and uncertain route to justice for individuals and groups experiencing discrimination. European institutions will continue to provide a useful reference point, but European law is also limited in its coverage and with the current emphasis on 'subsidiarity', giving member states a freer hand to decide on domestic issues without interference from Brussels, the ball is firmly back in the court of national governments.

## Dismantling Institutional Discrimination

The anti-discrimination laws created in the 1970s gave individuals the right to challenge discriminatory practices that affected them and to seek a legal remedy in the tribunals or courts (or in the case of religious discrimination, before the Fair Employment Agency). At the same time, specialist agencies were created, both to provide support for individuals and to perform a wider strategic and educational role in combating discrimination. Over the years, a considerable gulf has opened up between the aims of the legislation and its implementation in practice. In relation to individual litigation, the inordinate length of time taken to resolve cases, particularly if the appeals process is invoked, places an enormous strain on individuals and often makes the final decision irrelevant because of the changes occurring in the meantime. Also, the protection against victimisation of individuals involved in litigation has proved inadequate, partly due to the restrictive interpretation of the victimisation provisions by the courts and partly due to the practical difficulties of proving a link between the complaint and subsequent actions by the organisation, particularly in the case of 'low-level' victimisation.

In relation to the task of dismantling institutional discrimination, the powers given to the EOC and to the Commission for Racial Equality (CRE) to undertake formal investigations of companies or organisations suspected of discriminating have been severely curtailed by the courts, who were determined to prevent the Commissions from going on 'fishing expeditions'. Consequently, formal investigations became slow, cumbersome and expensive (Gregory, 1987; Ellis, 1988), resulting in an almost exclusive reliance on a reactive, complaint-driven strategy of enforcement. Where a discriminatory practice or payment system affects more than one person, everyone affected has to file a separate complaint, unless prior agreement on test cases can be reached with the other party. In the absence of collective remedies, a tribunal decision in an equal pay case can throw payment systems into disarray (Gregory, 1992). Before its abolition in 1986, the

Central Arbitration Committee played a useful role in scrutinising collective agreements and pay structures for possible discrimination. With the fragmentation of the labour market and the increasing complexity of payment systems, the need for some form of Equal Pay Commission has become overwhelming. As the implementation of a minimum wage will inevitably have a knock-on effect for equal pay, the logical solution is to widen the brief of the body entrusted with monitoring the implementation of the minimum wage to deal with equal pay issues as well (Hastings, 1997).

Only in relation to religious discrimination in Northern Ireland has there been any attempt within the United Kingdom to move away from an emphasis on individual complaints to a pro-active model. The Fair Employment (Northern Ireland) Act 1989 amended the 1976 legislation by substantially shifting the burden of tackling discrimination from individuals to employers. It requires employers to monitor the composition of their workforce and review recruitment, training and promotion practices to ensure fair participation of the two religious communities. A Fair Employment Commission was established to audit these procedures and where necessary to impose affirmative action, including setting goals and timetables for eliminating discrimination. In relation to equal pay, we have to look further afield for a useful model. The Ontario Pay Equity Act 1987 requires employers to examine their pay structures and to take steps to remove gender-based pay discrimination. As in Northern Ireland, there is a Commission (the Pay Equity Commission) to oversee this process.

Neither of these models offers a perfect solution; both were the product of political compromise, so that flaws and limitations have become increasingly apparent (SACHR, 1997; Fudge and McDermott, 1991). However, the policy of shifting responsibility for dismantling discrimination firmly onto the institutions that reproduce it, and away from the individuals who experience it, promises to be both a more efficient and fairer way of proceeding.

An increasing number of employers have adopted equal opportunities policies in recent years, both as a protection from litigation under the equality laws and as a public relations exercise. Almost all of them have been content to embrace the 'short agenda' of equal opportunities, such as introducing non-discriminatory practices into their human resource management systems; very few have progressed to the 'long agenda' which would require a radical overhaul of employment practices in close consultation with employees (Cockburn, 1991). After more than two decades of education and persuasion and a proliferation of Codes of Practice, the time has come for stronger sanctions against organisations that continue to ignore the expertise on offer. They should be required to undertake equality audits and pay audits and to develop programmes for the eradication of any inequalities revealed. An enforcement agency would need to be given the powers and resources to scrutinise this process and to take legal action where necessary.

## Transcending the Limits of Formal Equality

Both UK and EC sex equality laws take as their starting point the principle of equal treatment between men and women. There is an assumption of symmetry in this approach which suggests that men and women both suffer equally from discrimination, thus deflecting attention from the specific disadvantages experienced by women. A spurious gender neutrality in reality endorses a male norm and restricts the possibilities of remedial action designed to compensate for historical and structural disadvantages, on the grounds that such action discriminates against men. In practice, however, the application of the symmetry formula becomes unworkable and produces absurd results, as we saw in the early UK cases of pregnancy discrimination. The ECJ was able to avoid this pitfall by adopting a more interventionist stance, recognising that it is precisely because women become pregnant and men do not that pregnancy discrimination is a form of direct sex discrimination. Despite its initial emphasis on formal equality, European law has moved further than UK law in acknowledging the substantive inequalities preventing many women from competing in the labour market on equal terms with men. This is reflected in Article 2.4 of the Equal Treatment Directive which refers to the need to remove 'existing inequalities which affect women's opportunities' in access to employment. In December 1984, the Council of Ministers adopted a Recommendation on Positive Action which acknowledged that legal provisions on equal treatment were not in themselves sufficient to dismantle discrimination and that more action was needed by member states 'to counteract the prejudicial effects on women in employment which arise from social attitudes, behaviour and structures'. This was followed in the early 1990s by Recommendations on sexual harassment and on childcare.[10]

In relation to affirmative action, the ECJ has adopted a cautious approach, with a view to keeping the derogations from the equal treatment principle to a minimum. In *Kalanke* v *Freie Hansestadt Bremen* ([1995] IRLR 660 ECJ), the Court held that a rule giving women preference for promotion, where men and women candidates are equally qualified but where women are under-represented, is a form of discrimination not permitted under European law. The European Commission and the European Parliament responded with some alarm and sought to amend Article 2.4 to limit the potential damage to affirmative action programmes already underway in a number of member states. In the event, a new clause added to Article 119 in the draft Treaty of Amsterdam states that:

with a view to ensuring full equality in practice between men and women in working life, the principle of equal treatment shall not prevent any member state from maintaining or adopting measures providing for specific advantages in order to make it easier for the under-represented sex to pursue a vocational activity or to prevent or compensate for disadvantage in professional careers.

In *Marschall* v *Land Nordrheim-Westfalen* ([1998] IRLR 39), the ECJ found in favour of an affirmative action programme which was seemingly less rigid than the one under scrutiny in Kalanke, in so far as the rule gave priority to the promotion of the under-represented sex (women) 'unless reasons specific to an individual (male) candidate tilt the balance in his favour'. Women in Germany, the Netherlands and Scandinavia will be mainly affected by this decision; in the UK any form of preferential treatment in recruitment or promotion remains illegal under domestic law; since the Marschall decision, it has become possible to reconsider this position, but there is no requirement to do so.

Carol Bacchi (1996) has conducted a wide-ranging and comprehensive review of affirmative action programmes in a number of countries, illustrating the various ways in which it is co-opted and contained in practice. She argues in favour of a 'hard' or 'strong' version of affirmative action, defined as including reforms which make membership of a designated group (one of) the criterion for access to particular positions. However, it is clear from her own research that this is going to be difficult to achieve. It is also questionable whether the small gains to be made are worthwhile, in view of the hostility generated in the wider community by what is regarded as 'reverse discrimination'. Even the Dutch preferential treatment policies, whereby jobs are offered to ethnic minority applicants if their qualifications are equal to those of 'native' applicants (or in some cases if they have sufficient qualifications for the job), merely reduce the discrimination to zero and do not in fact favour minority applicants (Wrench, 1996). In Northern Ireland, the affirmative action provisions are very tentative and are much closer to formal equality than 'result equality' (McCrudden, 1991); they refer primarily to procedural changes 'confined to opening relevant doors, rather than ensuring that disadvantaged groups are in a position to reach the doorway' (Fredman, 1997).

There is much to be said in favour of a 'soft' version of affirmative action, or in other words, positive action, including the removal of structural impediments to access and strategies such as training schemes to help disadvantaged groups compete more effectively, despite Bacchi's rejection of it (Bacchi, 1996). Forms of affirmative action such as quotas are invariably perceived as temporary, one-off measures, in which (probably atypical) women would be expected to fit in with the existing culture and patterns of work. By contrast, an effective application of the 'soft' option could require organisations to re-examine their policies and practices and make radical structural changes which would be permanent. Unlike the current voluntary framework for positive action enshrined in the SDA, this process would need to be monitored and supported by legal sanctions.

In the political sphere, the arguments in favour of 'hard' affirmative action are more compelling and can be couched in terms of the need for social justice and fair representation. There is a strong lobby within the Council of Europe and the European Union pressing for 'parity democracy', insisting on the right of women to be represented in equal numbers on all decision-making bodies. In 1996, the Labour Party ran into difficulties over its policy of permitting women-only short-lists in the selection of candidates to stand for election in a limited number of constituencies. An industrial tribunal found this to be illegal under the SDA, although both the Labour Party and the EOC had been given legal advice to the contrary (*Jepson* and *Dyas-Elliot* v *The Labour Party* [1996] IRLR 116). As there was no appeal against this decision, the legal issues remain unresolved, posing a dilemma for political activists currently lobbying to ensure equal representation of women and men in the Welsh Assembly and the Scottish Parliament.

The way forward is first, to amend the domestic legislation so that strategies designed to make decision-making bodies more representative of the society in which we live are not constantly scuppered by an insistence on formal equality. Second, an alliance needs to be made with member states working on this issue at the European level to ensure that the exceptions to formal equality currently enshrined in European law are sufficiently strong and clear not to obstruct the goal of achieving equality of representation in the political sphere. In other areas too, a rigid insistence on formal equality has hampered developments designed to benefit women, such as women-only taxi services, special events at sports centres and 'priority to women' breakdown services. Again, it should be possible to accommodate a limited recognition of gender difference, for example on grounds of safety.

In making demands both for parity democracy and the recognition of gender difference, it is important to avoid creating a false antithesis between equality and difference in which the male norm remains as the standard in both cases. As Joan Scott argues, if individuals were all the same, there would be no need to ask for equality: 'Equality requires the recognition and inclusion of differences' (Scott, 1988, p. 48). This approach provides the framework for creating a much more flexible and imaginative set of social policies, in which neither men nor women are consigned to a straitjacket of pre-given social roles, nor penalised for the choices that they make. It opens up the possibility of acknowledging the diverse interests of women without in any way undermining the feminist project to speak on behalf of women. Indeed, feminism is strengthened by its recognition of the different experiences and interests of women and the need for a social movement which ensures that all of them have a voice.

A recognition of diversity does not necessarily lead to political paralysis; it can provide the basis for solidarity and common action on specific issues and has the merit of avoiding the 'horizontal' and 'elitist' focus of much existing policy on women (Hoskyns, 1996). As Rosi Braidotti has argued, the rejection of the falsely reassuring concept of 'global sisterhood' does not inevitably have to be replaced by a numbing cultural relativism. Political alliances can be forged on a firm foundation of mutual understanding, in which women are seen as 'locally situated' and consequently as offering different perspectives; these differences can be understood and mediated through the sense of responsibility of women to each other (Braidotti, 1992). Only by focusing on gender disadvantage rather than on gender difference can we seek to reverse the process of polarisation between those women who are currently benefiting from the processes of European integration and those who are losing out.

## Mainstreaming

Until recently, equal opportunities was regarded as a specialist issue, the exclusive concern of expert bodies created by government and of particular units within organisations. Mainstreaming seeks to integrate equality issues into the process of policy planning and decision-making and so 'make fairness and equity part of the social mainstream in which we all swim' (McCormack, 1996). At its most proactive, it is both anticipatory, in the sense that equality of opportunity is built into the process of policy formation, and participatory, involving meaningful consultation with disadvantaged groups before policies are put into effect (McCrudden, 1996). A minimal requirement would be an impact statement, assessing the likely effects of particular proposals on the relevant groups.

In most countries where mainstreaming has been attempted, inequalities based on gender have provided the central focus, although special attention is often paid to the particular needs of minority women. Among the first to consider the likely impact of policy proposals on women, the Australian government began producing an annual women's budget statement during the 1980s. More recently, the New South Wales (NSW) government has adopted a 'whole-of-government' approach, requiring each government department to take responsibility for meeting the needs of women (NSW Department for Women, 1996a and 1996b). New Zealand also has guidelines for gender analysis, directed at both public and private sector organisations (Ministry of Women's Affairs, 1996). The documentation from both NSW and New Zealand makes reference to international obligations and in particular the Platform for Action adopted at the Fourth United Nations World Conference for Women in Beijing in 1995. Under the heading 'institutional mechanisms', action is recommended to 'integrate gender perspectives in legislation, public policies, programmes and projects' (UN, 1995).

Significantly, the UK government made a specific commitment at Beijing to 'make an effort to integrate gender into policies and programmes' (Inter-Action's world wide web site).

These efforts were in fact already underway, as 'equality proofing' had been introduced into Britain in relation to gender and 'race' towards the end of the 1980s through the initiative of the Ministerial Group on Women's Issues. It involved building an equality check into the policy-making pro-cesses of all government departments, but remained a closely guarded secret. As the policy evolved and became known as Policy Appraisal and Fair Treatment (PAFT), there was no external consultation, no mechanism for co-ordination across departments and neither the guidelines nor evaluation reports were available in the public domain (Gallagher et al., 1996). In Northern Ireland, where equality proofing focused on gender and religion, criticisms of the process led to the withdrawal of the measures, followed by extensive consultations and the issuing of new guidelines which were both wide-ranging and ambitious. In 1996, a review of the implementation of PAFT in Northern Ireland concluded that adequate mechanisms were then in place but were not being used appropriately (Gallagher et al., 1996).

This demonstrates yet again the importance of political commitment. Mainstreaming is a brilliant idea whose time has come, but if it is regarded by those responsible for its implementation as little more than a paper exercise, providing the appearance but not the reality of equality, it becomes a sham. If it is adopted alongside policies which pull against it, any potential benefits will be lost. For example, in Northern Ireland, the trade union UNISON and the EOC(NI) campaigned vigorously for the PAFT guidelines to be applied to the tendering process for CCT, drawing attention to the damaging effects of 'contracting out' on women's employment.[11]

Similarly, if mainstreaming means dissolving or sidelining an existing body of expertise, leaving no one with a clear responsibility for delivering equality, its impact will be minimal. For example, the European Commission made a major commitment to mainstreaming in its Fourth Action Programme on Equal Opportunities (CEC, 1995), emphasising that an explicit equality dimension should be integrated into 'all policies, programmes, actions, finan-cial and support frameworks and evaluation systems of the Commission, as well as at national, regional and other appropriate levels' (ibid., p. B6). Unfortunately, the resources to make such a policy effective have so far not been forthcoming. As the Fourth Action Programme came into opera-tion, a number of important expert networks were wound up and the power shifted away from the Equal Opportunities Unit into the hierarchy of the Directorate-General for Employment, Industrial Relations and Social Affairs (Hoskyns, forthcoming).

The Labour government which came to power in 1997 fulfilled its commit-ment to appoint a Minister for Women with Cabinet status.[12] It also created a new Cabinet sub-committee involving Ministers from all the major government departments 'to co-ordinate and drive forward the women's agenda across government' (Women's Unit, undated). PAFT has become Policy Appraisal for Equal Treatment, defined as 'the process of assessing the impact of proposed or current policies and programmes on particular groups to ensure that everyone is treated fairly and that there is no unlawful discrimination' (Ministers for Women, 1998). Mainstreaming is seen as the process of 'putting women's interests at the heart of government, so that women's needs and interests are *first thoughts*, not *afterthoughts* for every department' (Women's Unit, undated; emphasis in the original). There is also a reference to opening up a new dialogue with women and to improving the representation of women in public life.

The new policy has the potential for being both anticipatory and participatory; also, it recognises the need for a specialist unit to oversee the process of mainstreaming. There will undoubtedly be resistance from many government departments and without frequent and effective monitoring, the policy could become no more than a bureaucratic exercise. The draft documentation currently available leaves a number of questions unanswered. For example, it is not clear whether the Ministers for Women have responsibilities in relation to all disadvantaged groups (and if so, how these groups are to be defined) or only to women. Also, the new Women's Unit reports to the Ministers for Women, while the EOC remains answerable to the Department for Education and Employment and deals with discrimination against both men and women. As the concept of equal opportunities widens and deepens, it becomes important to identify the structures most appropriate for the effective delivery of policy.

**Widening the Net**

The protection from discrimination enshrined in current equal opportunities legislation is patchy and incoherent, both in terms of the groups protected and the areas of activity covered. Discrimination on grounds of sex, 'race' and disability is outlawed throughout the United Kingdom, although the race relations legislation was only extended to Northern Ireland in 1997. These laws apply to discrimination in employment, education and the provision of goods, facilities and services. Discrimination on religious grounds is prohibited only in Northern Ireland and is restricted to employment. Age discrimination is currently not covered, nor is discrimination on grounds of sexuality.[13]

As the earlier part of this chapter revealed, EU law has provided a useful lever in both retaining and strengthening sex equality laws in the UK, but there has also been a downside to this process, owing to the exclusive focus of European law on gender inequalities and on employment. The beneficiaries of this approach are women who are able to participate in the labour market and whose main or sole disadvantage stems from their gender. Other issues of central concern to feminists, such as the undervaluing of women's unpaid work, male violence against women, the impact of racism and the exploitation of third country nationals without formal citizenship status, have proved more difficult to raise.

Alliances within the European Union have resulted in progress on some of these issues (see, for example, European Parliament, 1986 and 1990) and the Treaty of Amsterdam negotiated in June 1997 includes a new Article which would permit the development of policy 'to combat discrimination based on sex, racial or ethnic origin, religion or belief, disability, age or sexual orientation' (Article 6a). Article 14 of the European Convention on Human Rights also prohibits discrimination on a number of grounds. The government is committed to incorporating the Convention into UK law but apparently has no immediate plans to establish a Human Rights Commission. The Disability Discrimination Act 1995 is to be strengthened, including the creation of a Disability Rights Commission; in relation to age discrimination, a voluntary Code of Practice is to be tried before legislation is contemplated.

For the time being, then, it seems that the piecemeal approach is here to stay. This is confusing, both for complainants experiencing multiple discrimination and for organisations implementing equal opportunities policies, as the expertise they need is located in separate agencies. If these disparate bodies were to be brought together under an 'umbrella' Human Rights Commission, this could produce greater coherence and co-operation without losing the expertise and commitment of the component parts (IPPR, 1997). Whether such a structural change is implemented or not, the Commissions need to be given the legislative powers and resources adequate to the formidable task of dismantling institutional discrimination (see above; and Justice, 1997).

## CONCLUSION

After almost three decades of experience with equality laws, there is no shortage of recommendations for legislative reform (see, for example, Justice, 1997; and the most recent contributions from the agencies themselves: SACHR, 1997; EOC(NI), 1997; NDC, 1997; EOC, 1998; and CRE, 1998). A recurring theme in all these proposals is the importance of access to justice; sophisticated laws which are out of reach of the people most likely to need them, for reasons of legal complexity, cost, lack of awareness or fear of victimisation, are not worth the paper they are written on. In relation to the labour market, equality laws work best within the framework of a secure body of employment rights and trade union recognition rights; the progressive deregulation of the labour market during the past 20 years has led to a greater polarisation within the workforce, with the most vulnerable workers being the least likely to have access to equality rights. Before these laws can make a real contribution towards achieving social justice and combating social exclusion, it will be necessary to address this issue.

Effective legislation is an essential prerequisite for tackling discrimination, but it is only the beginning. The next step is to ensure that people are made aware of their rights and have access to expert advice and support. The implementation of policy appraisal and exemplary employment practices throughout the public sector, combined with strong legislation and strategies such as contract compliance[14] to promote similar practices in the private sector, will help to create an environment within which the principle of equality will at long last be swimming with the tide rather than against it.

## NOTES

1.  These were: 75/117/EEC, approximation of laws relating to equal pay for men and women (the Equal Pay Directive); 76/207/EEC, on the implementation of the principle of equal treatment for men and women as regards access to employment, vocational training and promotion, and working conditions (the Equal Treatment in Employment Directive) and 79/7/EEC, on the progressive implementation of the principle of equal treatment for men and women in matters of social security (the Social Security Directive).

2.  *Commission of the European Communities* v *United Kingdom of Great Britain and Northern Ireland* [1982] Industrial Relations Law Reports (IRLR) 333 ECJ (on the Equal Pay Act) and *Commission of the European Communities* v *United Kingdom of Great Britain and Northern Ireland* [1984] IRLR 29 ECJ (on the Sex Discrimination Act).

3.  This strategy was only available in relation to sex equality legislation, as European law was silent on other areas of discrimination (see section below on 'widening the net'). However, because of the parallels between the SDA and the Race Relations Act 1976, it was often possible to 'read across' from a decision in a sex equality case and so derive indirect benefit from European law (see Gregory, 1987, and the discussion of the Marshall case below).

4.  *Marshall* v *Southampton and South-West Hampshire Area Health Authority* [1986] IRLR 140 ECJ. As Ms Marshall was a public sector employee, she could rely directly on European law for a remedy. It required a change in UK law (Sex Discrimination Act 1986, Section 2) before private sector employees could also benefit from this ruling.

5.  The domestic cases were *Turley* v *Allders Department Stores Ltd.* [1980] IRLR 4 Employment Appeal Tribunal (EAT) and two cases heard together: *Hayes* v *Malleable Working Men's Club* and *Maughan* v *N.E. London Magistrates Court Committee* [1985] IRLR 367 (EAT). The first two ECJ cases were *Dekker* v *VJV Centrum* [1991] IRLR 27 ECJ (originating in the Netherlands) and *Handels-og Konorfunktionaererernes Forbund i Danmark* (acting for Hertz) v *Dansk Arbejds-*

*giverforening* (acting for Aldi Market K/S) [1991] IRLR 31 ECJ (a Danish case). The third ECJ case, involving the woman recruited to cover maternity leave (although significantly she had been recruited for an indefinite period), originated in the UK (*Webb* v *EMO Air Cargo (UK) Ltd* [1994] IRLR 482 ECJ).

6.  See for example the government white papers *Lifting the Burden* (1981), Cmnd 9571, and *Building Businesses...not Barriers* (1986), Cmnd 9794.

7.  Susan Scullard was the only woman employed as a unit manager for one of the Regional Councils; all twelve male unit managers at the other Councils were paid more than her. Applying the Defrenne test, she was permitted to pursue her claim (*Scullard* v *Knowles* [1996] IRLR 344 EAT). Similarly, dental surgery assistants were allowed to compare themselves with a senior dental technician employed by a different hospital trust. This merely helps to restore the status quo that existed prior to the break-up of the National Health Service, when pay was determined nationally through the Whitley Councils.

8.  The standard of justification was established in Bilka-Kaufhaus (see above), a case concerned with the exclusion of part-time workers from an occupational pension scheme. Other cases involved the exclusion of part-timers from German sick pay legislation (*Rinner-Kuhn* v *FWW Spezial-Gebaudereinigung GmbH* [1989] IRLR 493 ECJ) and from a collective agreement regarding a severance payment due on retirement (*Kowalska* v *Freie und Hansestadt Hamburg* [1990] IRLR 447 ECJ).

9.  Three major issues on the agenda at this time were the crisis over BSE or 'mad cow disease', 'quota-hopping' in the fishing industry and UK government opposition to the Working Time Directive, passed under the 'qualified majority' voting rules, thereby bypassing the UK veto.

10. The three Council Recommendations were: 84/635/EEC on the Promotion of Positive Action for Women (Official Journal of the European Communities L 331, p. 34), 92/131 /EEC on the Protection of the Dignity of Men and Women at Work (Official Journal C 27, p. 1) and 92/241/EEC on Childcare (Official Journal L 123, p. 16). Recommendations are a form of 'soft law', in the sense that, unlike Directives, they are non-binding, i.e. they do not impose such rigorous requirements on member states to comply. However, the ECJ has held that national courts are required to take Recommendations into consideration, particularly where they clarify the interpretation of national law or where they supplement binding measures (*Grimaldi* v *Fonds des Maladies Professionelles*, Case 322/88 [1990] IRLR 400).

11. In 1995 UNISON (NI) made an unsuccessful application for judicial review of the decision by a hospital trust not to suspend market testing of a number of services. The EOC(NI) conducted a formal investigation into the effects of CCT in relation to health and educational services and documented the adverse impact on women's employment (EOC(NI) 1996).

12. Harriet Harman, Secretary of State for Social Security, was appointed as Minister for Women in addition to her duties as Secretary of State. Joan Ruddock, MP was appointed as junior minister to assist her, but was given no salary for this role as the government had filled the allotted number of positions at this level (EOR 1997, No. 74). In the government reshuffle in July 1998 Baromess Jay was appointed Leader of the House of Lords and also became the new Minister for Women, replacing Harriet Harman and Joan Ruddock; Tessa Jowell became spokesperson on women's issues in the House of Commons. The women's unit moved from the Department of Social Security to the Cabinet Office, which should provide a better strategic location for co-ordinating policies across government departments.

13.   European and UK law provides limited coverage for lesbians and gay men
      from harassment (Gregory, 1995). The ECJ has ruled that discrimination on
      grounds of gender reassignment is covered by the Equal Treatment Directive (*P
      v S* [1996] IRLR 347 ECJ), but that discrimination against same sex couples is
      not (*Grant v South-West Trains Ltd* [1998] IRLR 188). At the time of writing, a
      decision from the ECJ in the case of a man dismissed from the armed forces for
      his sexual orientation is awaited (*R* v *Secretary of State for Defence ex parte
      Perkins* [1997] IRLR 297).

14.   Contract compliance is the practice of including clauses in contracts which
      impose standards on contractors in relation to employment practices. The
      Local Government Act 1988 which introduced CCT made it illegal for local
      authorities to impose 'non-commercial' conditions on contractors, with a nar-
      row exclusion for racial discrimination.

## REFERENCES

Allen, R. and Moon, G. (forthcoming) 'Strategic Litigation in Pursuit of Pay Equal-
    ity', in J. Gregory, A. Hegewisch and R. Sales (eds) *Women, Work and Inequality:
    the Challenge of Equal Pay in a Deregulated Labour Market*, Basingstoke:
    Macmillan.
Bacchi, C. L. (1996) *The Politics of Affirmative Action*, London: Sage.
Bevan, S. and Thompson, M. (1992) *Merit Pay, Performance Appraisal and Attitudes to
    Women's Work*, London: Institute of Manpower Studies Report No. 234.
Braidotti, R. (1992) 'The Exile, the Nomad and the Migrant – Reflections on Inter-
    national Feminism', *Women's Studies International Forum* Vol. 15(1), pp. 7–10.
Cockburn, C. (1991) *In the Way of Women: Men's Resistance to Sex Equality in
    Organizations*, Basingstoke: Macmillan.
Commission for Racial Equality (1998) *Reform of the Race Relations Act 1976: Propo-
    sals from the CRE*, London: CRE.
Commission of the European Communities (1995) *Proposal for a Council Decision on
    the Fourth Medium-term Community Action Programme on Equal Opportunities for
    Women and Men (1996–2000)* (Brussels COM(95) 381 final).
Docksey, C. (1991) 'The Principle of Equality between Women and Men as a Funda-
    mental Right under Community Law', *Industrial Law Journal* Vol. 20 (4) pp. 258–
    80.
Equal Opportunities Commission (1993) *Request to the Commission of the European
    Communities by the Equal Opportunities Commission of Great Britain in relation to the
    Implementation of the Principle of Equal Pay*, Manchester: EOC.
Equal Opportunities Commission (1998) *Equality in the 21st Century: A New Approach*,
    Manchester: EOC.
Equal Opportunities Commission (N. Ireland) (1996) *Report of Formal Investigation
    into Competitive Tendering in Health and Education Services in Northern Ireland*,
    Belfast: EOC (NI).
Equal Opportunities Commission (N. Ireland) (1997) *The Sex Discrimination Legisla-
    tion: Recommendations for Change*, Belfast: EOC(NI).
Ellis, E. (1988) *Sex Discrimination Law*, Aldershot: Gower.
Escott, K. and Whitfield, D. (1995) *The Gender Impact of CCT in Local Government*,
    EOC Research Discussion Series No. 12, Manchester: EOC.
European Parliament (1986) *Report drawn up on behalf of the Committee on Women's
    Rights on Violence against Women*, d'Ancona Report A2–44/86.

European Parliament (1990) *Report drawn up on behalf of the Committee of Inquiry into Racism and Xenophobia*, Ford Report A3–195/90.

Fudge, J. and McDermott, P. (eds) (1991) *Just Wages: a Feminist Assessment of Pay Equity*, Toronto: University of Toronto Press.

Fredman, S. (1997) 'Reversing Discrimination' *Law Quarterly Review*, vol. 113, pp. 575–600.

Gallagher, T., Osborne, B. and Cormack, B. (1996) 'The Operation of Policy Appraisal and Fair Treatment in Northern Ireland', conference paper, Belfast, University of Ulster.

Gregory, J. (1987) *Sex, Race and the Law: Legislating for Equality*, London: Sage.

Gregory, J. (1992) 'Equal Pay for Work of Equal Value: the Strengths and Weaknesses of Legislation', *Work, Employment and Society* Vol. 6 (3), pp. 461–73.

Gregory, J. (1995) 'Sexual Harassment: Making the Best Use of European Law', *The European Journal of Women's Studies*, Vol. 2, pp. 421–40.

Gregory, J. (1996) 'Dynamite or Damp Squib? – an Assessment of Equal Value Law', *International Journal of Discrimination Law* Vol. 1(4), pp. 313–33.

Hastings, S. (1997)'The National Minimum Wage and Equal Pay for Work of Equal Value: Will the One Achieve the Other?' Unpublished paper for the ESRC Economics of Equal Opportunities Series.

Hoskyns, C. (1996) *Integrating Gender: Women, Law and Politics in the European Union*, London: Verso.

Hoskyns, C. (forthcoming) 'Then and Now – Equal Pay in European Union Politics', in J. Gregory, A. Hegewisch and R. Sales (eds) *Women, Work and Inequality: the Challenge of Equal Pay in a Deregulated Labour Market*, Basingstoke: Macmillan.

Industrial Relations Services/Equal Opportunities Commission (1992) *Pay and Gender in Britain: 2* (second research report), London: IRS.

Institute for Public Policy Research (1997) *A Human Rights Commission for the UK: The Options*, London: IPPR.

Justice (1997) *Improving Equality Law: The Options*, London: Justice.

McCormack, I. (1996) Preface to C. McCrudden, *Mainstreaming Fairness?*, Belfast: CAJ.

McCrudden, C. (1991) 'The Evolution of the Fair Employment (Northern Ireland) Act 1989 in Parliament', in R.J. Cormack and R.D. Osborne (eds) *Discrimination and Public Policy in Northern Ireland*, Oxford: Clarendon Press.

McCrudden, C. (1996) *Mainstreaming Fairness? A discussion paper on 'Policy Appraisal and Fair Treatment'*, Belfast: Committee on the Administration of Justice.

Ministers for Women (1998) 'Policy Appraisal for Equal Treatment', London.

Ministry of Women's Affairs (1996) *The Full Picture: Guidelines for Gender Analysis*, Wellington, New Zealand.

National Disability Council (1997) *NDC Annual Report, April 1996 to March 1997*, London: HMSO.

New South Wales Department for Women (1996a) *Corporate Plan 1996–1997*.

New South Wales Department for Women (1996b) *Action Plan for Women*.

Scott, J. (1988) 'Deconstructing Equality-Versus-Difference: Or, the Uses of Post-structuralist Theory for Feminism', *Feminist Studies* Vol. 14 (1), pp. 33–50.

Standing Advisory Commission on Human Rights (1997) *Employment Equality: Building for the Future*, London: HMSO.

Trades Union Congress (1993) *Complaint to the Commission of the European Communities for Failure to Comply with Community Law*, London: TUC.

United Nations (1995) *Platform for Action, Fourth World Conference on Women, Beijing, China*, New York: UN Department of Public Information.

Women's Unit (1998) 'The Ministers for Women', London.

Wrench, J. (1996) *Preventing Racism at the Workplace: A report on 16 European countries for the European Foundation for the Improvement of Living and Working Conditions*, Luxembourg: Office for Official Publications of the European Communities.

# 8 Violence against Women: a Policy of Neglect or a Neglect of Policy?

## Liz Kelly

Britain was in the forefront of developing awareness of, and new responses to, violence against women in the early 1970s. Whilst many examples can still be found of creative and innovative work, these remain the outcome of the vision and determination of women across a range of sectors, rather than commitment from policy-makers or government. During the 1990s this neglect of an issue has been less evident in a number of other developed countries, where strong policy statements, strategic plans and research programmes[1] signal an acceptance that gender violence is a mainstream issue. As I write this chapter there is a prospect of a strategic and co-ordinated response from government, through a proposed policy document to be drafted by the government Women's Unit; it remains to be seen whether it will reflect the depth and breadth of the Canadian Panel (1993) report, or echo the courage of perspective which that report and the Australian National Strategy (1992) both display.

Violence against women has a different history and location within public policy from many of the areas addressed in this volume. Virtually all the theoretical and conceptual work, research, provision and campaigning has been undertaken by feminists, and its entry into the frame of mainstream policy debates is relatively recent. This chapter outlines the importance of violence to and for women, traces some of the ways it has been responded to in feminist theory and practice, sketches the current failures of public policy, and concludes with the challenges which responding effectively to violence against women raises for politicians, policy-makers and communities.

Violence against women is at one and the same time the issue which has generated some of the most intense debates between feminists[2] and some of the most profound theoretical and practical contributions of second-wave feminism. In less than 30 years we have moved from a situation where many of the forms of violence were not even named, let alone recognised, to gender violence having been defined as a fundamental violation of women's human rights and recognised as a major barrier to women's equality by the United Nations, World Health Organisation and the Council of Europe. The 1993 declaration from the UN world conference on human rights in Vienna stated:

gender-based violence and all forms of sexual harassment...are incompatible with the dignity and worth of the human person, and must be eliminated.

This was further developed in the Platform for Action from Beijing which calls upon all states not only to develop appropriate responses to a range of forms of violence, but to set targets for its prevention and elimination over the longer term. These strong statements of principle are the outcome of over a decade of coalition-building and skilled, strategic lobbying by feminist networks within and between every continent. Violence against women, exemplifies some of the many ironies of feminist history: work on violence against women, whilst being charged in many commentaries with essentialism, failing to address difference and constructing women as inevitable victims (see, for example, Roiphe, 1994) has produced the most long-lasting, effective and vibrant international coalitions, networks and exchanges; although it is an issue created by feminists, and the practical politics associated with it contain examples of the best efforts of women working with similarity and difference simultaneously, it remains a residual category in most women's studies courses.

The contributions and achievements of women's movements need to be acknowledged. But they also need to placed in context. Feminist perspectives are not monolithic, and debates (friendly and oppositional) abound, embracing both conceptual issues and practical strategies. Whilst the increased recognition of violence against women is undoubtedly a late twentieth-century success story, other stories attest to the multitude of ways in which feminist definitions, analyses and ambitions have either been ignored or reworked within a variety of professional and popular discourses (see, for example, Armstrong, 1994; Campbell, 1997; Dobash and Dobash, 1992; Lees, 1996).


## EVERY WOMAN'S ISSUE

The last three decades can accurately be described as decades of (re)discovery, uncovering: the range of forms of violence against women;[3] the contexts in which they occur; the extent of abuse in women's lives; its impacts and consequences; and the failures of public policy and agency practice to secure protection, justice or support.

It is only possible to give a flavour of the extensive knowledge base which has been created, but it is important to remember how limited knowledge was at the beginning of the 1970s. At this point rape and sexual abuse were understood as random, rare events committed by disordered strangers. The terms domestic violence, sexual harassment, genital mutilation and sexual exploitation had yet to be formulated. This absence of name and social definition meant that in terms of formal knowledge these realities of women's lives did not exist (Kelly, 1988). The creation of knowledge has, therefore, given social recognition to hidden and silenced experiences. In the process many of the mythologies which served as a veil to mask the extent and circumstances of men's violence in women's lives were challenged. It is precisely these facts, and the challenges they carry, which makes the issue of violence against women so profound and disturbing.

**Selected Data**

Presented here are data from Britain – both official statistics and social research, and findings from the most extensive and comprehensive international study to date. Box 1 contains data from official statistics relating to England and Wales. A number of caveats need to be borne in mind at this point: only a small proportion of assaults are reported; not all reports are recorded as crimes,[4] and therefore do not appear in crime statistics; some forms of violence against women, such as sexual harassment, are not legally defined as crimes; others, especially domestic violence, are covered under a range of generic categories (offences against the person, breach of the peace, criminal damage) and so no national figures are available. None the less, it is undoubtedly the case that reporting and recording of rape, domestic violence and sexual abuse in childhood (and more recently 'stalking') have all increased substantially in the last twenty years, with the most significant increases in the last decade.

One clear indicator of both a policy of neglect and a neglect of policy is that in 1975 the Select Committee on Violence in Marriage called for a mechanism whereby national statistics on reports of domestic violence to the police could be collated. Almost two decades later the same request was made by the Home Affairs Committee on Domestic Violence (1993). The mechanism still does not exist.

Social research provides more accurate data since it is able to uncover unreported assaults. Again some caveats need to made in order to place the findings in box 2 in context. Most research on the extent of violence against women measures prevalence – that is the proportion of the research sample who have *ever* experienced forms of assault. Traditional victimisation surveys, such as the British Crime Survey, focus on incidence – the number who have experienced victimisation within the last year; prevalence figures are, therefore, always considerably higher than incidence. This critical distinction is often not understood by practitioners and policy-makers, who frequently conflate the two. For example, the figure from our prevalence study (Kelly, Regan and Burton, 1991) that one in four girls will experience at least one incident of unwanted sexual intrusion before they are 18 has been wrongly

Box 1 Britain - Official statistics

**Rape**

| Year | No. of reports | Convictions | Conviction rate |
|------|----------------|-------------|-----------------|
| 1977 | 1015 | 324 | 32% |
| 1987 | 2471 | 445 | 18% |
| 1996 | 5759 | 573 | 10% |

*Source*: Home Office Statistics.

Reporting of rape has been increasing for two decades, but the conviction rate has dropped significantly from one in three in 1977, to one in ten in 1996.

**Domestic violence**

Since domestic violence is not a specific crime or a notifiable offence the only reliable national indicator is homicide figures.

| Year | Women killed by male ex/partner | Percent of total murders of women | Men killed by female ex/ partner | Percent of total murders of men |
|------|------|------|------|------|
| 1987 | 89 | 34% | 31 | 8% |
| 1991 | 122 | 42% | 28 | 8% |
| 1996 | 95 | 44% | 26 | 6% |

*Source*: Home Office Statistics

A current or ex-partner is the most likely murderer of women, which is not the case for men.

In recent years some local police forces have been compiling data on reported domestic violence cases. Greater Manchester Police Authority produces some of the most comprehensive.

| Year | Reported incidents | Female victims | Arrests |
|------|--------------------|----------------|---------|
| 1993 | 33,988 | 92% | 14% |
| 1994 | 35,084 | 91% | 14% |
| 1995 | 40,691 | 92% | 14% |
| 1996 | 50,291 | 89% | 12% |

*Source*: GMPA domestic violence reports, 1993, 1994, 1995, 1996.
*Note*: Police definitions include family members as well as current/ex partners.

Box 2 Britain: Findings from social research

---

**Domestic violence**

1 in 4 women have been victims of domestic violence
1 in 10 report an incident in the previous year (Mooney, 1993).

The 1992 British Crime Survey estimates a minimum of half a million domestic violence incidents per year, 80 per cent of which involve female victims (Mirrlees-Black, 1994).

**Rape**

1 in 4 women have experienced rape or attempted rape
The most common perpetrators are husbands/partners
Where rape is by a partner it is often a repeated experience (Painter, 1991).

**Sexual abuse of girls**

1 in 2 girls experience some form of unwanted sexual experience (includes non-contact forms such as flashing) before they are 18
The majority of assaults are committed by known males (Kelly, Regan and Burton, 1991).

**Sexual harassment**

More than 1 in 2 women report sexual harassment in the workplace (Her Majesty's Inspectorate of Constabulary, 1993; Industrial Society, 1993).

2 out of 3 of women report at least one experience of flashing (McNeil, 1987).

2 out of 3 women have received abusive/obscene phone calls (Glasgow Women's Support Project, 1990); 1 in 10 women receive at least one each year (Buck, Chatterton and Pease, 1995).

**Cumulative experiences and consequences**

Most women recall at least one incident of intimate intrusion in their lifetime and many report multiple experiences (Hanmer and Saunders, 1984; Kelly, 1988).
Women are more fearful about crime and restrict their movements and involvements in public life far more than men. Fear of sexual violence accounts for these gendered differences (Stanko, 1990).

used to suggest that in *any* classroom 1 in 4 children will be being abused. This prediction would not be accurate, even in a classroom of 18 year olds, most young people have left school before 18 so the class would not be representative.

There are no shared definitions of the various forms of violence against women, thus prevalence estimates will be higher or lower depending on the breadth or limitation of definition used. For example, in sexual abuse research the age cut off for childhood has been set at 15, 16 and 18, some researchers have excluded 'non-contact' abuse, including flashing, and some require an age difference of five years or more between victim and perpetrator where the perpetrator is also under 16/18. Debate also continues about the most effective methods for research into sensitive issues, and violence against women in particular. The promotion of qualitative methods, especially face-to-face interviews by women, as the preferred strategy has been tempered by the publication of quantitative studies which have drawn on lessons learnt from the smaller detailed studies which preceded them. Indeed, it has been the adoption of strategies developed in feminist qualitative research by government-sponsored victimisation surveys, like the BCS, which have led to improvements in their detection of violence against women, especially domestic violence and sexual assault.[5] What still discriminates between studies is the amount of attention paid to the form, wording and number of questions designed to invite disclosure (see Johnson and Sacco, 1995; Kelly, Burton and Regan, 1992, for more detailed discussion).

Unfortunately, in the UK, we still lack the depth and resourcing of prevalence research that has been evident in other developed countries. The majority of the studies cited in box 2 were conducted on small budgets and were, therefore, limited in sample size and geographical reach – most drawing on local community samples. It is, however, interesting to note that many of the prevalence estimates echo those found in the Statistics Canada study (see box 3); currently regarded as the most rigorous and methodologically sophisticated to date. Both the small-scale UK studies and the Canadian research record much higher rates of victimisation than have been detected by even the most recent British Crime Survey.

The accumulation of knowledge has produced a range of critical insights which challenge previous orthodoxies. Some of the most important are:

- Most women have suffered at least one form of gendered violence in their lifetime.
- Experiences span the commonality of sexual harassment to sexual and domestic murder.
- Women and girls are most likely to be victimised by a male known to them.
- Whilst differences of class, race, age, sexuality and disability do not protect women, there are both variations in vulnerability across the life course and

some assaults where women are targeted because of their difference (Kelly and Radford, forthcoming).

- The home, far from being 'a safe haven' for women and girls, is frequently the location for brutal physical and sexual assaults.
- Almost any setting which women and girls frequent can be the location for abuse, but some settings generate cultures of abuse, these include workplaces which have a predominantly male labour force and many residential settings, including those in which disabled children and adults live.
- Whilst single experiences are reported, many forms of violence against women – especially sexual harassment, sexual assault, sexual abuse in childhood and domestic violence – involve repeat victimisation.
- Assaults that begin in one setting can spill over into others – from the home into the street, to the houses of a woman's supporters and even to her employment. Harassment may focus on work, but also involve phone calls at home, tracking of, and even interference in, women's private lives.
- Both the cumulation of experiences in individual women's lives, and their knowledge of violence locally and generally have consequences ranging from factoring personal safety into routine decision-making to long-term mental health problems.

Whilst the extent of particular forms of violence against women and children – such as rape, sexual harassment or domestic violence – is sometimes acknowledged, it is the fact that they can be cumulative, and that women's sense of danger encompasses many potentials for violence, and affects everyday routine behaviour, which accounts for the overall impact on women's lives. The Canadian panel note:

> All women pay the price of male violence: while not every woman has directly experienced violence, there are few who do not fear it and whose lives are not in some way affected and restricted by its pervasive presence in our society. (1993, p. 6)

That violence is an issue for every woman is illuminated not just by the findings of prevalence research, but also through a number of surveys and local authority consultations in which violence against women features as one of, if not the, issue which women are concerned about.

The prevalence and cumulative nature of violence against women makes it a citizenship issue. The right to personal security and bodily integrity is systematically denied more often to women than men. For men the threat to basic security primarily concerns the public sphere, whereas for women and children the home (the private) is one of the most likely settings in which violence occurs. The fear and threat of violence limits not only women's sense of security and safety, but also their behaviour. A number of studies demonstrate that women restrict the places they go to and the times they

## Box 3 Statistics Canada Study: Selected findings

---

**Methodology**
*Conducted in 1993 following extensive consultation on both methods and content of survey instrument*

*National random sample of 12,300 women*

*Telephone interviews*

**Physical and sexual assault**
  1 in 2 (51%) women have experienced at least one assault since age 16.
  45% by current/ex partner, 23% other known men, 23% by strangers

**Domestic violence**
  1 in 4 (29%) of ever married or cohabiting women have experienced violence from a current or ex partner
  • 1 in 3 (34%) had feared at some point for their life
  • 2 out of 3 (63%) reported repeat assaults
  • 1 in 2 (48%) separated women reported violence from ex/partners
  • 1 in 5 (19%) of this group were assaulted after separation, and in a third of these cases the violence was more severe.
  • 1 in 6 (15%) of currently married women reported violence from their partner
  • 1 in 10 (13%) women of this group reported fearing for their lives

**Rape and sexual assault**
  4 in 10 (39%) women report a sexual assault
  More than half (57%) of women sexually assaulted by someone other than a spouse reported repeat victimisation, 1 in 4 (26%) reported four or more assaults.

**Sexual harassment**
  9 out of 10 (87%) women report sexual harassment, the most common forms being street harassment, obscene phone calls and flashing.
  85% of reported incidents involving strangers
  50% reported incidents involving known men, a large proportion of which were work related

**Personal safety**
  More than 2 out of 3 women reported concerns for their safety in a variety of public settings and many reported using precautionary strategies.
  Heightened fears were linked to socio-economic status and previous experiences of intrusion and assault.

**Reporting**
  Domestic violence        1 in 4 women reported at least one
                           incident to the police
  Sexual assaults          1 in 20 were reported to the police
  Assaults by intimates are least likely to be reported

*Source: Canadian Journal of Criminology Special Issue: Focus on the Violence Against Women Survey, July 1995.*

---

travel; a 1988 Harris survey found that women's travel patterns were strongly influenced by the need to avoid danger (Crime Concern, 1993) and the 1992 British Crime Survey confirmed that women restrict their movements far more than men do. Indeed there is no place that women and children are safe from the possibility of abuse – the home, educational institutions, work-places, leisure facilities, places of religious worship, hospitals and residential homes, public transport, streets and public spaces are all locations where violence occurs. This lack of a safe haven has significant impacts on women's quality of life.

Ruth Lister, in her exploration of feminist perspectives on citizenship (1997), notes how traditional conceptions of 'the citizen' have been disembodied abstract individuals:

> women enter public space as *embodied* individuals; their citizenship can be jeopardised by sexual violence and its threat, sexual harassment and pornographic or derogatory sexual representations. Women's bodily experiences still tend to be 'constructed as problematic, abnormal, or outwith the realm of politics' as 'a barrier to citizenship', against the norm of male bodily experience which is taken for granted. (p. 71, original emphasis)

Lister also points to the failure nationally and internationally to ensure that the autonomy which has been seen as one of the prerequisites of citizenship encompasses physical autonomy:

> If women cannot move and act freely in the public sphere and/or are intimidated in the private sphere because of the threat of violence, then their ability to act as citizens is curtailed, as is that of Black and gay men as well as women, in the face of racist and homophobic violence. Where women have fled their country to escape sexual violence, the lack of recognition of the right of bodily integrity in international human rights law has served to deny them refugee status (p. 113).[6]

Violence has extensive and profound implications for women's quality of life and life chances; it has direct and indirect consequences in terms of employment, relationships, health, leisure, and political participation. Unfortunately the linkage between violence and most areas of social policy are seldom anticipated by either policy-makers or policy analysts.

## SISTERS DOING IT FOR THEMSELVES

The emergence of innovative and creative responses to violence against women is one of the lasting contributions of feminist action. The last three decades have been witness to the creation and maintenance of new approaches to explanation, practical support and policy.

The 1970s was a decade of protests and transformations; protests at legal judgments and judicial thinking and Reclaim the Night marches; transformation in responses to women through the establishment of new services run by women for women. A network of refuges and rape crisis lines emerged, often run on shoe-string budgets with volunteers. The 1980s was a time of expansion and consolidation alongside the emergence of strong challenges to professional discourses and practices. The most evident of these were the questioning of police responses to both domestic violence and rape, and towards the end of the decade feminist intervention into debates about child sexual abuse. During this period some attention was paid to sexual harassment and women's safety more broadly. The former was narrowed down to an employment issue and became the preserve of trade unions and employers, the later was addressed by some local authorities especially in relation to street lighting, planning and transport. The 1990s has been the decade of domestic violence, with some local areas attempting to develop more integrated approaches, including corporate policies and work with violent men (see Mullender, 1996, for more detailed discussion). Most local areas now have inter-agency domestic violence fora, which are supposed to ensure co-ordinated and consistent responses (Hague, Malos and Dear, 1996). The ascendancy of domestic violence can be seen in the frequency with which policy-makers and politicians use the term as if it were equivalent to violence against women. That said, however, the 1900s also saw the return of explicitly feminist campaigning, both about particular issues[7] and through the first crime prevention campaign addressing violence against women, Zero Tolerance.

This gloss suggests a story of progress, and in the sense of placing the issue of violence on policy, research and other agendas this is true. But it is a story of uneven progress; of change being driven by women inside and outside organisations. Overall, the implementation of changes has been patchy and inconsistent, and has to be set in the context of government policy more generally in terms of increasing poverty especially for women and young people, decreased access to safe, affordable housing, cutbacks in welfare benefits and access to justice.

As recognition of violence against women in general, and specific forms of it, were gradually acknowledged, debates about definition emerged. Such debates are not just struggles about meaning and conceptualisation, they invariably include contests about who has the power to define social reality. Celia Kitzinger (1994) notes that new social problems are always contested since they constitute a challenge to taken for granted meanings and definitions. She further outlines the most common definitional strategies which are marshalled to resist challenges to taken for granted knowledge: 'the frequency game' – if it is rare, then it is not a serious problem; if it is common, then it is normal rather than problematic; victim blame; reference to unwarranted incursions of the state into private life; reversals – such as an over-emphasis on abuse by women; and boundary disputes. All of these can be discerned, and could be mapped out through time in the responses to suggestions that current legal frameworks and the methods used in previous research were inadequate to the task of recognising violence against women.

## THEORETICAL MILESTONES AND/OR MINEFIELDS

Both definitions and prevalence estimates influence what requires explanation. If sexual violence is defined narrowly and therefore relatively rare, it is the exceptional which requires explanation. If on the other hand it is defined more broadly, and is a common experience in the lives of women and girls, then the opposite is the case:

> that sexual violence is so pervasive supports the view that the locus of violence rests squarely in the middle of what our culture defines as 'normal' interaction between men and women. (Johnson, 1988, p. 146)

Extending this approach Lori Heise (1994), in a report published by the World Bank, comments:

> Violence against women is an extremely complex phenomenon, deeply rooted in gender-based power relations, sexuality, self-identity, and social institutions. Any strategy to eliminate gender violence must therefore confront the underlying cultural beliefs and social structures that perpetuate it. (p. 29)

How the extensiveness of violence against women is to be understood and explained has been an issue of contention for much of the history of contemporary women's movements. Using the conventional distinction between liberal, socialist and radical feminist perspectives,[8] it is the latter which has both had the most to say and been best equipped to accommodate the issue. Evidence of widespread victimisation, especially within 'intimate' relations, cannot easily be located within a liberal framework focused on discrimination in the public sphere. The emphasis on economics and class relations in socialist feminism was also challenged by the evidence that privileged women were not immune from assault, and that working-class men were often positioned as the persecutors, rather than protectors, of the women and children in their families and communities.

The vast majority of violence and abuse of women and children is committed by men. Although each individual makes a choice to use violence, explanations which focus only on individual traits cannot account for either the scale of the problem or what has been called the 'male monopoly'. It is the implication of men as individuals, and as a social group, which has made violence against women such a contentious area of investigation. As feminist research and practice has revealed the systematic, planned and organised nature of much abuse of women and children, the deliberateness of the infliction of pain and harm, many found the evidence disturbing and threatening. That women were most likely to be assaulted by men that they knew, current and former intimates and family members, lent support to critical feminist analysis of the family and heterosexuality. Discomfort with the fundamental questions violence against women poses is one reason why the connections between it and other areas of women's inequality have been inadequately theorised.

Any serious attempt to tackle violence against women must combine a short- and long-term strategy; the former aimed at addressing current victimisation and the legacies of the past, the latter at eliminating it. Neither can make significant progress if the fundamental questions are avoided – but this is precisely what happens when social policy initiatives are discussed with no reference to violence against women. What, for example, are the implications of policies on the family, the rights and responsibilities of fatherhood, divorce which eschew recognition of the extent of domestic violence, of child sexual abuse within the family? The point is not that the ambitions of government policy-makers – to build stronger families and more lasting links between men and their children – are wrong, but that without an accompanying awareness of the extent to which the family remains a context in which men's use of violence is commonplace the outcome is likely to further disempower women and children. The best intentions may create the worst of outcomes. Similar arguments can be made about plans to increase young men's contact with children through the childcare initiative (both babysitting and nurseries are contexts in which young children are sexually abused) and welfare to work where limited, if any, attention is being paid to sexual harassment.

The locating of male violence as a key form of male domination has been an issue of contention within feminist theory, as has the inclusion of pornography and prostitution as forms of violence against women. The most recent charge made against those who have chosen to focus on sexual violence is that they are guilty of essentialism; constructing women as inevitable victims and men as predetermined abusers. The accusation is often supported by selective and literal readings of rhetorical statements. For example, the statement that 'all men are potential rapists' does not state that all men *are* rapists (although this is often how it is interpreted), but was intended to draw attention to the fact that rapists can be any man, that rapists are, in the main, not strangers, not 'deviant' others who can be easily identified and avoided.

The reproach that work on violence against women has created a 'victimhood' feminism sits uneasily with the rejection by most women's organisations of the term victim, and its replacement with the concept of 'survivor', which is intended to draw attention to women's agency in coping with both victimisation and its consequences. 'Victimhood' is usually referred to in the abstract; applying it to real lives is problematic and frequently involves eliding feminist analysis with therapeutic responses (see Armstrong, 1994; Kelly, Burton and Regan, 1996). At a recent conference in Calcutta the story of five girls from Nepal who were trafficked to India was told.[9] The girls jumped out of a window to escape being prostituted, all are now back in Nepal, but three have major disabilities and one will never walk again. Research and practice has documented how many young women with histories of sexual abuse populate our prisons and children's homes; many self-harm, disfiguring their arms, legs and faces. All these young women are agents, they act to establish some control over their destinies and emotions. But the context in which their actions take place involves victimisation. To minimise their abuse is to remove from consideration the material realities through which their actions become explicable.

At the same time as being contested within feminism, theoretical and conceptual developments with respect to violence against women have resulted in some of the most profound challenges to professional and academic discursive frameworks. Feminist perspectives have had extensive influence in such disparate fields as social work, probation, law and the humanities more broadly. Indeed, some of the most intense debates within academic life over the last two decades have concerned issues such as pornography, whether and how to work with violent men and sex offenders and how to understand the family.

One clear example is the scholarship in feminist jurisprudence on violence against women. The work of women like Catharine MacKinnon and Robyn West has questioned the fundamental canons of liberal democratic law, and generated more debate than any other contemporary legal theorists. Robyn West's recent book *Caring for Justice* attempts to find a route through a variety of theoretical minefields which arise in both feminist thought and legal argument. Her central enterprise is to establish that an ethic of care need not be precluded from the practice of law, and that the practice of care would be less problematic for women if it were just. In the process she outlines how the current framework of law cannot accommodate a range of gender-based harms, including violence against women.

> physically, women suffer harms of *invasion* not suffered by men; emotionally, women suffer greater harms of *separation* and isolation than men do; psychically, women suffer distinctive harms to their subjectivity, or sense and reality of *selfhood* that have no correlate in men's lives; and politically, women suffer distinctive harms of patriarchal *subjection* ... (p. 100; original emphasis)

In a framework of formal equality the rights women share with men 'are rights and entitlements to be free of harms largely suffered by men' (p. 8). Thus, to address gendered harms effectively some of the accepted – but not necessary – foundations of law have to be transformed.

Engaging with violence against women at the level of theory, and in terms of policy development, is not an arena where fundamental questions can be easily fudged. The field contains theoretical milestones and minefields; negotiating them, rather than choosing an alternative route, is one substantial challenge for policy development.

## COUNTING THE COSTS

There are enduring repercussions of violence for *all* women. The threat and reality of violence can limit choices in virtually every sphere of life including work, social life and relationships. In surveys women are most likely to express this in terms of fear in the public sphere, and particularly fear of rape, more detailed explorations – either in research or just in conversation reveal that many of women's routine actions in a range of settings are informed by the wish to minimise/avoid harassment, abuse and violence.

Failure to integrate violence against women in public policy means the huge personal, interpersonal and social costs of violence continue to be borne by women and their supporters. There are also substantial financial costs to the public purse, and some work quantifying this has recently been undertaken. The Canadian Panel Report notes:

> The cost benefits of violence prevention ... have not been clear to many because such costs have never been realistically or comprehensively tabulated in Canada. Even a rough estimate of the cost of one crime of violence provides some appreciation of the need to prevent violence from happening in the first place. The cost of one sexual offence where the offender serves three years in prison can be conservatively estimated at $200,000. (p. 12)

A recent report *Violence Against Women: the Hidden Health Burden* (Heise, 1994) includes the following:

- in the US women who have been raped or beaten incur two and a half times the medical costs of women who have not been victimised;
- the most significant predictor of psychiatric treatment, suicide attempts, criminal convictions and involvement in the sex industry is prior victimisation;
- globally 1 in 5 of women's loss of healthy years of life (calculated as DALYs – Disability-Adjusted Life Years) are due to domestic violence and rape.

Lori Heise (p. 17) concludes: 'rape and domestic violence emerge as a significant cause of disability and death among women of reproductive age in both the industrial and developing world.'

Minimal work of this nature has been conducted in the UK, and most international studies to date have focused on domestic violence. The one published UK study echoes this trend in estimating selected costs to the public purse of domestic violence in the London borough of Hackney (Stanko et al., 1998). It concludes that £7.9 million was spent, in 1996, on an ineffective and poorly co-ordinated response.

These kinds of calculations can be important tools in discussions about resource allocation, but they also run the risk of prioritising financial expenditure at the expense of the fundamental principle of women's right to personal and bodily integrity. The toll of violence and abuse defies accounting measures. Years of abuse or a single incident can result in nightmares and have profound impacts on trust in, and intimacy with, others. The physical costs can also be tremendous in terms of scars, broken bones, lacerations, internal injury. For some women permanent disabilities result, for others miscarriages, HIV infection and a range of other consequences are continual reminders of past victimisation.

Experiences of violence often involve other losses in women/children's lives, including: loss of control; loss of independence; loss of memories; loss of confidence; loss of housing and property; loss of support networks including family and friends; loss of status; loss of children; loss of jobs and educational opportunities; loss of freedom; and even loss of life itself. Two authors have recently drawn attention to the damage men's violence does not only to women's sense of self but also their connections to others (Herman, 1993; West, 1997). Robyn West links her insights to the recent emphasis in social theory on subjectivity. She argues that victimisation threatens, and even at times severs, elements of the liberal individualist concept of selfhood, that women's subjectivity is limited, diminished and even at times destroyed by sexual violence.

## THE NEGLECT OF POLICY AND POLICY OF NEGLECT

Developing policy on violence against women requires engaging, even if only minimally, with the difficult questions it raises. It necessitates, at least in passing, noting the extent to which substantial numbers of men inflict damage on women and children. It requires recognising and understanding why intervention has failed to support, protect or deliver justice to countless women and children. In one sense it is unsurprising that governments and organisations have preferred to avoid these complex and challenging tasks.

There have been moments when the force of public pressure has prompted change, and opportunities which women's organisations and their supporters have used to move agendas forward. But these have always been restricted to particular forms of violence; neither the opportunity to develop integrated policies nor the connections between forms of violence against women have been grasped. In the remainder of this section I seek to draw attention to the absence of strategic thinking, to trumpeted changes which over time have proved to be chimera. At the same time it is undoubtedly the case that some changes in attitudes and individuals have occurred, and many women and children have benefited from their encounters with committed advocates in the statutory and voluntary sectors. But this remains a matter of good fortune, respectful and effective responses cannot be guaranteed, and there has clearly been little if any impact on the scale of violence women and children suffer.

In what follows I use the criminal justice system as an exemplar of both the neglect of policy and the policy of neglect. It has been an important principle of women's activism to have violence against women recognised as a criminal act, since this both validates women and children's sense of violation and makes strong statements about the unacceptability of violence through sanctions on perpetrators. Responses to domestic violence and rape are explored in depth, as in this instance the failures are as much in the detail as the overall framework.

## Case Studies in Policy Failure

Over the last two decades the numbers of women and children reporting domestic violence, rape and sexual abuse has increased markedly. Research projects, women's organisations and occasional media attention have, for over two decades, highlighted the failures of the justice system and resulted in calls for change. But in the 1990s there is little evidence that policy has made more than a minimal difference.

Police responses to domestic violence have long been a target of criticism; a reluctance to intervene in the 'private' and attitudes which defined assaults in the home as 'just a domestic' were finally acknowledged in 1990 by the Home Office, which issued a circular (60/1990) calling for a more interventionist policy. Whilst not a mandatory arrest policy there was a strong statement that where an offence had been committed arrest should follow. Stress was also placed on recording and investigating domestic violence in the same way as other violent crimes. The potential of Domestic Violence Units (DVUs) within the police to encourage good practice was also noted.

An internal Home Office study (Grace, 1995) to assess the impact of the circular found that whilst some change was evident, it was inconsistent within and between forces. Many officers were unaware of the circular or local policies based upon it, arrest was still limited to a minority of cases (12–14 per cent), with a far lower proportion proceeding to prosecution, and the most likely outcomes of court cases were fines or bindovers. Thus whilst a positive policy was created, monitoring its implementation was neglected, both within the police and by government. The absence of substantial change was reflected in the actions (and inactions) of other players in the criminal justice system, especially the Crown Prosecution Service (CPS), magistrates and judges.

Several little publicised policy decisions had precisely the opposite effect. Charging standards and case disposal were agreements between the police and CPS in the mid-1990s, designed to create a shared framework for the laying of charges (see Kelly, 1996a, for more detailed discussion). Charging standards involved redefining a variety of crimes, including assaults. Various injuries which previously would have fallen within the remit of Actual Bodily Harm (ABH) were located in the lesser charge of Common Assault. Many of these are the likely injuries in an incident of domestic violence. The implications for domestic violence cases include: that whilst ABH is an 'arrestable offence' common assault is not; the likely sentence for a conviction for common assault is far lower than for ABH; and in some areas local agreements were made between the police and CPS to not prosecute common assaults, using other strategies such as cautions. Case disposal requires police officers following an arrest to complete a form before making the decision whether to lay a charge. The process involves assessing a variety of aggravating and mitigating factors; a calculation where one is subtracted from the other produces a number which in turn determines whether a charge should be laid. A number of the mitigating factors can be read through the traditional reasons for non-intervention in domestic violence. Both of these policies were developed in relation to a wide variety of crimes; but it is evident that at all levels the implications for domestic violence were neglected. It is yet another illustration of a policy of neglect that no attempt has been made to assess the impact of these changes on responses to domestic violence.[10] The consequence was not simply that a Home Office policy on policing domestic violence was seriously undermined by organisational decision-making, but also that these decisions were being implemented at the same time as the Home Office and Scottish Office were running short-lived public education campaigns based on the message that domestic violence is a crime.

The evolution of DVUs within the police further illustrates inconsistency and lack of follow-through. The original model in Tottenham aimed to improve police responses in responding to domestic violence as a crime. Two female officers monitored all domestic violence cases and followed up those where officers had failed to enforce the law. The DVU officers acted as advocates for a law enforcement response. The model was adopted by many forces and divisions, but with subtle differences. By the mid-1990s most DVUs were operating as a clearing-house, collating information on cases and offering some form of victim support. Towards the end of the decade, despite no evidence that practice had changed substantially (in fact, most research on policing shows minimal if any change), some forces are either disbanding their DVU or combining them into larger Women and Child Units or Vulnerable Person Units. These decisions reflect both the culture of change for change's sake within the police, and a perception – all evidence to the contrary – that they have so improved their responses to domestic violence that specialist units are no longer needed.

What has happened over the last two decades with respect to rape is an even clearer example of neglect. The figures presented in box 2 illustrate the attrition rate for reported rapes. Governments have presided over a worsening situation for almost two decades: in 1977 one in three reported rapes resulted in a conviction, by 1996 this had slumped to under one in ten. Yet there was no attention paid to this crisis in the legal processing of rape until the figures were analysed by feminists and published in the Labour Party consultation document *Peace at Home*. This prompted questions in the House of Commons, and a study commissioned by the Home Office to investigate. This is due to be completed at the end of 1998, but the interim report (Harris, 1998) reveals that despite instructions to the contrary large numbers of rape complaints are still being 'no crimed' by the police (see also Lees and Gregory, 1993). Over a third of reported rapes do not pass the first hurdle, either because the police decide that it is a 'false' complaint or women decide to withdraw the complaint. At each further stage of the process cases are lost, including acquittals in court.

Policy changes designed to prevent further victimisation of women during the investigation and trying of rape cases have clearly failed. Circulars issued to the police following the revelations in a documentary featuring Thames Valley police in 1982 were intended to prevent the type of interrogation which caused public outrage. Yet Jennifer Tempkin recorded the following almost ten years later from a detective with responsibility for investigating rape complaints:

I am not a great believer in pussyfooting around and mollycoddling the woman because she won't get that in court. She has got to understand that, all right, she has given this story, but its got to be watertight. It's got to be absolutely bomb proof ... My role would be to make sure that what she is saying will hold up. There has to be a certain amount of coming back to her time and time again to say, 'Look this is what he says has happened, can you negate that or can you prove this?' You have got to sift through the bits which can sometimes appear quite nasty when you are doing it, but it does save the woman some trouble when it gets to court ... You've got, to a certain extent, to put her through the mill to make her understand what she is going to go through in court .... I always, always without fail tell a woman that rape is the most difficult offence to prove and the easiest one to allege. (pp. 516–17)

This police officer proceeds to recount how much attitudes have improved since he joined the force, but that some of the older officers are still chauvinists! This small qualitative study sought to explore how far reporting rape had changed by the early 1990s. It did reveal that initial contact with a trained sympathetic female officer is seen positively by women. However, the investigation is then invariably transferred to CID, whose officers are generally male, and women's experiences from this point on vary.

The provisions of Section 2 of the Sexual Offences (Amendment) Act 1976 were intended to limit the extent to which women were subjected to degrading, and arguably irrelevant, questioning about their previous sexual history in court. It was clear that applications under Section 2 were expected to be granted only in 'exceptional' circumstances. Sue Lees' research (1996) demonstrates that permission to cross-examine on these issues is frequently given, and that many counsel do not bother seeking judicial approval before raising these issues. Similarly, rather than removing the corroboration warning altogether, as many other common law jurisdictions have done, it took until 1994 for it to be made discretionary in England and Wales.

The right of accused men to cross-examine the person who has accused them of rape is but the latest example of policy failure. The most publicised case involved Julia Mason, who chose to forgo her right to anonymity in order to campaign against this aspect of law. At the time of her case the then Home Secretary, Michael Howard, asserted that this would not be allowed to happen again. Cross-party support made reform unproblematic in parliamentary terms. Nothing was done. The issue was one of the few explicit commitments about violence against women in the Labour Party's policies on women in the run-up to the 1997 general election. Yet at least two other cases have taken place in 1997, which prompted similar concerned statements from the new Home Secretary Jack Straw, but no action has been forthcoming.[11]

There was also encouragement in the mid-1980s for police and health authorities to explore establishing sexual assault centres, drawing on an Australian model, where investigative requirements could be conducted in a context which took more account of the needs of victims. The St Mary's Centre in Manchester was the flagship example of this kind of provision. A decade later there are only two other centres which provide similar services, both in the north-east of England. Many police forces did develop 'rape examination suites', but it is unclear how many of them remain, and in forces which cover a large area it is often impossible to transport women to them, especially at night. It remains the case that women reporting rape still cannot be guaranteed that the forensic medical examination will be conducted by a woman doctor (Tempkin, 1996).

## The Politics of Reaction and Redefinition

A similar picture of policy failure could be painted with respect to child sexual abuse, sexual harassment, pornography and prostitution. A pattern emerges: a neglect of the issue for long periods of time; a trigger to action, usually a media 'scandal'; a reactive response to defuse public pressure. Such changes seldom get to the root of the problem, and are often not even considered important enough to be systematically monitored. In the case of child sexual abuse the scandal was not the extent of abuse of children, but events in Cleveland in the mid-1980s. A consensus discourse emerged, questioned only by feminists (see Campbell, 1997, for a detailed account), that the problem was poor professional practice. Similar events drove policy frameworks in other industrialised countries. One outcome has been a proliferation of literature and official guidance focused on appropriate methods of investigation, assessment and treatment responses. Debates in the field are increasingly limited to matters related to legal processes and requirements (see, for example, Department of Health, 1995; Myers, 1994) rather than the wider social implications which raise complex questions about masculinity, childhood and the family (Driver and Droisen, 1989; MacLeod and Saraga, 1988). This avoidance of the key issues has been further fuelled by the 'return of the paedophile' (see Kelly, 1996b), which is rapidly returning us to perceptions of abusers as deviant monsters, outsiders who have no place in children's daily lives. This media-driven agenda has been ably abetted by successive governments, and has seriously undermined the understanding that children are most at risk from men that they know. Whilst policy on sex offenders has developed rapidly in recent years it is grounded in a fundamental flaw, and has yet to engage honestly with the contradictions between, for example, a proposal that convicted sex offenders be barred from paid and voluntary work with children and the fact that the presumption of contact for children with parents means that rapist fathers are frequently awarded contact by the courts.[12]

As awareness of the extent of sexual violence has developed, so have professional responses to it. In many western societies this response has become increasingly therapeutic and individualised (Dobash and Dobash, 1992); displacing feminist frameworks which stressed collective support and response, through self-help groups and political activism. The last decade could be described as a 'decade of disorders' in relation to the impacts of sexual violence. A range of syndromes and disorders have been proposed, researched and debated, with some being formally recognised as 'diagnoses' in the Diagnostic and Statistical Manual (DSM). All, have, however, proved inadequate in encompassing the range of victimisation and its consequences (see, for example, Finkelhor, 1986; Herman, 1992). Judith Herman (1992) has recently proposed an integrated traumatic response model which includes single events, repeated assaults and the potential for cumulative impacts. Whilst undoubtedly a more inclusive framework, the emphasis on damage and personal healing has eclipsed an earlier stress on social justice and collective action (see Armstrong, 1995, for an analysis of this transformation in relation to incest). It is something of a bitter irony, that whilst a medicalised response is increasingly evident (a brief perusal of the 'self-help' section of any bookshop will prove the point) the area where the least policy development is evident in the UK is the health sector. Limited recognition exists of violence and abuse as a significant cause of physical and mental health problems. Mis- or wrong diagnoses represent significant costs to health care systems, individuals themselves and their social networks. Prescription of medication, and/or repeated use of mental health services are the most obvious examples of inappropriate responses, but lack of intervention also means that in a significant number of cases violence and abuse will continue and subsequent injuries will be incurred.

No government has developed policy which secures the network of provision developed in the voluntary sector. Thus the few organisations that offer specialist support are constantly seeking replacement sources of funding, simply to stand still. The preference of funding bodies for 'new' projects places inordinate pressure on maintaining core functions. Women and children who have suffered violence and/or abuse have the right to expect adequate support. There is currently no consistency in the level and form of provision, and women and children are unknowing players in a geographical and/or interpersonal lottery. Policy must also seek to ensure equality of access and redress to *all* women who have experienced victimisation. The barriers which are created for black and migrant women, disabled women, young and elderly women, lesbians, women in the sex industry, women with mental health problems must be explored and addressed at all levels.

Whilst policy failures are evident with respect to provision, protection and justice they are even more stark with respect to prevention. The scale of violence against women means it is as serious a public policy issue as HIV/AIDS or drink driving. But the only serious attempt at prevention of violence against women through public education, Zero Tolerance, has emerged from a small women's organisation, and local authorities have to choose to run it. Rather than adopt the campaign, senior Labour Party politicians, including the soon to be Prime Minister, Tony Blair, co-opted the slogan for a range of other issues (from crime in general to failing schools) and in the process did considerable damage to the profile of a small, but effective, women's group.

Official responses to prevention have been a proliferation in 'safety advice' to women (Stanko, 1993) and assertiveness training for women has become the predominant response of organisations to sexual harassment. Both implicitly reassert women's responsibility for policing men's behaviour, and suggest that is the content of individual interactions which is the issue rather than gender inequality. Similar arguments can be made in relation to child sexual abuse prevention programmes which centre on teaching children strategies to escape/ avoid assaults – strategies which many have already used (Kelly, Regan and Burton, 1993; Reppucci and Hauggard, 1989). Few prevention efforts to date have taken up the challenge of 'primary prevention'; interventions which are intended to stop men and boys from using sexual aggression.

## TOWARDS A POLICY FRAMEWORK

The failure of the state and public services to curb violence against women and children has created a context in which women do not have equal access to justice, employment, leisure, community and political participation, freedom of movement – all of which are basic to modern concepts of citizenship. Unchecked violence encourages and maintains social discrimination and social exclusion.[13] In the short term this means developing responses which state the unacceptability of abuse, and in the longer term developing strategies which target the underlying causes.

Protection from violence is something citizens have the right to expect from the national and local state, particularly legal protection. Protection should support and empower those who have been victimised, so that the state becomes a resource in the active empowerment of individuals and groups and the guardian of equity. This would require better access for women to resources, justice and services than at present. Currently the legal framework hinders, rather than enables, in part because most of the statute law in place is inadequate at best, and at worst serves to reinforce outdated notions of women's sexuality, and women's and children's credibility as witnesses. Any attempt to address violence against women in a coherent and integrated way must begin with a fundamental review of criminal and civil law, including the reporting process and procedural issues. In the process the kinds of far-reaching reforms which have been introduced in other jurisdictions must be canvassed.[14]

The wide-scale nature and consequences of violence against women and children makes it relevant to employment and incomes policy, poverty, immigration policy, law and order, housing, transport and planning, health care and education. It should also be a thread in equalities work with regard to racism, disability, the elderly and lesbian and gay rights. It is also relevant to defence and foreign policy, not only in terms of the recent attention to 'war rape' but also evidence of sexual violence perpetrated by UN 'peace keeping' forces, amongst whom will number UK nationals (Enloe, 1994). In foreign policy attention must be given to the involvement of British nationals in sex tourism and trafficking, outside the UK, and whether and how governments in developing countries are addressing the issue ought to inform overseas development.

An integrated approach would require all government departments – at national, regional and local levels – to consider violence against women, to audit all decisions and policies to ensure that they are consistent with a broad set of principles. Those outlined below (adapted from the Canadian Panel on Violence Against Women for a Council of Europe report [Kelly, 1997]) would be a useful starting point, and draw on the principle of zero tolerance.

---

National and local government should provide a leading role in the elimination of violence against women and children. For this to be effective other organisations and all communities and individuals need to become involved in developing a social climate of zero tolerance. These principles, adapted from the Canadian Panel report would be a starting point.

Equality and freedom from violence are rights of all women and children, and it is the responsibility of every individual, community, government and institution to work towards securing those rights.

- The elimination of violence will best be achieved through the adoption and rigorous application of a policy of zero tolerance.
- No amount of violence is acceptable, and the elimination of violence against women and children must be an absolute priority.
- Those with responsibility for public safety have an obligation to take the most comprehensive and effective action possible to prevent violence from happening and limit the harms from violence when it has occurred.
- Sexist and racist practices and other forms of discrimination and bias which encourage or support acts of violence must be eliminated.
- The rights of the victims in the legal system must be at least equal to the rights of the accused.
- Victims must not be blamed for the violence committed against them.
- Governments and institutions have a primary responsibility to demonstrate leadership and provide resources to achieve equality and end violence.
- Individuals and all communities within society have a responsibility to work towards ending violence and achieving equality for all.

---

Whilst making clear the responsibilities of government and organisations, there is a recognition in these principles that any serious attempt to eradicate violence against women necessitates changes at the community and individual levels too.

Working with such principles will require insight and courage from government; insight into the range[15] and connections between forms of violence against women and children[16] and courage in addressing the complexity which the issue creates for existing policy commitments. For example, whilst there were two pages in the Labour Party's election document on women addressing violence against women its connections to the other policy areas was not developed, and the issue is noticeable in its absence from policy documents on both the family and crime. I am not suggesting that existing commitments or policy has to be abandoned, but rather that it must be qualified and/or enhanced by recognition of the difference that integrating violence against women makes. Below are a few examples of the ways in which existing policy areas could be developed.

### Crime and Disorder

Much has been said about being tough on crime and on the causes of crime. Yet little, if anything, has been made of the fact that the vast majority of *all* crime is committed by males. How would understanding of the causes of crime, crime control and crime prevention be enhanced if began from a critical engagement with the current constructions of masculinity? Such a shift would bring violence against women from margin to centre, since work in this area is already well developed.

### The Family

For almost twenty years government policy has sought to promote and support the family. It is undoubtedly the case that the Labour government has, at the level of rhetoric at least, a more inclusive model of families, but it too has been silent about the fact that the family is a site of danger for many women and children. Rather than promoting 'the family', policy should seek to promote relationships between adults and children based on democracy and equity, 'democratic families'.

## BEYOND SOUND BITE POLICY

A potential stumbling block to the kind of integrated approach, which has as its guiding principle an ambition to decrease, and eventually eliminate, violence against women, is that there are no simple, sound-bite messages through which to create a wide consensus. The issues are contentious in themselves, and encapsulate many of the recurring tensions and debates of the last three decades – this is not an arena for the faint-hearted, and fudging hard choices results in women and children continuing to suffer at the hands of men. Yet the experience of the Zero Tolerance campaign tells an instructive story: that communities respond to an uncompromising feminist message, women were empowered by it and men challenged. In most of the evaluations to date local people have been fairly unanimous; expenditure on Zero Tolerance by local authorities is money well spent and they would support a national campaign (Kelly, 1998). But beyond this, many also make clear that they want more than public education, they want a responsive and equitable justice system which protects victims and sanctions offenders, they want extensive provision of quality services, they want children and young people to have access to different models of relationships. It remains to be seen whether the Labour Party has the courage and conviction to respond to these aspirations.

## NOTES

1.  For example, Canada established five regional research centres in the early 1990s, conducted the most extensive national consultation on the issue (National Panel 1993) and the most rigorous and extensive prevalence study (Johnson and Sacco, 1995). Australia issued a national strategy in 1992, which has been supplemented by later documents in individual states. Norway has for over a decade funded a feminist research programme, now in its third phase, on sexualised violence.

2.  Many commentators site the 'sex wars' of the 1980s as the primary cause of fractures within feminist theory and women's organisations (see, for example, Vance, 1984), choosing to downplay that from the outset debate and disagreement existed alongside support and sisterhood within the Women's Liberation Movement (WLM). Indeed, Lynn Segal (1990) goes as far as to claim that it was the group of women who worked to have a demand on violence against women added to the then six demands of the UK Women's Liberation Movement who were responsible for the abandonment of national WLM conferences in 1978.

3.  Also rediscovered has been documentation of violence against women and children by previous generations of feminists and in official records of courts and philanthropic organisations. See, for example, Clark (1987); Dobash and Dobash (1979); Gordon (1988); Hendessi (1992); Pleck (1987).

4.  A police practice of 'no criming' continues, it is done when after initial investigation the case is dropped, either because it is deemed a 'false' or malicious complaint or the complaint is withdrawn.

5.  Jayne Mooney (1993) notes that whilst there has been some acceptance that the BCS underestimates the prevalence of domestic violence and sexual assault the scale of the gap is not acknowledged (p. 33). She notes that within the BCS in 1984 19 sexual offences were reported in a sample of 6,000 women, in 1988 the figure was 15 from a sample of 5,500.

6.   This anomaly has been addressed in a number of countries through explicit recognition of gender discrimination and/or sexual violence as grounds for asylum. Examples here include Canada and most of the Scandinavian countries.

7.   Examples here include Justice for Women and Southall Black Sisters who developed high profile campaigns around individual cases of women convicted of murder for killing their abusive partners, the Best Interests Campaign which highlights the dangers of child contact arrangements where domestic violence is an issue, the Campaign Against Pornography, and the most recent Campaign to End Rape.

8.   Whilst useful as a heuristic guide to the connections between ideas and actions, this conceptualisation is often deployed in ways which draw distinctions too strongly, and thus fails to reflect connections and alliances – especially at the levels of local networks and national campaigns (see Radford, 1994). It is also inaccurate given the diversity of feminist perspectives which emerged in the 1980s and 1990s (see Kelly, Burton and Regan, 1996).

9.   Regional Workshop on Violence Against Women, organised by the British Council, 18–20 March 1998.

10.  I have been told by police officers from a variety of forces that they drastically reduced their options, and decreased the arrest rate.

11.  The Home Office report on Vulnerable and Intimidated Witnesses, published in June 1998, proposes a blanket ban on cross-examination by rape defendants, and the Home Secretary has reiterated an intention to act on this matter. It looks likely, however, that the legislation necessary will not be introduced until the crime bill in the next parliamentary session. This limited protection promised in the run-up to the 1997 general election, and immediately after it, will have taken at least two years to be introduced, let alone implemented.

12.  At least three women have served prison sentences in the last three years (for contempt of court) because they refused to hand their children over to ex-partners who had abused them.

13.  The concept of social exclusion has not been applied to either women, as a group, or survivors of sexual violence. But what greater kind of exclusions can there be than to have one's movements, activities and social contacts controlled by another person, or to be so terrorised by the damage of the past that one finds trusting another human being the most frightening prospect?

14.  Examples here include: specific legislation on domestic violence, which names and defines it as a specific area of crime and includes psychological abuse; integration of criminal and civil processes so that prosecution and protection are automatically connected; the recent review of all sexual offences undertaken in Australia; special prosecutors and dedicated courts; both statute law about public sexual harassment and mandatory guidelines on sexual harassment at work as have been introduced recently in India.

15.  Forms of violence against women which prompt little outrage or media coverage frequently disappear from view. Sexual harassment is an example; it has become limited to employment contexts and even here is increasingly subsumed into a broader and gender neutral focus on 'bullying', despite a directive from the EU which emphasises the importance of sexual harassment to equality of work and expects serious progress from member countries in effectively addressing it. Limited attention is paid to forms of violence which are less prevalent in the UK, such as female genital mutilation.

16.  Whilst forms of violence against women and children may be easy to separate as analytic concepts they are not so clearly demarcated in lived experience. For example: domestic violence and various forms of child abuse frequently coin-

cide (Bifulco and Moran, 1998; Department of Health, 1995; Foreman, 1993; Mullender and Morley, 1994); significant proportions of young people involved in the sex industry have histories of sexual abuse (Kelly et al., 1996); prostituted women face elevated risks of violence in both public and private (McNeill, 1995); what has been named 'elder abuse' is disproportionately abuse of women, usually by men and often by sons, some of whom return to live with their mothers following exclusion from the marital home due to domestic violence (Mastrocola-Morris, 1989).

## REFERENCES

Armstrong, Louise (1994) *Rocking the Cradle of Sexual Politics: What Happened When Women Said Incest*, New York: Addison Wesley.

Bifulco, Antonia and Moran, Patricia (1998) *Wednesday's Child: Abuse and Neglect in the Lives of Women*, London: Routledge.

Buck, Wendy, Chatterton, Michael and Pease, Ken (1995) *Obscene, Threatening and Other Troublesome Phone Calls to Women in England and Wales: 1982–1992*, London: Home Office Research and Planning Unit Paper 92.

Campbell, B. (1997) *Unofficial Secrets*, London: Virago (revised edition).

*Canadian Journal of Criminology (1995)* Special Issue: Focus on the Violence against Women Survey, July.

Canadian Panel on Violence Against Women (1993) *Changing the Landscape: Ending Violence – Achieving Equality*, Ottawa: Minister of Supplies and Services.

Clark, Anna (1987) *Men's Violence, Women's Silence*, London: Pandora.

Crime Concern (1993) *Women's Safety: Briefing Papers*, Swindon: Crime Concern.

Department of Health (1995) *Child Protection: Messages from Research*, London: HMSO.

Dobash, Rebecca and Dobash, Russell (1979) *Violence against Wives: a Case against the Patriarchy*, New York: Free Press.

Dobash, Rebecca and Dobash, Russell (1992) *Women, Violence and Social Change*, London: Routledge.

Driver, Emily and Droisen, Audrey (1988) *Child Sexual Abuse: Feminist Perspectives*, London: Macmillan.

European Parliament (1997) *Report on the Need to Establish a European Union-wide Campaign for Zero Tolerance of Violence against Women*, A4–0250/97.

Finkelhor, David (1986) *A Sourcebook on Child Sexual Abuse*, Beverly Hills: Sage.

Forman, Janette (1995) *Is There a Correlation between Child Sexual Abuse and Domestic Violence?*, Glasgow: Glasgow Women's Support Project.

Gordon, Linda (1988) *Heroes in Their Own Lives: the Politics and History of Family Violence, Boston 1880–1960*, New York: Viking Press.

Grace, Sharon (1995) *Policing Domestic Violence in the 1990s*, Home Office Research Study 139, London: HMSO.

Greater Manchester Police, (1993/4/5/6) *Domestic Violence Statistics*, Force Headquarters, Manchester.

Glasgow Women's Support Project (1990) Summary of findings from newspaper survey on 'Women's Safety', Glasgow Women's Support Project, unpublished.

Hague, Gill, Malos, Ellen and Dear, Wendy (1996) *Multi-agency Work and Domestic Violence: a National Study of Inter-agency Initiatives*, Bristol: Policy Press.

Hanmer, Jalna and Saunders, Sheila (1984) *Well-Founded Fear*, London: Hutchinson.

Harris, Jessica (1997) *The Processing of Rape Cases by the Criminal Justice System: Interim Report*, London: Home Office Research and Statistics Directorate.

Herman, Judith (1992) *Trauma and Recovery: From Domestic Abuse to Political Terror*, London: Pandora.

Her Majesty's Inspectorate of Constabulary (1993) *Equal Opportunities in the Police Service*, London: Her Majesty's Inspectorate of Constabulary.

Heise, Lori (1994) *Violence Against Women: The Hidden Health Burden*, World Bank Discussion Paper 255, Washington DC: World Bank.

Hendessi, Mandana (1992) *4 in 10: Report on Young Women Who Become Homeless as a Result of Sexual Abuse*, London: CHAR.

Industrial Society (1993) *No Offence? Sexual Harassment, How it Happens and How to Beat it*, London: Industrial Society.

Johnson, Holly and Sacco Victor (1995) 'Researching Violence against Women: Statistics Canada's National Study', *Canadian Journal of Criminology: Special Issue: Focus on the Violence against Women Survey*, vol. XXXX, pp. 281–304.

Kelly, Liz (1988) *Surviving Sexual Violence*, Cambridge: Polity Press.

Kelly, Liz (1996a) 'Zero Commitment: Legal Changes Affecting the Treatment of Domestic Violence', *Trouble and Strife*, 32, pp. 9–16.

Kelly, Liz (1996b) 'Weasel Words: Paedophilia and Cycles of Abuse' *Trouble and Strife*, 33, pp. 44–9.

Kelly, Liz (1997) *Final Report of the Activities of the EG-S- VL Including a Plan of Action for Combating Violence against Women*, Strasbourg: Council of Europe.

Kelly, Liz (1998) *Research and Evaluation: a Briefing Document for the Zero Tolerance Trust*, Edinburgh: Zero Tolerance.

Kelly, Liz, Burton, Sheila and Regan, Linda (1992) 'Defending the Indefensible? Quantitative Methods and Feminist Research', in Hilary Hinds et al. (eds) *Working Out: New Directions for Women's Studies*, London: Falmer Press.

Kelly, Liz, Burton Sheila and Regan, Linda (1996) 'Beyond Victim or Survivor: Sexual Violence, Identity and Feminist Theory and Practice', in L. Adkins and V. Merchant (eds) *Sexualizing the Social: Power and the Organization of Sexuality*, London: Macmillan.

Kelly, Liz and Radford, Jill (forthcoming) 'Sexual Violence against Women and Girls: an Approach to an International Overview', in Rebecca Dobash and Russell Dobash (eds) *Rethinking Violence against Women*, London: Sage.

Kelly, Liz, Regan, Linda and Burton, Sheila (1991) *An Exploratory Study of the Prevalence of Sexual Abuse in a Sample of 1244 16–21 year olds*, Final Report to the Economic and Social Research Council.

Kelly, Liz, Regan, Linda and Burton, Sheila (1993) 'Beyond Victim to Survivor: the Implications of Knowledge about Children's Resistance and Survival Strategies', in Harry Ferguson et al. (eds) *Surviving Childhood Adversity: Issues for Policy and Practice*, Dublin: Social Studies Press.

Kelly, Liz, Wingfield, Rachel, Regan, Linda and Burton, Sheila (1995) *Splintered Lives: Sexual Exploitation of Children in the Context of Children's Rights and Child Protection*, Ilford: Barnardo's.

Kitzinger, Celia (1994) 'Anti-lesbian Harassment', in Clare Brant and Yun Lee Too (eds) *Rethinking Sexual Harassment*, London: Pluto Press.

Koss, Mary and Harvey, Mary (1991) *The Rape Victim: Clinical and Community Interventions*, London: Sage.

Labour Party (1995) *Peace at Home: A Labour Party Consultation on the Elimination of Domestic and Sexual Violence against Women*, London: Labour Party.

Lees, Sue (1996) *Carnal Knowledge: Rape on Trial*, London: Hamish Hamilton.

Lees, Sue and Gregory, Jeanne (1993) *Rape and Sexual Assault: a Study of Rape Attrition*, London: London Borough of Islington.

Lister, Ruth (1997) *Citizenship: Feminist Perspectives*, London: Macmillan.

Mastrocola-Morris, Estelle (1989), 'Woman Abuse: the Relationship between Wife Assault and Elder Abuse', Canadian National Clearinghouse on Family Violence.

Mayhew, Patricia et al. (1993) *The 1992 British Crime Survey*. Home Office Research Study 132, London: HMSO.

MacLeod, Mary and Saraga, Esther (1988) 'Challenging the Orthodoxy: Towards a Feminist Theory and Practice', *Feminist Review* 28, pp. 16–55.

McNeil, Sandra (1987), 'Flashing – its Effect on Women', in Jalna Hanmer and Mary Maynard (eds) *Women, Violence and Social Control*, London: Macmillan.

Mirrlees-Black, Catriona (1994) 'Estimating the Extent of Domestic Violence: Findings from the 1992 BCS', *Home Office Research Bulletin* No. 37, London: Home Office Research and Statistics Department.

Mooney, Jayne (1993) *The Hidden Figure: Domestic Violence in North London*, London: Islington Council.

Mullender, Audrey (1996) *Re-thinking Domestic Violence: the Social Work and Probation Response*, London: Routledge.

Mullender, Audrey and Morley, Rebecca (1994) *Children Living with Domestic Violence: Putting Men's Abuse of Women on the Child Care Agenda*, London: Whiting and Birch.

Myers, John (ed.) (1994) *The Backlash: Child Protection under Fire*, Beverly Hills: Sage.

National Committee on Violence Against Women (1992) *National Strategy on Violence Against Women*, Canberra, Australia: Office of the Status of Women.

O'Neill, Maggie (1995) 'Researching Prostitution and Violence: Towards a Feminist Praxis' in Marianne Hester, Liz Kelly and Jill Radford (eds) *Women, Violence and Male Power*, Buckingham: Open University Press.

Painter, Kate (1991) *Wife Rape, Marriage and Law: Survey Report, Key Findings and Recommendations*, Manchester: Manchester University, Department of Social Policy and Social Work.

Pleck, Elizabeth (1987) *Domestic Tyranny: the Making of Social Policy against Family Violence from Colonial Times to the Present*, Oxford: Oxford University Press.

Radford, Jill (1994) 'The History of Women's Liberation Movements in Britain: Reflective Personal History' in G. Griffin, M. Hester, S. Rai and S. Roseneil (eds) *Stirring it: Challenges for Feminism*, London: Taylor and Francis.

Roiphe, Katie (1994) *The Morning After: Sex, Fear and Feminism*, London: Hamish Hamilton.

Segal, Lynne (1990) *Slow Motion: Changing Masculinities, Changing Men*, London: Virago.

Stanko, Elizabeth (1990) *Everyday Violence: How Women and Men Experience Sexual and Physical Danger*, London: Pandora.

Stanko, Elizabeth, Crisp, Debbie, Hale, Chris and Lucraft, Hebe (1998) *Counting the Cost: Estimating the Impact of Domestic Violence in the London Borough of Hackney*, London: Crime Concern.

Statistics Canada (1993) *The Violence Against Women Survey, The Daily*, 18 November, Statistics Canada.

Tempkin, Jennifer (1996) 'Doctors, Rape and Criminal Justice', *Howard Journal of Criminal Justice*, 35, pp. 1–20

Tempkin, Jennifer (1997) 'Plus ca change: Reporting Rape in the 1990s', *British Journal of Criminology*, 37(4), pp. 507–28.

*Times Higher Education Supplement* (1992) 'Sexual Harassment Survey of Students at Durham University', 27 November.

Vance, Carol (ed.) (1984) *Pleasure and Danger: Exploring Female Sexuality*, London: Routledge Kegan and Paul.

West, Robyn (1997) *Caring for Justice*, New York: New York University Press.

# 9 A Crisis in Masculinity, or New Agendas for Men?

Jeff Hearn

## INTRODUCTION

Recent years have seen the *naming of men as men*. Men have become the subject of growing political, academic and policy debates; in some respects this is *not* new; there have been previous periods of debate on men, and then, in a different sense, much of politics, research and policy has always been about men, often overwhelmingly so. What is new, however, is that these debates are now more explicit, more gendered, more varied and sometimes more critical. At their base is the assumption that men, like women, are not 'just naturally like this' or 'just bound to be that way', but rather are the result of historical, political, economic, social and cultural forces.

One social change that is now in place is that men and masculinities can at least be talked about as problematic. We can now ask such questions as: What is a man? How do men maintain power? Is there a crisis of masculinity? Or is there a crisis of men in a more fundamental way? Do we know what the future of men looks like or should be? What policy and practice implications follow both in relation to men and boys, and for men and boys? Importantly, there has also been a process of internal critique and autocritique (Hearn, 1994) within these discussions. For example, the idea of crisis may well be overstating what is happening (Brittan, 1989), not least because for many men life may continue very much the same as before.

So what form do these changes take? In what ways do these changes mean significant and substantial change in relations between men, women and children? And what are their policy implications for government, policy-making and polity? Indeed, just as there are new agendas for women, are there new agendas for men?

## FEMINISM, NEW SEXUAL MOVEMENTS AND MEN

Several influences have brought this renewed focus on men and masculinities. First and foremost is impact on men of second-, and now third- (or 1000th?), wave feminisms. Questions have been asked of all aspects of men and men's actions by feminists and feminisms. Different feminist initiatives have focused on different aspects of men, and have suggested different analyses of men and different ways forward for men. Feminism has also demonstrated many theoretical and practical lessons for men, though most men seem to to be able to ignore or forget most of them. One is that the understanding of gender relations, women and men has to involve attention to questions of power. Another is that to transform gender relations, and specifically men's continued dominance of much social life, means not only changes in what women do and what women are but also that men will have to change too. This may be hard for many men to hear, and even harder to act on. These are vital issues for politics, policy development and personal practice.

Other forces for change include the gay movements, queer politics, other 'new sexual movements' and the proliferation of sexual discourses more generally. While it is difficult to generalise about the form and direction of these critiques, they have often emphasised the desirability of (some) men to each other, the more public recognition of men through same-sex desire, and the associated or implied critique of heterosexual men's practices. However, the exact directions of these 'new sexual movements' remains diverse and difficult to predict.

Men's responses to feminism have also been various. Since the early 1970s there have been 'anti-sexist men' and 'pro-feminist men', to be followed in the 1980s by 'wild men' and 'mythopoetic men', and the media creation of 'new men'. The 1990s have brought 'newish man', 'new lads', 'men's rightists' (some now very confusingly called The Men's Movement, as opposed to the anti-sexist and the mythopoetic ones), and now 'post-new men' too. In the US there are extremely worrying moves to gender-conscious, more or less anti-feminist, political organising by men, such as the Coalition of Free Men (men's rights), the Million Man March (Nation of Islam) and the Promise Keepers (Christian) (Minkowicz, 1995). In different ways, other, often composite, groups of men have been more willing and able to identify themselves as men, for example, as 'older men' or 'black gay men'.

## THEORY AND ACADEMIA

Something similar has happened in academia. In some senses there are as many ways of studying men and masculinities as there are approaches to the social sciences. They range from examinations of 'masculine psychology' and psychodynamics (Craib, 1987) to broad societal, structural and collective analyses of men (Hearn, 1987); they have interrogated the operation of different masculinities – hegemonic, complicit, subordinated, marginalised, resistant (Carrigan et al., 1985; Connell, 1995) – and the interrelations of unities and differences between men (Hearn and Collinson, 1994); they have included detailed ethnographic descriptions of particular men or men's activity as well as investigations of the constructions of specific masculinites in specific discourses (Edley and Wetherell, 1995). The International Association for Studies on Men has been established as a research network for several years and is currently co-ordinated from Norway.

The study of men and masculinities, whether critical or otherwise, is no longer considered so esoteric. It is now established, if rather tentatively, for teaching and research. While it has examined boys' and men's lives in schools, families, management, the military and elsewhere, many aspects remain unexplored. As research has progressed, it has become more complex, less concerned with just one 'level' of analysis, and more concerned to link previously separated fields and approaches. These kinds of critique of men also imply drastic rewritings of *academic disciplines* themselves, and their frequently pre-scientific ignoring of the fact that their 'science' has been dominantly done by men, for men, and even primarily about men (Morgan, 1981).

## CULTURE, MEDIA AND REPRESENTATION

Contemporary namings of men have been accompanied by greater interest in men in the global worlds of consumption, advertising, journalism and popular culture. New global technology has created the possibility of more powerful images of men and women that can be transferred around the world. Imaging men is now a matter of both fiercely reaffirming boring old Rambos and their like, in film, computer games and comics, and presenting ever-more ambiguous homo-het, man-woman pictures of 'men' in both mainstream and alternative media. An increasingly important feature of media is the portrayal of men in sport. At the present rate of change, there are likely to be all manner of surprising associations to be drawn in the future in image and text around the sign of men or masculinity as signs (Saco, 1992). The critical examination of images can also be used as a powerful way of informing discussion of men in political, educational and other practical settings.

## ECONOMIC, SOCIAL AND CULTURAL CHANGE

If we compare women and men in the nineteenth and the twentieth centuries, both major changes and major continuities are obvious. While changes abound in law, work, citizenship, personal relations, and so on, there has been a widespread, stubborn persistence in men's dominance – in politics, business, finance, war, diplomacy, the state, policing, crime, violence generally, heterosexual institutions and practices, science, technology, culture, media, and many other social arenas. What is perhaps most interesting is that while men's general power as a (the) dominant social category remains virtually unchanged and may even have become intensified in some respects, men's power is constantly being challenged, fragmented and even transformed. Men are more than ever being affirmed as 'men'; whilst at the same time the experience of being a man is subject to questioning and acute fracturing (Hearn, 1992a). Men's situation, and particularly men's power, is a complex mixture of change and no change. Indeed the presence of change for men should not be confused with any general assertion of a so-called 'crisis in masculinity'.

Specific changes, or potential changes, of individual men and groups of men should be contextualised by social change more generally. The current talk in the UK may all be of 'boys' under-achievement' but social contexts and social changes that affect men are very much wider. In the UK there has been the End of Empire and men's sense of a certain place in the world (Tolson, 1977); rapid transformations of capitalism and capitalist enterprises; and huge losses of men's manufacturing jobs and growing service employment. Individual fathers' authority, no longer automatic, is in possible tension with the state. Separations, divorces and remarriages have increased. There is now a growing recognition that ways of being men are culturally and ethnically variable. All of these changes do not just affect but actively construct ordinary men in myriad ways. Furthermore, whatever change in men and men's power occurs, or indeed is advocated, can affect *all* areas of social life. These include: education, class, work, employment, race, sexuality, violence, the family, childcare, the state, personal and private life, sport, care, health and illness, age and ageing, birth and death, the body, and so on. To put this another way, all the various changes addressed elsewhere in this book with regard to women can be re-read as suggesting both social changes and possible policy changes in relation to men.

Just as men's relationships to feminism is likely to remain problematic (Hearn, 1992b), so change in men is likely to be problematic and uneven (Walby, 1986, 1990). It is highly unlikely that a radically new 'sexual contract' (Pateman, 1988) or 'gender contract' (Hirdmann, 1988, 1990) will *suddenly* arrive; rather, we can expect a series of temporary 'settlements' or 'truces' within a difficult long-term process, burdened by the weight and oppressions of history.

There is also the need increasingly to consider the changing global context for men's lives and power. While for most men life remains local in the way it is lived, the forces that affect it are certainly becoming more transnational in character; globalisation is in place and becoming ever more developed. This is a very complex and often contradictory picture. At its simplest it means that the fate of men and women is increasingly in the hands of economic, social and cultural processes that transcend the nation. These processes often involve racialisation, sexualisation and the reproduction of other massive inequalities between 'North' and 'South' and between various 'cores' and 'peripheries' (see, for example, *Human Development Report*, 1995). The idea of the self-contained 'unit', be it the nation or indeed the individual man, is breaking down (Hearn, 1996).

In thinking about the future of men, there is, however, a need for some gendered caution. Many of the 'grand narratives' of the future – globalisation, environmental destruction, population growth, food and water scarcity, information explosion, reproductive engineering, technological advance generally – typically remain presented as inevitable and strangely rather genderless, rather than largely controlled by relatively small groups of men: the real 'men of the world' (Hearn, 1996), with their own brand of 'transnational business masculinity' (Connell, 1997). These global and international changes have major implications for men and masculinities. The well-charted shift from private patriarchy to public patriarchy (Walby, 1989, 1990; Hearn, 1992a) is itself being superseded by another shift, this time towards what might conveniently be called global patriarchy, which is itself likely to be a diffuse and multi-centred social formation (Hearn, 1996). Any would-be crisis in masculinity needs to be considered within that context, and the loss of both immediate, and even national, control and power that men may be experiencing.

Having said that future change will probably be relatively mundane for most men. Some of men's future is likely to follow existing trends; other aspects are difficult to discern, unpredictable or unknown; much, short of global catastrophe, will not change. Many men will probably still find ways of holding on to various powers; of being violent, threatening, shouting, seeking to get their own way, whilst leading rather circumscribed lives, working fewer hours and getting paid more than women, living less healthily, dying younger and 'hanging out' with other men. Meanwhile, changes are inevitable. Much of the way men are will necessarily change, in terms of specific conjunctions of age, body, class, culture, (dis)ability, dress, ethnicity, kinship, language, nationality, race, religion, sexuality and other social divisions that make someone a man, and some people men. Being a man is historically and culturally contingent.

## WORK, EMPLOYMENT AND UNEMPLOYMENT

The central importance of 'work', still usually meaning specifically paid work, for many men has been well established (for example, Cockburn, 1984, 1991;

Collinson and Hearn, 1996b). Work is a source of power and resources, a central life interest, and a medium of identity, as well as being a source of worry and concern. When men are unemployed or are inappropriately employed, extra problems may follow for them, such as for their health, and indeed for women too. Gender segregation persists, and much of men's activity at work is homosocial: why do so many (heterosexual) men seem to prefer men, and their cosy company?

The recent transformation of work, through major structural change in employment and unemployment, has been extremely significant for many men. During the two decades, from 1973 to 1993, the number of men in employment shrank from 13.1 million to 10.7 million. The shift in the sectoral makeup was even more dramatic: with changes from 39.7 per cent to 27.9 per cent in manufacturing; from 12.4 per cent to 17.9 per cent in retail, wholesale, consumption, catering and leisure; and from 5.4 per cent to 11.9 per cent in finance, insurance, estate agency and business services. Women's employment is also changing, with more women joining the labour market; there are already more young women than young men in the 16–19 age range in employment. Particularly significant increases in women's employment, especially part-time employment, have occurred in the financial sector and in community, social and personal services (see chapter 3; Dickens, 1995). Work changes for women also necessarily impact on men.

These structural changes mean that many men have experienced personal change in their working lives. No longer is life-long security of employment guaranteed, not even for the relatively successful and well qualified; so-called 'traditional' working-class based masculinities, most obviously around heavy manufacturing and mining, can no longer be easily sustained unchallenged (Dicks et al., 1998; Waddington et al., 1998); meanwhile corporate reorganisation is commonplace; post-Fordist flexibility demands flexibility of men. In the first five years of the 1990s 44 per cent of the male workforce experienced unemployment at some point. And, of course, for many men, especially young, less qualified men, the prospect of unemployment remains. This is a particularly urgent problem in certain inner-city localities and large city-edge 'council estates', and for some young black men, especially in London and other urban centres. Policies for work generation remain a particularly high priority for young, working-class and black men.

Men's work and (un)employment also interact closely with domestic and family life. Despite and perhaps because of the transformations in men's work, men who are in employment tend to work longer hours than almost all other men in the EU. The phenomenon of presentism is a serious problem in some sectors, and difficult to resist for men whose jobs remain insecure. There are urgent needs for government and employers to facilitate ways and means for men to reconcile (un)employed life and family life in a much more positive way – in employment and income support policies, and in managerial practices. These include attention to more job-sharing, voluntary reduced work time (whilst being 'full-time'), flexible working hours, term-time working, working from home, and other approaches promoted by New Ways to Work (1993, 1995) and similar initiatives. It also means men adjusting socially and psychologically to not necessarily being the 'breadwinner'. Indeed, greater equality in employment depends on greater equality in unpaid work in the home. There is thus a need to consider how men can contribute to both overall levels of household income and a more equal gendered division of labour both in and outside the home.

While employment changes have transformed many men's relation to work, men remain in control of most powerful organisations, whether state, capitalist or third sector. This is especially so in terms of men's continued domination of top management (Collinson and Hearn, 1996a) in capital and the state. Men in management are important *political* actors; while management certainly can be a facilitating process, managers may reproduce uncaring, sexually oppressive and even violent and abusive actions, without much comeback. They also have the task of overseeing and underwriting the behaviour of other men in their charge. Equal opportunities policies can themselves be a way of both implementing greater equality and containing more radical demands for change. It is in organisations that the public doing of gender is predominantly done and re-done. Furthermore, organisations and their control are fundamentally important, and becoming even more so, with the development of globalisation through multinationals, transnational governmental institutions, worldwide media and information networks, and so on. These are also vital in the changing men's relationship to the personal and 'the private'. Men in management have a special responsibility to facilitate men's caring for others, as do men in government.

## FAMILIES, FATHERS AND CARE

Although patriarchy has certainly changed in form over the last century or more, especially through the growth of the state, men's power still resides at least in part in the family and the institution of fatherhood (Hearn, 1987). Historically, fatherhood is both a means of possession of and care for young people, and an arrangement between men. It has also been and still is a way for some men of living with, being with, being violent to, sexually abusing, caring for and loving *particular* young people (those that are called 'your own'), and a way of avoiding connection, care and contact with other young people more generally. Even nice fathers can switch to become nasty ones. Fatherhood has often involved getting something for nothing, an assumption of rights and authority over others, principally women and children, rather than responsibilities for them. The problems of both father absence and father distance are now recognised more than ever (Williams, 1998). For some men, becoming fathers can and obviously does involve major changes in responsibilities and more work.

State intervention in the rights and responsibilities of fatherhood – most obviously through the Child Support Agency and the Children Act of 1989, but also more subtly through state control of reproductive technology, such as IVF – has increased. The last few years have also, and paradoxically, seen signs of a growth in the rights of fathers, as well as in the assumption that such power and authority are 'natural' and 'normal'. Even a glance through history and across cultures will show this to be extremely problematic. These issues become more complicated as men's relationships to families develop over time – how to be positive and responsible to others in families, without asserting the power and authority of the father. This is especially important in long-term relationships, whether with or without marriage, and with the increasing number of men involved in separation, divorce and reconstituted families of various kinds. The number of women petitioning for divorce has doubled in the last 20 years. There is a clear need for a 'post-marriage' ethics for men. In addition there are long-term changes in the number of men living alone.

So a challenge for men is how is to respond to these difficult questions – to love, care for and be friends with young people without drawing on the power of the father. This may even involve working towards the abolition of that power of fatherhood whilst recognising the reality of responsibilities in men's lives (Hearn, 1983, 1984, 1987). Social and educational policies need to be directed towards assisting those who are carers, and not the so-called 'rights' of 'natural fathers', just by virtue of biological fatherhood. Such policies should support carers and encourage boys and men to participate much more fully in the activity of caring. One primary way of doing this is for a massive increase in state funding of support for childcarers. Provision of publicly funded childcare in the UK remains derisory; at present it is available for only 2 per cent of children under three (Daycare Trust, cited in Toynbee, 1998), one of the lowest rates in Europe. As such, this lack of funding is a clear governmental underwriting of the dominant system of unpaid care, largely by women.

Questions of care and caring are central in how boys and men change their practice in relation to others, both physically and emotionally. So often men's avoidance of caring has been the defining feature of 'being men'. This is very much a *structural* question in terms of women doing more caring work, both in private and in public. There have been some increases in men's active participation in childcare and domestic work, but the baseline from which change is beginning is low. In addition, specific changes of this kind need to be placed against other changes – for example, women's employment, domestic technology and women's leisure. Men's activity may be focused on particular tasks, such as weekly shopping, or at particular periods, such as around childbirth. However, fathers with young children are particularly likely to work long hours in employment (Fagan, 1996). This could be for a variety of reasons, including compensation for loss of women's earnings, the contribution of extra working to help establish men's careers, avoidance of childcare, and the reproduction of gender divisions in the family.

There is some evidence of a tendency for men with more education to do more housework, but again this broad trend should be treated with caution, not least because of the impact of 'greedy occupations' (see Moyes, 1995; Lunneberg, 1997). There are also gradually growing numbers of lone fathers – from about 70,000 in 1970 to about 110,000 by 1990. On the other hand, the increase in men's unemployment in the 1980s did not generally lead to increases in men's work in the home, and may well have involved dispro-portionately negative effects for wives and other women partners (for example, McKee and Bell, 1985, 1986).

The 1996 British Social Attitudes Survey found that in 79 per cent of households women did the washing and ironing alone, and in 48 per cent women looked after sick family members alone while men never did so alone (Lunneberg, 1997). The Mintel 2000 Survey found only 2 per cent of men did all the household tasks or shared them equally (Mintel, 1994). Men with wives who are in employment may be changing, but only slowly. Men with wives in full-time employment may in some cases take on more house-hold work, but this may more likely involve a shift in the tasks that they are doing rather than devoting more time in total to housework (Anderson et al., 1994).

Boys and men learn *not* to care for others, and changing this is an important part of the project of socialisation, for example, in the education of boys at home and in school. This should be a major policy development – in nurseries and schools, by government and education authorities, and in higher education – not as an afterthought or something left to the whims and wishes of individual teachers. Like fatherhood and the family, caring is both a very personal issue and one built into wider societal structures and political institutions. It is not 'solved' by increasing daycare provision, vital as that is – the problem goes to the very structuring of how men behave, feel, are. It is an area of life that can bring fundamental change in men's experience of themselves; it can also bring about both direct antagonisms (deciding who will stay in or look after someone who is ill) and direct improvements in the quality of relationships. The question of caring also raises the challenge of how men become and do more caring, without just taking over.

A special challenge is how to encourage boys and young men to become more used to the bodily care of others in a way that does not lead to further dominance. This has to be attempted, yet with great care and caution – perhaps initially by the encouragement of care in their own families and in schools by the teaching of safety and first aid, and the care of pets and animals, and then moving on, under supervision, to the care of babies, young children, older people, those with disabilities elsewhere. Nurturing can be redefined as normal for boys, young men and men. More specifically, it involves teaching boys gentleness and non-erotic forms of touch. However, throughout, we need to be alive to the problems with this scenario, for example, in terms of potential abuse. It is not enough just to leave the dominant forces to define boys and men and then pick up the urgent need for positive initiatives that assist the redefinition of boys and men towards care and nurture as central defining features (Salisbury and Jackson, 1994). Educational policy and practice should be directed towards teaching boys how to care; boys' caring should be expected, valued and, indeed, rewarded.

## EDUCATION

In the last few years education has had a high profile in public debates about boys and young men. In considering this it is important, however, to remember that men's general domination of education persists. This is clear in the occupation of headships and other senior staff positions in upper schools, in national and local educational policy-making, and in the universities and academia. Meanwhile many boys, particularly poor, working-class boys, are not achieving well at school. In 1994 43 per cent of girls gained five or more GCSEs at grades A to C, compared with 34 per cent of boys (Pratt, 1996). More specifically, a recent report for the Equal Opportunities Commission found that girls outperformed boys at GCSE in English, modern languages, technology, history and art; and at A level in geography, social studies, art, chemistry and biology (Arnot et al., 1996).

Boys' performance in schools is a complex issue. This policy issue of boys' (under)achievement can be understood in many different ways. The issue can be framed in terms of human capital, class inequality, equal opportunities or social justice. Links can be drawn between the low educational attainment of some boys and the low employment rates of some young men. There is also for some boys an antagonism between educational attainment, even attentiveness, and the performance and achievement of particular and valued masculinities. But most importantly, it should not be seen as a problem of girls doing too well; rather as boys not doing well enough. As Madeleine Arnot, one of the leading researchers in this field, has put it: 'We have a success story here. This is an excellent sign of the work schools have done to improve girls 'performance. So that they are now catching up' (quoted in Judd, 1996, p. 1).

The way forward on this question is certainly not by way of any kind of backlash against girls' achievements. Nor, in the long run, are boys likely to be encouraged to take education more seriously by trying to involve them through resort to further officially sanctioned use of competitive and aggressive methods and materials. Instead, formal attention needs to be given to the very basis of how boys are meant to be. Boys are considerably more likely to damage themselves through risk-taking behaviour than are girls (see pp. 162–4). Just as the problem of 'normal manhood' remains a problem for many men, so does that of 'normal boyhood'. Perhaps it is, in fact, more accurate to speak of a crisis in boyhood than it is to assert a crisis in masculinity. Schools and other educational arenas are major sites for the possible reinforcement or challenge to dominant and subordinated ways of being boys. There is thus a need for thoroughgoing strategies on all aspects of gender relations in those institutions that assist the fostering of less oppressive ways of being boys and thus men (Connell, 1996). There is great scope here for more focused 'boys' work', youth work and educational work with boys and young men, not only on educational questions, but also on all the issues raised here. Such work needs to be undertaken within a pro-feminist framework if it is not to merely reproduce some of the inequalities of past single-sex education.

The irony is that it is men's general social power that may underwrite the choice of some boys and young men not to devote themselves to schooling and learning. In the past this may not have been a special problem for young men because of the structure of the labour market; that is no longer the case in many localities. More generally, with such difficulties around education and employment, as well as father absence/distance, crime, violence and so on, young men have been increasingly defined in recent years as a problem category (see Hearn, 1998a).

## SEXUALITY

Men's sexuality has often been neglected as a focus for change, except as a reaction to the initiatives of the Right. Dominant forms of 'normal male sexuality' – characterised as power, aggression, penis-orientation, separation of sex from loving emotion, objectification, fetishism, and supposed 'uncontrollability' (Coveney et al., 1984) – have been described and critiqued as highly problematic. For some, perhaps most, men, the connection of sexuality with violence is fundamental, as violence is eroticised, most obviously in pornography. This is not the way men's sexuality is or has to be all the time.

Sexuality may feel like that which is the most personal, the most 'one's own'; yet it is also structural. For example, heterosexuality is as much a social institution as marriage. Heterosexist culture and homophobia continue to abound. Men's domination of sex and sexuality, and the reduction of sex to intercourse, to ejaculation, to orgasm are still represented as 'just normal, aren't they?' Heterosexual men may often be misogynist: the object of love can be the object of hate. Gay men are not necessarily pro-feminist. Homophobic men may inhabit homosocial pubs, clubs, organisations and work-groups – so what exactly are these sexual loyalties *between* men?

More broadly, it is important to emphasise that the pressures on the construction of men's sexuality seem to be diverging more and more – the forces of reaction, of the glorification of sexual violence, of internet sex, of anti-gay politics (most obviously around HIV/AIDS) are ever stronger – while at the same time there is a gathering public confidence around sexual progressivism, queer politics, lesbian and gay rights, 'outing' (Reynolds, 1999), and even a small anti-sexist politics of heterosexuality. There is, of course, a specific and urgent need for law reform, to abolish discriminatory legislation against young gays (around age of consent), same-sex sexuality more generally (Local Government Act 1988, Section 28), and older gays (around pensions, tenure and property rights, and so on).

Furthermore, anti-gay politics can damage both gay men and heterosexual men. They can be physically dangerous and personally undermining for gay men. Heterosexual men may come out or change to being gay; less obviously to some, there is the gay part or gayness of heterosexual men. So hetero-sexual men need to support gay men, partly for political principles of equality and justice, and partly for self-interest (Hearn, 1992a).

In all of this, there is a need to develop an important educational debate and practice around sex and sexuality – not least around what is understood by sex and sexuality, and the practice of safe(r) sex. This has to affirm different sexualities, work towards non-oppressive sexualities, support young gays and engage with the real dilemmas that young people face in their everyday lives. For young men, this means promoting, in schools and elsewhere, intimate and sexual relationships that are non-threatening, non-oppressive and responsible (Salisbury and Jackson, 1996). Men's and boys' sexuality is as much a matter for public debate, policy development and social change as is violence. A major challenge is how men can acknowledge their sexuality, even be proud of it, without being oppressively sexual or sexually oppressive. What chance is there for real change in men without that?

## VIOLENCE AND CRIME

As will already be apparent from the previous discussion, it is not possible to make a strict separation between men's sexuality and men's violence, in this society at least. A lot of what men do needs to be relabelled as violence. This would include child abuse, child sexual abuse, domestic violence, rioting, crime, policing, soldiering, wars, football hooliganism, public disorder. It might seem hard to talk about crime and violence without talking about men, and yet this has been done quite successfully for a long time (see

tehead, 1992; Newburn and Stanko, 1994; Collier, 1995).
ence are very largely a problem for men, and they are also
show certain masculinities to others (Messerschmidt, 1993).
e, debates on crime, violence and indeed punishment and impri-
s͟   ͟need to be conducted carefully in relation not just to gender, but
also ͟  age, class, locality and racialisation (Gilroy, 1987; Jefferson, 1991).

Much of men's violence needs to be understood as conscious, deliberate actions and as forms or examples of particular masculinities (Hearn, 1998b). Men's violence to women, children, young people and each other needs, indeed demands, not just patching up the problem, but the changing of men and 'normal masculinity' (Hearn, 1990). Examples here might include what is seen as the 'normal' behaviour of certain men and boys, as fathers, teachers, workmates, school mates, and so on, in reproducing ordinary, everyday violence to others and each other.

Men's violence is thus about both violence to women, children and young people, and often less obviously, violence to the self – in self-brutalisation and the denial and 'victory over' the non-violent parts of ourselves (Kaufman, 1987). Violence may bring power and dominance, but it may also bring unhappiness and self-destruction. Men who are violent are generally not happy men (Maiuro et al., 1988), even if they 'enjoy' the violence.

This suggests the need for men both to recognise men's own violence and potential violence, whilst opposing and stopping men's violence – in war, armies, initiation ceremonies, bullying, unsafe working conditions, personal relationships and being on the street. Campaigns against such initiations, lack of safety in workplaces, bullying and violence at work are all good ways of bringing together men concerned to work against sexism, trade unions and anti-racist and other interested groups. These are thereby necessary concerns of equal opportunities policies and responsibilities of managements.

In reducing and opposing men's violence, a necessary first thing to do is to make a *national* commitment against violence. This should be an absolutely central plank of the policies of government and the political parties. A Gulbenkian Foundation Commission Report (1995), *Children and Violence*, made as its first priority recommendation: 'Individuals, communities and government at all levels should adopt a "Commitment to non-violence", of similar standing, to existing commitments to "equal opportunities".' The Report continued:

> The aims of the commitment are to work towards a society in which individuals, communities and government share non-violent values and resolve conflict by non-violent means. Building such a society involves in particular reducing and preventing violence involving children, by developing:

- understanding of the factors which interact to increase the potential for violence involving children, and those which prevent children from becoming violent
- action to prevent violence involving children in all services and work with families and children
- consistent disavowal of all forms of inter-personal violence – in particular by opinion-leaders. (p. 18)

Thus governmental and other policies and strategies should take a clear position that opposes violence, should tell boys and men not to be violent, should advocate policies that encourage men to behave in ways that facilitate women's equality, and make it clear that the realisation of such changes depends partly on men in politics and policy-making, and their own understanding of their gendered actions. So the vision here is a world without men's violence, without men as we know them.

There is increasing interest in policies that try to stop men's violence directly, such as programmes for men who have been violent to known women (Gondolf, 1985; Pence and Paymar, 1986; Adams, 1988; Caesar and Hamberger, 1989; Edelson and Tolman, 1992; Lees and Lloyd, 1994). Such programmes remain controversial in terms of underlying philosophy, methods of change and resource basis. In recent years there has been a developing critique of approaches that are narrowly psychological or focused on anger management, and instead a movement towards those based on a 'power and control' model that is pro-feminist in orientation. The latter kinds of programmes can be a significant and effective initiative, especially when linked to wider educational and political change (Dobash et al., 1996). A crucial and current issue is whether such programmes should become court-mandated and a responsibility of the probation service rather than accessed on a voluntary basis. Any such development needs to carefully screen out men who have no interest whatsoever in change and who may even use programme to learn new forms of violence and control. Even more important, any innovations for men have to be supplements to broaden major public policy changes – including, consistent police prosecution policy and practice; inter-agency work for women experiencing violence; improved housing provision for women; and full state support for Women's Aid and other projects for women.

Finally, discussion of violence would be incomplete without a mention of sport, itself often a major public arena of legitimated violence, often of a severe kind. Sport also remains a major point of influence in creating and changing boys and young men, and thus men. It can also be a source of considerable anxiety since it is still often a pre-eminent activity for establishing masculine identity. And 'retirement' from sport can bring further difficulties for men and others around them. Sporting events and loyalties could be effective places to oppose men's violence, perhaps through a modified version of the Zero Tolerance campaigns, just as they have been to counter racism in professional football in the 'Kick Racism out of football' campaign.


## HEALTH

If there is one policy arena that has attracted attention from a wide range of constituencies and interests in recent years, it is that of men's health. The concern for men's health has been mobilised as if it is a common, cross-generational concern – perhaps a kind of mythical consensus. 'Men's health' can be represented as an issue for all men, and indeed women too. For different reasons, the question of men's health has attracted involvement from government, employers, trade unions, pharmaceutical and medical industries, medical professionals, and health educators and activists. Significantly, in the last few years there have been a number of conferences bringing together such diverse groups; in some cases these have been high-status occasions with sponsorship from the financial and industrial sectors. The concern with men's health can be appealing both to men promoting a backlash against feminism and who are insistent on the disadvantages of being male and to men who wish to develop a pro-feminist politics and change their relationship to women and children (see, for example, *HFA 2000 News*, 1994; Bruckenwell et al., 1995; Bradford, 1995; see also Sabo and Gordon, 1995). In particular, discussions of men's health should not be read as necessarily antagonistic to those on women's health.

The central issue that has attracted concern is the fact that at every stage of the life of a boy or man, he is more likely to die than a girl or woman of equivalent age. At different stages different hazards affect boys and men, and different risks are taken by them – accidents as a child, suicide and motor vehicles as young men, and the effects of diet, smoking, drinking and sexual habits later in life. For example, in the 15–34-year-old male age group, 21 per cent of deaths are from road vehicle accidents, 20 per cent are from other causes of injury and poisoning, and 17 per cent are from suicides (OPCS, 1992, quoted in Calman, 1993, p. 212). Life expectancy for those born between 1985 and 1990 is 78.1 years for women, and 72.4 years for men. Throughout most of the twentieth century, there has been at least a five-year difference between men and women. The EU difference is slightly higher still at 7.1 years (OHE Compendium of Health Statistics, 1992). One part of this discrepancy comes from men's higher level of suicide, which stands at more than three times the rate of women's suicide. Furthermore, over the last ten years there has been an 80 per cent increase in suicide by males. Particular concern has been the increase in the suicide of young men (Charlton et al., 1993; Befrienders International, 1995).

These issues of the health, mortality and suicide of young men are not peculiar to the UK, and indeed similar trends are attracting attention in France and elsewhere in Europe (Jougla, 1994). Furthermore, the physical health debate has recently been extended into the realm of mental health. For example, the Royal College of Psychiatrists' (1996) report publicised the relatively hidden question of men's depression, and the lack of recognition of this problem both amongst men, as evidenced in their low levels of help-seeking, and more generally in medical and policy development. The Samaritans have reported an 80 per cent increase in male suicide in the last ten years (Cohen, 1996).

The problem of men's health has now been recognised in the statements of the Chief Medical Officer, Kenneth Calman (1993, pp. 6, 106):

> Although some diseases, such as prostatism, are obviously unique to men, the main differences in mortality and morbidity relate to variations in exposure to risk factors. Thus, there should be great potential for improvement in health in many areas, for example CHD and accidents. Further work is particularly needed on targeting health messages to men. Women seem to be more aware of their own bodies and pay more attention to health messages. Health messages for men may be more effectively transmitted through mothers or sisters, wives or girlfriends, but men must now be brought up to be more aware of their own bodies and not be reluctant to seek help.... It is to be hoped that Regions and Districts will investigate ways to promote the health of men over the next few years.
>
> Despite an apparent difference, if not resistance, to health promotion messages among men it must be brought home to them that many of the risk factors to their health – such as smoking, physical inactivity, poor diet, excess alcohol consumption, unsafe sexual practices and risky behaviour likely to lead to accidents – are preventable. Thus the scope for men to improve their health, and to prolong active, healthy life, is considerable.

Despite these kinds of observations, the policy debate on men's health has not dwelt extensively on the social divisions between men, by class, race, locality, sexuality, and so on. These divisions are important, for the state of men's health is subject to a range of social influences – some associated with power and control, and some with attempts to extend (or appear to extend) power and control by those with relatively less power and control but who are still members of a powerful social category.

Many men in relatively less powerful social positions may survive, attempt to survive or fail to survive by passive coping, for example, in depression, social withdrawal, watching television, drinking or whatever. Yet active assertions of power, especially over women and children, and passive resistance can go hand in hand. Real uncertainties remain on how some men may actively resist capitalist, managerial and other men's oppressions without perpetuating practices that oppress women: how to be tough on men who are oppressive to women and men, without at the same time oppressing women. Similarly, improving men's health involves developing policies and practices that support men without further oppressing women. For example, boys and men frequent learning that it is socially desirable to ignore pain and avoid doctors (Briscoe, 1989) needs to be demystified and unlearnt.


## CONCLUSION: POLITICS AND PRACTICE

Men's societal dominance continues; yet at the same time certain groups of men are facing considerable change from previous social patterns and arrangements – at home, work and elsewhere. Despite the extent of the changes and challenges outlined, it is premature to talk of a widespread 'crisis of masculinity'. Individual men and certain groups of men may be facing, even confronting, change, like it or not, and they may indeed be changing, but this has to be put in the context of the stubborn stability of men's structural power. For *some* relatively less powerful groups of men, the combination of lack of educational success, reduction in traditional jobs, avoidance of 'women's' work, and their own more damaging actions (to both themselves and others) may indeed constitute a *material* crisis for them and others around them. But this generally may not (yet) match closely with an ideological crisis in how men are assumed to be. The contradictions between the material and the ideological state of men and masculinities may be growing but are not yet at crisis point for most men, and certainly not for men in general.

All the issues that I have discussed here are important for what it means to be a 'man' in this society. They have, however, all often remained neglected in what is generally defined as 'politics'. Transforming what is understood by politics is part of transforming men. All these issues are also both profoundly structural and intensely personal. Each can also prompt great depths of negativity – feelings of hopelessness, terribleness, desperation – as well as being arenas of possible positive change and hope. Each is a way of unifying men *as a class*, with different interests to women and *dividing* men from each other – old from young, heterosexual from gay, healthy from unwell, and so on. Each is a way of oppressing women, children and young people, and a way of relating to other men. And each represents an avenue for men opposing oppression, supporting feminist initiatives, and changing men.

Policies and practices are needed that address these issues in all policy arenas; they need to name men and the persistence of men's powers, without stereotyping men. In doing this, there are dangers that an increased focus on men may divert attention from women and women's agendas by arguing that men should have even more resources for solving these problems. So vigilance is necessary in this respect.

However, it is useful to bear in mind that a critical focus on men is not in men's general interest, just as it is not in the interests of other dominant groups to focus critically on them. This will involve debate, clear policy statements, publications and other materials, education and teaching, professional interventions, pro-feminist 'mens' work' and 'boys' work', and research. It is time that government had a strategy on changing men away from power and oppression as *part* of its strategy for women and gender justice. In particular a distinction needs to be drawn between support between and for men that encourages domination and support between and for men that diminishes domination. The latter kind of initiatives are necessary not only in the state but throughout all areas of social life society, in business, community, media, religion, sport and other public and indeed private forums.

Finally, one further likely and paradoxical implication of the naming of men is that the deconstruction of men may be opened up more fully. Changing future agendas for women involves changing men; changing men involves deconstructing men and reducing men's power; and, in the longer term still, this may even involve the abolition of 'men' as such a ubiquitously important social category. Is it time at last for men to change, and both to develop and be subject to new agendas?

# REFERENCES

Adams, David (1988) 'Treatment Models of Men who Batter: a Profeminist Analysis', in Kersti Yllö and Michelle Bograd (eds) *Feminist Perspectives on Wife Abuse*, Newbury Park, Ca. and London: Sage.

Anderson, Michael, Bechhofer, Frank and Gershuny, Jonathan (1995) *The Social and Political Economy of the Household*, Oxford: Oxford University Press.

Arnot, Madelaine, David, Miriam and Weiner, Gaby (1996) *Educational Reforms and Gender Equality in Schools*, Manchester: Equal Opportunities Commission.

Befrienders International (1995) *Study of Suicide Prevention within the European Community*, London: Befrienders International.

Bradford, Nicki (1995) *Men's Health Matters*, London: Vermilion.

Briscoe, M. E. (1989) 'Sex Differences in Mental Health', *Update*, 1 November, pp. 834–9.

Brittan, Arthur (1989) *Masculinity and Power*, Oxford: Blackwell.

Bruckenwell, Peter, Jackson, David, Luck, Mike, Wallace, Jim, Watts, Jonk (1995) *The Crisis in Men's Health*, Bath: Community Health UK.

Caesar, Peter L. and Hamberger, L. K. (eds) (1989) *Treating Men who Batter*, New York: Springer.

Calman, Kenneth (1993) *On the State of the Public Health 1992*, London: HMSO.

Carrigan, Tim, Connell, R. W. and Lee, John (1985) 'Toward a New Sociology of Masculinity', *Theory and Society*, 14(5), pp. 551–604.

Charlton, John et al. (1993) 'Suicide Deaths in England and Wales: Trends in Factors Associated with Suicide Deaths', *Population Trends*, No. 71, Spring, pp. 34–43.

*Children and Violence* (1995) Report of the Gulbenkian Foundation Commission, London: Calouste Gulbenkian Foundation.

Cockburn, Cynthia (1983) *Brothers*, London: Pluto.

Cockburn, Cynthia (1991) *In the Way of Women*, London: Macmillan.

Cohen, David (1996) 'It's a Guy Thing', *The Guardian Weekend*, 4, May pp. 26–30.

Collier, Richard (1995) *Masculinity, Law and the Family*, London: Routledge.

Collinson, David and Hearn, Jeff (eds) (1996a) *Men as Managers, Managers as Men*, London and Thousand Oaks, Ca.: Sage.

Collinson, David L. and Hearn, Jeff (1996b) "Men" at "work": Multiple Masculinities/Multiple Workplaces', in Mairtin Mac an Ghaill (ed.) *Understanding Masculinities. Social Relations and Cultural Arenas*, Buckingham: Open University Press, pp. 61–76.

Connell, R.W. (1995) *Masculinities*, Cambridge: Polity.

Connell, R.W. (1996) 'Teaching the Boys: New Research on Masculinity, and Gender Strategies for Schools', *Teachers College Record* (USA), Vol. 98(2), pp. 206–35.

Connell R.W. (1997) 'Arms and the Man: Using the New Research on Masculinity to Understand and Promote Peace in the Contemporary World', paper at Norwegian National Commission for UNESCO, Expert Group Meeting, Oslo, September. Mimeo, University of Sydney.

Cordery, Jack and Whitehead, Antony (1992) ' "Boys Don't Cry": Empathy, Warmth, Collusion and Crime', in Paul Senior and David Woodhill (eds) *Gender, Crime and Probation Practice*, Sheffield: Sheffield City Polytechnic, PAVIC Publications.

Coveney, Lal, Jackson, Margaret, Jeffreys, Sheila, Kaye, Linda and Mahoney, Pat (1984) *The Sexuality Papers*, London: Hutchinson.

Craib, Ian (1987) 'Masculinity and Male Dominance', *Sociological Review*, 35(4), pp. 721–43.

Dickens, Linda (1995) 'UK, Part-time employees and the Law – Recent and Potential Developments', *Gender, Work and Organization*, Vol. 2(4), pp. 207–15.

Dicks, Bella, Waddington, David and Critcher, Chas (1998) 'Redundant Men and Overburdened Women: Local Service Providers and the Construction of Gender in Ex-mining Communities', in Jennie Popay, Jeff Hearn and Jeanette Edwards (eds) *Men, Gender Divisions and Welfare*, London: Routledge, pp. 287–311.

Dobash, Russell, Dobash, Rebecca, Cavanagh, Kate and Lewis (1996) *Research Evaluation of Programmes for Violent Men*, Edinburgh: Scottish Office.

Edelson, Jeffrey L. and Tolman, Richard M. (1992), *Intervention for Men who Batter*, Newbury Park, Ca. and London: Sage.

Edley, Nigel and Wetherell, Margaret (1995) *Men in Perspective*, Hemel Hempstead: Harvester Wheatsheaf.

Fagan, Colette (1996) 'Gendered Time Schedules: Paid Work in Great Britain', *Social Politics*, 3(1), pp. 72–106.

Gilroy, Paul (1987) *There Ain't No Black in the Union Jack*, London: Hutchinson.

Gondolf, Edward W. (1985), *Men who Batter*, Holmes Beach, Fl.: Learning Publications.

Hearn, Jeff (1983) *Birth and Afterbirth: A Materialist Account*, London: Achilles' Heel.

Hearn, Jeff (1984) 'Childbirth, Men and the Problem of Fatherhood', *Radical Community Medicine*, 15, pp. 9–19.

Hearn, Jeff (1987) *The Gender of Oppression*, Brighton: Wheatsheaf; New York: St. Martin's Press.

Hearn, Jeff (1990) 'Men's Violence and "Child Abuse" in Violence Against Children Study Group, *Taking Child Abuse Seriously*, London: Unwin Hyman, pp. 63–85.

Hearn, Jeff (1992a) *Men in the Public Eye*, London and New York: Routledge.

Hearn, Jeff (1992b) 'The Personal, the Political, the Theoretical: the Case of Men's Sexuality and Sexual Violence' in David Porter (ed.) *Between Men and Feminism*, London and New York: Routledge, pp. 161–81.

Hearn, Jeff (1994) 'Researching Men and Masculinities. Some Sociological Issues and Possibilities', *Australian and New Zealand Journal of Sociology*, Vol. 30(1), pp. 40–60.

Hearn, Jeff (1996) 'Deconstructing the Dominant: Making the One(s) the Other(s)', *Organization*, Vol. 3(4), pp. 611–26.

Hearn, Jeff (1998a) 'Troubled Masculinities in Social Policy Discourses: Young Men', in Jennie Popay, Jeff Hearn and Jeanette Edwards (eds) *Men, Gender Divisions and Welfare*, London: Routledge, pp. 37–62.

Hearn, Jeff (1998b) *The Violences of Men*, London: Sage.

*Health 2000 News* (1994) Special Issue 'Men's Health', No. 29, Winter, ed. David Marks.

Hirdman, Yvonne (1988) 'Genussystemet – reflexioner kring kvinnors sociala under-ordning', *Kvinnovetenskaplig Tidskrift*, 3, pp. 49–63.

Hirdman, Yvonne (1990) 'Genussystemet', in *Demokrati och Makt i Sverige*, Stock-holm: Statens Offentliga Utredningar.

*Human Development Report 1995* (1995) New York/Oxford: Oxford University Press for the United Nations Development Programme.

Jefferson, Tony (1991) 'Discrimination, Disadvantage and Police Work', in Ellis Cashmore and E. McLaughlin (eds) *Out of Order? Policing Black People*, London: Routledge, pp. 166–88.

Jougla, Eric, Hatton, Françoise and Le Toullec, Alain (1994) 'The Increase in Mor-tality for Young Males in France between 1981 and 1991', *HFA 2000 News* No. 29, Winter, pp. 6–8.

Judd, Judith (1996) 'Girls Sweep Past Boys in Exam Race', *The Independent*, 22 April, p. 1.

Kaufman, Michael (1987) 'The Construction of Masculinity and the Triad of Men's Violence', in Michael Kaufman (ed.) *Beyond Patriarchy*, Toronto: Oxford University Press.

Lees, John and Lloyd, Trefor (1994) *Working With Men Who Batter Their Partners*, London: WWM/The B Team.

Patricia Lunneberg (1997) *OU Men: Work through Lifelong Learning*, Cambridge: Lutterworth.

McKee, Linda and Bell, Colin (1985) 'Marital and Family Relations in Times of Male Unemployment', in Bryan Roberts, Ruth Finnegan and Duncan Gallie (eds) *New Approaches to Economic Life*, Manchester: Manchester University Press.

McKee, Linda and Bell, Colin (1986) 'His Unemployment: Her Problem. The Domes-tic and Marital Consequences of Male Unemployment', in Sheila Allen, Kate Purcell, Alan Waton and Stephen Wood (eds) *The Experience of Unemployment*, London: Macmillan.

Maiuro, R. D., Cahn, T. S., Vitiliano, P. P., Wagner, B.C. and Zegree, J. B. (1988) 'Anger, Hostility and Depression in Domestically Violent versus Generally Assaul-tive Men and Nonviolent Control Subjects', *Journal of Consulting and Clinical Psychology*, 56, pp. 17–23.

Messerschmidt, James (1993) *Masculinities and Crime*, Lanham, Md.: Rowman and Littlefield.

Minkowitz, Donna (1995) 'In the Name of the Father', *Ms.* November/December, pp. 64–71.

Mintel (1994) *Men 2000*, London: Mintel.

Moyes, Jojo (1995) 'Long Hours Culture Hits Productivity', *The Independent*, 26 October, p. 4.

Newburn, Tim and Stanko, Elizabeth (eds) (1994) *'Just Boys Doing Business' Men, Masculinities and Crime*, London: Routledge.

New Ways to Work (1993) *Change at the Top: Working Flexibly at Senior and Managerial Levels in Organisations*, London: NWTW.

New Ways to Work (1995) *Balanced Lives: Changing Work Patterns for Men*, London: NWTW.

*OHE Compendium of Health Statistics* (1992), 8th edition.

OPCS (1992) cited in Calman (1993) *On the State of the Public Health*, London: HMSO.

Pateman, Carole (1988) *The Sexual Contract*, Cambridge: Polity.

Pence, Ellen and Paymar, M. (1986) *Power and Control: Tactics of Men Who Batter. An Educational Curriculum*, Duluth, Mn.: Minnesota Program Development.

Pratt, Simon (1996) 'Could Do Better', *Achilles' Heel*, No. 20, pp. 20–1.

Reynolds, Paul (1999) 'In Defence of Outing', in Paul Bagguley and Jeff Hearn (eds) *Transforming Politics: Power and Resistance*, London: Macmillan.

Royal College of Psychiatrists (1996) *Depressed Men: Why Don't They Speak Out*, London, April.

Saco, Diana (1993) 'Masculinity as Signs', in Steve Craig (ed.) *Men, Masculinity and the Media*, London: Sage.

Sabo, Don and Gordon, David Frederick (eds) (1995) *Men's Health and Illness. Gender, Power and the Body*, Thousand Oaks, Ca: Sage.

Salisbury, Jonathan and Jackson, David (1996) *Changing Macho Values. Practical Ways of Working with Adolescent Boys*, Basingstoke: Falmer.

Tolson, Andrew (1977) *The Limits of Masculinity*, London: Tavistock.

Toynbee, Polly (1998) 'Mothers in the Moral Maze', *The Guardian*, 11, March p. 10.

Waddington, David, Critcher, Chas and Dicks, Bella (1998) '"All jumbled up": Employed Women and Unemployed Husbands', in Jennie Popay, Jeff Hearn and Jeanette Edwards (eds) *Men, Gender Divisions and Welfare*, London: Routledge, pp. 231–56.

Walby, Sylvia (1986) *Patriarchy at Work*, Cambridge: Polity.

Walby, Sylvia (1989) 'Theorizing Patriarchy', *Sociology*, Vol. 23(2), pp. 213–34.

Walby, Sylvia (1990) *Theorizing Patriarchy*, Oxford: Blackwell.

Williams, Fiona (1998) 'Troubled Masculinities in Social Policy Discourse: Fatherhood', in Jennie Popay, Jeff Hearn and Jeanette Edwards (eds) *Men, Gender Divisions and Welfare*, London: Routledge, pp. 63–97.

# 10 Rethinking the Boundaries of Political Representation
## Judith Squires

### INTRODUCTION

> Blair...took over leadership of the Labour Party with a promise to 'reconnect politics' by making it more inclusive and authentic. (Wilkinson and Diplock, 1996, p. 5)

A MORI poll to accompany the 75th anniversary of women's rights showed that 76 per cent of women were not involved in any form of party political activity. Alienation from the political system is widespread throughout society, but particularly deep amongst specific social groups. Research indicates that the young, the black and the female are significantly less likely to be politically active than the middle-aged, the white and the male: 'For many young people in Britain today politics has become something of a dirty word...In effect, an entire generation has opted out of party politics' (Wilkinson and Mulgan 1995, p.98) The fact that it is the more oppressed groups within society that feel most alienated from the political process signals that the liberal democratic rhetoric of political equality is yet to become a reality. Given that an increasing number of people fail to see any direct link between the government and government institutions and their own lives, what form of representative structures might inspire more active support and participation?

The extent to which the changes now being considered will begin to negotiate and ameliorate the manifest disengagement from party politics will depend in no small part upon the degree to which key political players are willing to engage with the profound critiques of the very basics of our current political structures that are emerging. It is not only the style of debate and content of policies that will need to change (though these are clearly substantial agendas in their own right), politicians need to be willing to 'think the unthinkable' in terms of electoral systems and representative structures.

Unlikely as it may seem, it would repay mainstream politicians to be attentive to debates within feminist theory. Many, if not all, of the issues now emerging around social exclusion and political participation have been theorised and debated from various feminist perspectives which deserve to receive more consideration than they have to date both from abstract reasons

169

of justice and from pragmatic reasons of efficacy. The mainstream is no longer so secure that it can afford to block its ears to the voices of its critics. If we are to entertain a paradigm shift in terms of our political thinking we must be willing to consider all existing perspectives with an open mind. The current period of political flux created by the forces of globalisation may bring with it many negative developments, but it might also present us with a precious opportunity to rethink the nature of political representation: to restructure our representative structures in ways which, for the first time, neither formally exclude nor actually marginalise a substantial range of groups, including women.

In asking 'what does feminist theory contribute to the practical task of restructuring our actual mechanisms of political representation?' I am aware that I am attempting to bridge a rather large gulf. As one political scientist has noted:

> Feminist theory and empirical gender politics research have surely not been deliberately estranged, but it seems that they have had unfortunately narrow epistemological grounds and almost no methodological ground, in common. (Tolleson Rinehard, 1992, p.16)

This works to the detriment of each, empirical gender politics frequently retaining cumbersome and counter-productive theoretical premises and feminist theory rarely making explicit what the practical implications of its abstract assertions are. I hope to bring these two approaches into closer proximity. Both have important contributions to make, not only to each other but, crucially, to policy-makers and constitutional reformers contemplating possibilities for electoral reform.


## WITHIN THE BOUNDARY

In Britain, since 1918 when women aged 30 and over won the vote (it being extended to women over 21 in 1928), the parliamentary political system has not formally excluded women. Yet in practice the interests and voices of women have remained marginal to mainstream debates and they have notoriously failed to enter parliament in anything like 'representative' numbers.

It is generally assumed that women have lower levels of interest in politics than men. The Government's Central Statistical Office report on women stated that 'women are not particularly interested in politics' (quoted in Stephenson, 1996, p.15). This assumption would seem to be supported by empirical research: a recent government survey showed that only 7 per cent of women claimed to be 'very interested' in politics. Women are more likely than men to be floating voters: 16 per cent of women as opposed to 11 per cent of men stating that they only made up their mind 'in the last few days' of the 1992 election campaign, and 75 per cent of men as opposed to 71 per cent of women claiming to have made up their mind 'a long time ago' (Stephenson, 1996, p.15). Women also formed the majority of 'don't knows' in Gallup's pre-election poll. There would seem to be a clear gender gap regarding interest in and identification with mainstream party politics.

But it is not just that the female electorate is less engaged than the male in party politics in terms of levels of voting and membership. When women do engage, they do so differently. 'Since 1945', a recent report notes, 'opinion polls have recorded a difference in voting between men and women, with women more likely to vote Conservative, and less likely to vote Labour than men' (though this reverses in the 18–34-year-old group, see Stephenson 1996, p.4). This gender gap exists not only in voting intentions but also in political priorities and perspectives. A July 1996 MORI poll revealed clear gender differences regarding political priorities. Although comparable numbers ranked health (54 per cent men, 65 per cent women), unemployment (49 per cent men, 47 per cent women) and education (49 per cent men and 53 per cent women) as the most important policy areas, there were significant differences within these broad areas. Women were more likely to be concerned with balancing work and family life, flexible working hours, low pay and part-time work than were men, who prioritised 'being out of work' as a concern (Stephenson, 1996).

How one interprets these facts depends on whether one is inclined to see women as having a less developed interest in and knowledge of politics, or as holding a distinctive perspective on and conception of politics. The argument that women simply have a less developed interest in politics leads one to be primarily concerned to assist women to find their voice within the political system as currently conceived. The argument that they show a different perspective on the political might on the other hand lead to a concern to learn more about this political perspective and to allow for its concrete articulation by changing political structures themselves.

Current empirical gender politics research tends to the latter approach. If women are more undecided than men (and it is always possible that they are simply more willing to admit to it), this should not be read as a failing, but as a positive statement of disillusionment and discontent. It is worth being attentive to recent research that reveals that women find the current form of party politics particularly unappealing, failing to represent their concerns or priorities. According to the 'Vision and Values Survey', women were more likely to display a cynical and less trusting attitude to political parties, finding it to be dominated by men who only go into politics for themselves (Stephenson, 1996, p.15). 52 per cent of women, as compared to 35 per cent men, said they did not know which of the parties could be trusted the most.

Such findings have provided useful resources to those who wish to challenge a traditional political science presumption that explanations of women's relative absence from politics should be sought by addressing the failings of women. The notion that this might reflect a considered cynicism arising from a realistic perception that their policy priorities are not adequately reflected in mainstream party agendas requires that one shifts one's attention away from the failings of women towards the failings of mainstream party politics itself.

## ON THE OUTSIDE

> Since the agenda of politics is defined and articulated primarily by men, many women are bound to be disconnected from traditional politics. (Wilkinson and Diplock, 1996, p. 10)

The argument that women are suspicious of traditional forms of party politics and choose not to engage with them provides one explanation for their relative absence (self-selection along with the selection and election processes being the three most frequently cited explanations explored). This thesis is given credence by the long history of ambivalence about the wisdom of entering the mainstream manifest within both feminist activism and theory.

There are three common yet distinct ways of attempting to reconnect women and politics involving, respectively: a rejection of the narrow representative conception of politics in favour of a participatory movement-based politics (such as the Greenham Common protest); calls for inclusion in existing political structures (often relying on purely rhetorical encouragement of women to enter into the system as it is); and attempts to augment and modify the latter to make them less exclusionary and more open to the participation for women (including positive action such as training, positive discrimination and the adoption of quotas).

Those engaged in the participatory form of political action have typically organised outside of state structures in such things as women's peace movements and ecology movements (Mies and Shiva, 1993). Many of their activities are concentrated below the level of the state and are often geared towards agitating against oppressive state structures and policies and have also tended to involve issues and movements that cut across state boundaries (Peterson and Sisson Runyan, 1993). During the peak of the second-wave women's movement many different protest strategies were adopted, including spontaneous action, well-organised campaigns of sit-ins, marches and demonstrations. All these forms of political protest were 'movement events', working outside the formal mechanisms of procedural politics. The political participation which was advocated during this period by many within the women's movement was direct participation in women's autonomous organisations. These organisation aspired to be open to all, non-hierarchical and informal (Phillips, 1991).

However, for all their strengths in terms of consciousness-raising, confidence-building and coalition-formation, these forms of radical participatory politics were not without their problems. Although claiming to be open to all, women's groups were largely unrepresentative of the diversity between women. The emphasis on participation was too demanding for many who were already juggling the 'dual burden' of work and family responsibilities, and the lack of representative structures raised serious questions of accountability (see Phillips, 1991). In recognition of these factors, many women prefer to pursue a strategy of modifying the institutional, representative mechanisms of politics rather than rejecting them altogether. If self-selection ceases to a primary concern, attention inevitably shifts to the barriers to entry posed by the selection and election processes. Party reforms, including new systems of candidate selection, new means of policy-making, and the establishment of new structures of government (such as ministries for women) have all been explored as means to increase women's political participation in the legislature (Lovenduski and Norris, 1993). What has not taken place is a systematic review of the principles and objectives of political representation itself. Intent on increasing the number of women in parliament, many have drawn pragmatically upon a series of frequently distinct and sometimes contradictory theoretical claims.

Most forms of feminist activism during the 1990s have asserted an explicit claim for an increased presence of women in decision-making structures. These demands tend to be based on a presumption that women have interests which are best represented by women. Yet as one commentator notes, 'that understanding has been fiercely contested by feminists, their sympathisers and their opponents in a continuing and sometimes acrimonious debate' (Lovenduski, 1996, 1). Given that women, even those claiming the title feminist, currently articulate such distinct political positions (in terms of both political goals and conceptions of the political itself) it is difficult to determine the extent to which such strategies actually 'represent women's interests'. It is simply no longer clear from a feminist perspective whether one should seek to represent women, or their interests, or indeed whether one can invoke the category of 'women' at all without repressing some significant other. In these circumstances it is far from clear that simply (though, of course, it has not been simple) increasing the number of women in the legislature will actually work to 'reconnect politics' to women and/or their interests or beliefs.

It is here that reflection on recent developments within feminist theory will help to elucidate the rationale and implications of the various proposals for change currently under consideration. There are many arguments made and campaigns waged to increase the representation of women in parliament, each making appeal to a diverse range of theoretical assumptions concerning both gender and politics, many mutually incompatible. To clarify the notoriously fraught and complex debates within feminist theory, I shall outline three distinct schools of feminist thought: equality, identity and difference. These different schools of thought are worth briefly surveying because each entails a distinct approach to the questions of women and political representation. That few people actually adopt and articulate one position unambiguously is perhaps inevitable and even laudable, but the failure to perceive the analytic distinctiveness of the agendas does lead to confusion as to 'what women want' and how best to achieve it in this context of political representation.

## EQUALITY, IDENTITY AND DIFFERENCE

When does legal recognition become an instrument of regulation and political recognition become an instrument of subordination? (Brown, 1995, p. 99)

Equality, identity and difference perspectives adopt distinct theoretical positions and endorse contrasting political arrangements. Each is concerned to recognise the political claims of those who are marginalized, but in contradictory ways. Equality politics assumes politics to be about the equal access of individuals to decision-making arenas for the pursuit of pre-existing political interests. If women's interests have not been adequately pursued within the current system it is presumed to be a result of contingent sexism on the part of individuals within a system that is itself just in principle and which needs to be held more fully accountable to its own professed ideals. Given the current discrimination against women, it is assumed that women might have interests that are best represented by women (given the likelihood of shared experience), but could be pursued by anyone who understood and sympathised with them. The important point is that one engages in politics to pursue interests not to articulate identities, aiming to transcend one's female specificity not emphasise it. Representation is assumed to be about the representation of interests.

Identity politics assumes women to be oppressed on the basis of being female and urges that one recognise as social and systematic what was formerly perceived as isolated and individual. For those engaged in identity politics, membership of a group both helps to explain the nature of oppression experienced by members of that group and serves as a source of strength, community and intellectual development. Engaging in identity politics entails finding one's true, unrepressed identity and then constructing a politics upon this. The consciousness-raising process adopted within the women's movement is a classic example of this. Politics is made to express a group loyalty: one engages in politics to achieve recognition for one's distinct voice. The claim is that there is a 'woman's perspective' which is currently repressed and that requires greater political recognition.

In the context of feminist theory, this identity politics perspective takes the form of a 'maternalist politics', drawing heavily upon the writings of Carol Gilligan, whose claim that women's experience of interconnection shapes their moral domain and gives rise to a different moral voice has been widely used as a basis for feminist politics (Gilligan, 1982, pp.151–76). In criticising Lawrence Kohlberg's research into moral development on the basis that it privileged an 'ethic of justice' over an 'ethic of caring', Gilligan offers feminists a framework within which they might critique the individualism and universalism of liberal political institutions. As Benhabib notes, 'Gilligan's critique of Kohlberg radically questions the 'juridical' or 'justice bias' of universalist moral theories' (Benhabib, 1992, p. 146). *Contra* Kohlberg, whose model of moral development assumed that the highest level of moral development involves the ability to abstract and universalise moral rules, Gilligan argued that we can distinguish between two ethical orientations: that of justice and rights on the one hand, and that of care and responsibility on the other. The latter requires a contextuality, narrativity and specificity not valued in the former. Gilligan made the further claim that women were more likely to manifest the latter than were men, giving them a different – but not inferior – moral sense. This claim is echoed in the writings of the 'maternalists' who argue for a feminised version of citizenship (Ruddick, 1980; Elshtain, 1981) and articulate a female political consciousness that is grounded in the virtues of women's private sphere – primarily mothering. Distributive justice, it is asserted, is not sufficient to generate a morally acceptable polity, we also need to adopt the maternal mode of caring as a basis for public interactions. The claim is that women's experiences as mothers within the private sphere provides them with certain insights and concerns which are valuable to the public sphere but currently absent from it.

From this perspective, then, it is argued, not primarily that women have different interests, but that women articulate their interest in a different voice: that they have a different perspective on politics. The reason why it might be important to have more women involved in the political arena on this account is because women will do politics differently, they will transform the style of debate and moral framework underpinning politics. In order to achieve this women will have to be present themselves: one cannot delegate the task of representing identities in the way one can delegate the task of representing interests. The representation of women is here the representation of women's identities.

On the other hand those who advocate a difference politics claim that we need to question the viability of the subject as the ultimate candidate for representation. In the context of feminist theory, this difference perspective takes the form of a postmodern feminism, drawing heavily on the writings of Judith Butler. It too offers feminists a framework within which they might critique the individualism and universalism of liberal political institutions, but from a very different basis. Rather than claiming a distinct female identity and ethic, Butler's approach questions the notion of a stable identity *per se*: 'there are those', she argues, 'who seek recourse to Gilligan and others who establish a feminine specificity that makes itself clear in women's communities or ways of knowing. But every time that specificity is articulated, there is resistance and factionalization within the very constituency that is supposed to be unified by the articulation of its common element' (Butler, 1995, p.49) The recognition of this resistance, leading to a political emphasis upon plural rather than dichotomous differences, arises from a performative notion of identity, constituted by language and produced within a given network of power/discourse. This approach emphasises the subject's historicity and susceptibility to change, thereby allowing for the possibility of disruption of constricting identities. Politics here, to the extent that it is accepted that this is a politics at all, is made to question group loyalty and subvert group identities. From this perspective then, one's political objective should be to undermine rather than entrench existing identities. One should seek to challenge the prevailing understanding of what it is to be a woman, rather than (as with equality politics) pursue the interests of 'women', or (as with identity politics) voice a 'woman's' perspective. Given this, it is simply not clear that the difference perspective offers any rationale for pursuing the 'representation of women' at all.

Critiques of identity politics from a difference perspective include the claim that it frequently conflates or ignores intra-group differences: to talk of 'women' as a unified group is to deny the significant differences between women thereby fuelling injustices rather than overcoming them. In other words, the perspective claimed to be that of 'women' will always be that of particular (probably relatively privileged) women and, in failing to acknowledge its specificity, will silence the voices of some women in the very process of claiming to speak for them. This is precisely the charge made by many black women in relation to dominant groupings within the women's movement. Furthermore when identity as reified politics is constrained: to view politics as a means for gaining recognition for existing 'identities' is to entrench what is itself a product of oppression and ultimately to perpetuate one's victim status (Brown, 1995, p. 120). For instance, to claim an ethic of care as a distinctly female perspective is to accept as natural an identity that was actually imposed upon women by a highly specific set of historical circumstances (see Tronto, 1993). It is also to celebrate as virtuous all those aspects of the identity of the oppressed which are associated with strategic self-preservation in a condition of weakness: acuity of perception of the other's feelings; the masking of assertive and direct modes of leadership in those of indirect suggestion and persuasion; the assertion of power through goodness where this works to occlude the subject's interest in power and makes it appear that all they are doing is operating on behalf of the need of others. (Yeatman, 1997, p. 148)

The result of the assertion of this form of identity politics is, its difference critics claim, that rights claims are deployed to protect historically and contextually contingent identities, such that the former operates inadvertently to resubordinate by renaturalizing that which it was intended to emancipate by articulating (see Riley, 1988; Butler, 1990; Yeatman, 1994; Brown, 1995).

On the other hand, critiques of difference politics from an identity perspective argue that the approach is nihilistic: there is no ethical apparatus with which to acknowledge social injustice or to negotiate relations of dominance. The celebration of heterogeneity and the proliferation of identities combined with the assertion that one need never (ought never) accept the limits of identity, have the effect of negating birth, history, privilege and social responsibility (Jones, 1993). What is more, at this point in history, advocates of identity politics argue, a strong case can be made that the most critical resistance strategy for disempowered groups is to occupy and defend a politics of social location rather than to vacate and destroy it (see Jones, 1993; and Stanley, 1990).

So, when considering our question: 'What does feminist theory contribute to the practical task of restructuring our actual mechanisms of political representation?' one part of the answer will be, perhaps inevitably given the nature of theoretical debates, 'It depends'. I have indicated that there will be at least three quite distinct responses according to the type of feminist theory adopted. This point has political, as opposed to purely theoretical, significance in that it highlights the extent to which there are radically distinct conceptions of women, their interests and their perspectives, even amongst those who call themselves feminist, and that these differences translate into quite distinct proposals for political change. Failing to perceive the antagonisms between them has led and will lead to a tendency to adopt a confused and confusing mixture of often incompatible political strategies. When considering proposals for restructuring mechanisms of political representation the last thing needed is further confusion. Things are already muddled enough.

## REPRESENTATIVE MUDDLES

That representation is a muddle is accepted by most political theorists. (Phillips, 1995, p. 41)

Should our elected representatives represent their supporters, their ideological allies within their party, their own conscience, their constituents... or some combination of the above? Are these compatible or contradictory roles? Much of the muddle surrounding the nature of representation can be traced to the historical tension between various distinct forms of representation which have developed alongside, but not replaced, pre-existing representative mechanisms. Medieval roots within our representative systems can be witnessed in the notion that parliament functions as a geographic forum where representatives speak for districts. Then again immediately prior to the late eighteenth century it was commonly assumed that government represented not districts but property owners. The mass suffrage movements, demanding working-class male and then women's suffrage, challenged this notion of representation ushering in the adoption of the party system in which representatives represent ideological perspectives and class interest. In short, there has been no clear, unchanging conception of what it is that we require our 'representatives' to represent. For as long as representation has been a key feature in our model of liberal democracy, the issue of what it is that is to count as being politically worthy of representation and who deemed able to represent others has itself been the object of political battle. Britain, with its emphasis on stability and tradition, manages to assume a particularly confused cluster of working definitions of what representation is.

So, before looking at the particular insights and proposals emerging from feminist theory regarding a more just representative system, a brief clarification of the analytically distinct conceptions of representation may be helpful. There are four questions worth considering: When claiming to be a representative what is one representing? How does one represent it? Where does one represent it? What is the purpose of representation? My argument is that theoretical exploration and clarification of the what, how, where and why of representation will bring the key normative issues at stake into clearer relief.

In answer to the first question – What is one representing? – there would seem to be four distinct sorts of answer: identities, beliefs, constituencies and interests. According to which of these one chooses to prioritise, one will advocate social, ideological, geographic or functional representation respectively (Marsh and Norris, 1997). In answer to the second question – How does one represent it? – there are generally thought to be three means: symbolic, microcosmic and principal/agent (see Phillips, 1995). In answer to the third question – Where does representation take place? – the traditional answer of local and national arenas has been supplemented by the new site of Europe. The answer to the fourth question – What is the purpose of representation? – is actually very complex, but hinges on the issue of justice. I shall argue, rather schematically, that what is distinctive within the identity version of feminist theory is an emphasis upon justice as requiring recognition not just redistribution (Fraser, 1997).

We can, therefore, distinguish between distinct conceptions of representation according to what is being represented, how, where and why. Each of these factors will have a significant impact on the form of representative mechanisms. Take, for instance, the ideological, geographic, functional and social distinction. The ideological axis involves collective representation via parties. It is the 'responsible party government' model which requires disciplined parties with alternative programmes on major issues facing the country, voter choice on the basis of evaluations of government record or policy platforms and free and fair elections. This is 'representation from above' (Marsh and Norris, 1997, p. 154) in that there is a highly centralised, party-led decision-making structure. Collective responsibility and party discipline work to ensure that representatives do not represent differences other than those of belief – be they geographic, interest group or identity-based.[1] The geographic axis involves district-based delegates. Here representatives are to act in ways consistent with the opinions of citizens from areas which elect them. This is 'representation from below' (Marsh and Norris, 1997, p. 155) with low levels of party discipline and minimal ideological manifestos. The functional axis involves representatives acting as spokespeople for interest groups and new social movements. On this model representatives respond not primarily to party or constituents but to pressure from organised interests (such as farmers or the gun lobby). Such functional representation is often viewed as compensating for weak parties, operating to the extent that ideological representation does not. The social axis involves representatives reflecting the social composition of the electorate in terms of presence as secured by quotas policies or reserved places. On this model representation occurs when the legislature include the same proportion of each relevant subgroup as the population from which it is drawn. Rather than looking to the decisions of the legislature to determine its representativeness one looks to its composition .[2]

Where, then, does feminist theory stand in terms of these alternatives? Which forms of representation would be most sensitive to the interests of women and/or which most likely to secure the presence of women in our decision-making bodies? There is, of course, no consensus on this issue. Current theoretical debate is focused on the question of whether, as women, we want our identities or our interests represented; whether we want social or functional representation; and whether it is politically acceptable to continue invoking the 'we' of a single category of women at all.

## PLURALISING REPRESENTATION

To re-site the political is to recognise the multiple terrains and spaces producing and produced by politics. (Dean, 1997, p. 2)

It should be evident from the categorisations above that equality politics focuses on ideological or functional representation: on what one theorist calls 'the politics of ideas' (Phillips, 1995) whereas the current 'politics of identity' literature focuses exclusively on social representation (or a 'politics of presence') at the expense of other forms. Difference politics would seem to entail a critique of each of the above but offer little positive in their place. The fact that one commonly finds appeal to all three perspectives as a means for improving gender justice may go some way to explaining the lack of consensus surrounding strategies for political change.

The equality approach is manifest in many of the arguments for equal opportunities to engage in ideological or functional representative practices. This is usually accompanied by a direct rejection of both positive discrimination and of social representation as an ideal. Liberal Democratic spokesperson Diana Maddock, for instance, denounced the Labour Party quotas policy saying: 'We want equal treatment for women not special treatment. Our aim is equality of opportunity not equality of outcome' (*The Times*, 7 March 1995). The assumption underpinning such claims is that the existing criteria of selection and election are themselves fair and need to be more fully realised rather than structurally amended. It should be noted that this approach, by far the most common within British party politics, has largely failed to increase the representation of women, their interests or perspectives.

Those who advocate identity politics, on the other hand, have a relatively clear (if highly ambitious) agenda: women are a discernible identity group; women 'do' politics differently; they manifest a care rather than a justice perspective; the recognition of women's distinctive identities requires political representation of women as women. Representation is assumed to be of the mirror form. The effect upon political representation of adopting an identity politics is to introduce the issue of 'presence' and group recognition[3] with group rights and quotas as appropriate mechanisms. We can perhaps see elements of such thinking in the NEC statement following the Annual Conference of 1994:

> Conference reaffirms its view that if the Labour Party is truly to reflect the communities it seeks to represent there must be a significant improvement in the level of women's representation in Parliament.

In endorsing a women-only quotas policy for the selection of Labour parliamentary candidates the Labour Party revealed a willingness (albeit only briefly, as it transpired) to integrate a form of social representation into representative structures which are primarily developed to represent differences of interests and beliefs not identities. The possibility for considering social representation is greater within the Labour Party than either the Liberal or Conservative Parties due to the differing party cultures: Labour politicians have traditionally been more likely to see themselves as social representatives than have members of other parties (given the close connection between class identity, economic interests and ideological beliefs surrounding the Party's formation: see Norris and Lovenduski, 1995, pp. 168–9). So identity theorists advocating mirror representation found some success in modifying the selection process prior to the last general election, resulting in what some have called 'the long awaited breakthrough for women's representation in the House of Commons' (Lovenduski, 1997).

Those who advocate a difference politics have a more challenging task in negotiating the connection between their abstract theoretical insights and their practical political proposals. There is a tension between constituting political procedures (which inevitably posit some stability of identity and require exclusions of certain differences) and celebrating the fluidity of heterogeneous difference. What the effect upon political representation of adopting a difference politics would be is thus far not clear. Given that the project of a difference politics is to challenge the normalising rules that seek to constitute, govern and control various behaviours, to question and denaturalise all that is entrenched in politics, both individual and group representation look problematic. Arguments for quotas for women would seem to reinforce that which a difference politics would have us deconstruct: to the extent that quotas are argued for as a means of bringing an alternative, female perspective to political debate and decision-making, they institutionalise the notion that politics is about expressing pre-existing identities and entrench the presumption that male and female identities are distinct. In other words, calls for social representation could, it is argued, reify that which should be undermined and made fluid. This being the case a politics  of difference perspective may have little positive to contribute to the task of rethinking political representation, but does provide an invaluable framework for understanding many contemporary single-issue campaigns, acts of individual transgression and subversion of existing orthodoxies as 'political' challenges to current representative politics. It draws one's attention to the ways in which any mechanism for political representation works to constitute and/or entrench identities which may themselves come to be constraining or even oppressive. Advocates of identity politics should, therefore, think long and hard about the precise proposals for representing women for, if adopted, these will also become mechanisms for constituting women.[4] The representative structures we adopt and operate not only determine the inclusiveness and justice of the political system with respect to existing marginalised groups, they will also work to construct future group identities.

To return to our opening question: 'What does feminist theory contribute to the practical task of restructuring our actual mechanisms of political representation?' I would argue that it reveals that extent to which anyone seeking to redraw the boundaries of political representation will need to reconfigure the relationship between ideological, functional, geographic and social representation. Anne Phillips has argued that ideological representation makes sense 'when politics is organised around binary oppositions, or when political beliefs and objectives fall into coherent clusters of congruent ideas' (Phillips, 1995, p. 41) – a presumption that looked more plausible when class was the central organising principle defining the political spectrum than it does today. Debates within feminist theory have been structured around equality, identity and difference perspectives, with the identity and difference perspectives coming to dominate in recent years. The equality perspective continues to focus attention on ideological representation in terms of concentrating upon the question of mechanisms for encouraging individual women to enter into parliament as a member of an existing political party. The turn towards an identity perspective, however, shifts the focus of attention towards a consideration of the pros and cons of functional and social representation. The women's movement generated both a large social movement and a huge number of small, focused interest groups both of which used the functional form of representation to impress their interests upon representatives across the ideological spectrum. It has also placed the issue of social representation firmly on the mainstream political agenda in the form of the introduction of quotas into our political institutions. As Phillips argues, this necessitates that we consider the 'politics of presence' as well as the 'politics of ideas'.

The imperatives of a reconceptualised radical democracy would seem to require a commitment to representative pluralism. To be a radical democrat, one social theorist has commented, is to appreciate two different kinds of impediments to democratic participation: social inequality and misrecognition of difference (Fraser, 1997, p. 173). The current structuring of representative mechanisms around ideological differences emphasises the social inequality aspect of politics, but fails to address the 'misrecognition of difference' aspects. Feminist theory has in recent years tended towards the other extreme. If anything, there has been a tendency within feminist theory to focus 'one-sidedly on cultural politics to the neglect of political economy' (Fraser, 1997, p. 174). The impasse between identity and difference theorists has preoccupied many feminist theorists to such an extent that they have focused exclusively upon the merits or dangers of social representation rather than contemplating its possible relation to functional and ideological representation. However, when placed in the context of party political debates, the agenda of feminist theory is enlightening if only because it is so different. The gulf between the two could (though as yet has not) work to highlight the omissions of each to the benefit of both.

Current feminist theory tends to be characterised by debate about the merits and failings of identity politics, rendering debates over women's representation into debates about the nature of 'woman'. When politics becomes about identities, interests and beliefs tend to be marginalised. This makes a certain sense given that the current institutional privileging of ideological representation is increasingly at odds with popular conceptions of political identification, turning many away from representative politics altogether. However, arguing for the replacement of this system with one which only emphasises identity differences by privileging social representation immediately runs into problems associated with essentialism, ghettoisation and a politics of 'ressentiment'.[5] The old ideological notion of representation may indeed no longer be adequate but a simple replacement of it with social representation will not suffice. It is not, after all, the (only) function of the state to affirm people in their differences. Indeed, given that identities are themselves arguably a historical product, it is not clear why one should feel compelled by the argument that politics should be about the representation of all those identities that already exist. The mere existence of social difference is not sufficient to justify recognition in the form of group representation, some other criteria of political pertinence will need to be deployed. For this we will need to invoke a critical theoretical perspective which brings questions of functional interests and ideological beliefs back in. One of the most perceptive of thinkers on these matters has argued persuasively:

> while the politics of ideas is an inadequate vehicle for dealing with political exclusion, there is little to be gained by simply switching to a politics of presence. Taken in isolation, the weaknesses of the one are as dramatic as the failings of the other... It is in the relationship between ideas and presence that we can best hope to find a fairer system of representation, not in a false opposition between one or the other. (Phillips, 1995, pp. 24–5)

Negotiation of the two different agendas will, of course, be complex. Women are subject both to economic and cultural injustice. Yet the redistribution which responds to the former promotes group de-differentiation, and the recognition which responds to the latter promotes group differentiation. Nancy Fraser argues that women, therefore, need both to deny and claim their specificity, to fight to abolish gender differentiation and to valorise gender specificity (Fraser, 1997). If this is the case, they will need both functional and social representation: functional to act as interest groups and new social movements mobilising for particular decisions and policies, social to gain recognition as a distinct cultural grouping with distinct perspectives and identities. If one were to adopt this pragmatic endorsement of what have often been viewed as antithetical stances within feminist theory (as many in practice do), representative pluralism may be the only realistic way forward.

It is simply not realistic to expect a single representative system to capture the complexity of the current political subject. The trick will be to find distinct forms of political structure in which each might be appropriate to distinct representative moments. Perhaps no single representative system can do all the work entailed in this demand. Recall that the ideological axis involves collective representation via parties, which implies 'representation from above' in a highly centralised, party-led decision-making structure, whereas the geographic axis involving district-based delegates, the functional axis involving representatives acting as spokespeople for interest groups and the social axis involving representatives reflecting the social composition of the electorate in terms of presence, all imply a 'representation from below' with low levels of party discipline and minimal ideological manifestos.

Given that the majority of women across all ages are uninterested in and cynical about party politics the ideological axis of political representation with its emphasis on representation from above would seem to have proved to be particularly unappealing to the female electorate to date. Allowing that this is probably a result of historically specific structural gender relations which are currently subject to transformation (Walby 1997) this is not in itself reason to give up on this form of politics. However, recent research indicates that young women are politically volatile, non-ideological and pragmatic (Wilkinson and Mulgan, 1994), indicating that the 'representation from below' models of political inclusion will prove more appealing in the future. If this is the shape of things to come, perhaps it makes sense to realign our mechanisms of representation such that they too are pragmatic and non-ideological.

Moves in this direction are already afoot. Constitutional reform, including devolution for Scotland and Wales and the proposals for devolving power to the regions, reintroduces a recognition of the role of geographic representation in contemporary representative structures. Moreover, the pluralisation of the sites of political representation would itself allow for a significant diversification of the characteristics deemed politically pertinent. Multiple sites of representation would allow for multiple criteria of political difference to be accommodated. In this context it is significant that proposals for the electoral system to operate for the coming Scottish Parliament build in an element of social representation in proposing that every constituency have both a male and a female representative.

Proposals for electoral reform also break the hold of ideological representation and allow for a more flexible recognition of functional and social issues. It has been shown that the nature of the electoral process adopted makes a big difference to the actual composition of legislatures. As Pippa Norris has revealed, multi-member constituencies and a 'party lists' system allow greater recognition of difference within one's political structures (Norris, 1996, pp. 89–103). Proportional representation allows for a greater inclusiveness of candidates for election by making under-representation in the nomination process both more visible and more accountable. Countries with proportional representation and large numbers of representatives in districts are the leaders among democracies in the proportions of women in parliament. For the equality and difference theorists, wary of the consequences of the identity perspective's focus on social representation, proportional representation may be a vitally important way forward. In allowing for diversification and fragmentation generally, PR systems are able to address the relative absence of women and minorities within the political system, without resorting to the entrenchment of such identities within existing party selection procedures.

No single form of representation will be sophisticated enough to represent complex subjects in all their aspects. If we are genuinely concerned to make our political institutions more representative, maybe we should be thinking of creating a number of distinct structures each of which operates upon a distinct model of representation. The problem posed by the current preoccupation with ideological representation is that its 'top-down' approach to representation works to deny the possibility of a pragmatic disaggregation of the geographic, functional and social representative moments.

Finally, it might also be worth considering moving away from representation altogether. The difficulties inherent in claiming to speak for another are notorious. To speak for a group, whether it be a geographical constituency, interest group or social movement, without silencing some within the group or some aspects of the group is probably an impossibility. It is likely that selection, as opposed to election, could be more sensitive to functional and social differences than current electoral representation. The current consideration of the possible merits of citizens' juries is one further move in the direction of radically rethinking the boundaries of representation such that it might 'reconnect politics' by making it more inclusive.

In this it would appear that Tony Blair's willingness to consider fundamental constitutional and electoral reform might indeed make politics more inclusive of women. But I would propose that we remain sceptical about his second aspiration: to make politics more 'authentic'. Representative politics does not simply re-present what we are. It not simply a mechanism for more or less accurately capturing and articulating pre-existing identities and/or interests. It is never solely a means of voicing 'authentic' selves. Politics is also performative and constituting. In engaging in the political we actually gain identities and interests. Clearly, it is a function of representative politics to be expressive of that which already exists. But this should not blind us to the significant role that politics, including representative politics, plays in *perpetuating* certain identities and interests whilst denying others, and actually *creating* that which does not yet exist. The selection of future mechanisms of representation entails not only the pursuit of a pure expression of authentic selves, but also the modification of the art of government in which subjects are shaped. Rethinking the boundaries of political representation might well allow for a more inclusive politics, but it will also generate a new set of criteria as to what is to be deemed politically pertinent, which identities and interests perceived as authentic. We would do well to reflect on this and consider which exclusions are implicit in the new forms of inclusiveness proposed.

## CONCLUSION

What, then, are the practical implications of these theoretical debates in terms of women's representation? The first point is that there is no single theoretical perspective to which one might appeal for guidance within the feminist literature. I have schematically labelled distinctive positions as equality, identity and difference perspectives. Equality politics endorses a vision of representation as the representation of beliefs and interests (ideological and functional representation). Identity politics endorses a vision of representation as the representation of identities (social representation). Difference politics largely adopts a critical perspective, highlighting the potential dangers of each of these two perspectives, but has few of the theoretical tools necessary to assert a practical alternative.

If we are to negotiate new boundaries of political representation we should be attentive to each of these perspectives whilst recognising the impossibility of simply conflating them. Adding a demand for social representation onto our already overburdened existing representative system (which already attempts to realise functional, ideological and geographic representation) will simply reduce the likelihood that any of these forms will be realised sufficiently to impress the electorate. Recognition of the complexity and fluidity of contemporary subjects will require a more radical restructuring of our representative structures than this. A disaggregation of distinct representative forms may now be needed. Perhaps the dominance of ideological representation and party politics has had its day?

## NOTES

1.   The extent to which parties discipline 'representatives' such that they represent the party before they represent their constituents, their group identities or their conscience was clearly shown in the case of the overwhelming majority of new women MPs in the current government voting for the reduction of benefits to lone-parents.

2.   Whilst ideological and functional representation are clearly distinct, they both share the same 'principal/agent' mechanisms for representation. Social

representation, on the other hand, requires microcosm or 'mirror' mechanisms to ensure representativeness.

3.    One can, of course, argue for special representation rights without invoking identity politics. The equality politics perspective can be modified to incorporate group representation, where special representation rights are used as a mechanism to rectify past exclusions not as a means of celebrating differences *per se*.

4.    '...the feminist subject turns out to be discursively constituted by the very political system that is supposed to facilitate its emancipation' (Butler, 1990, p. 2)

5.    The tendency simply to affirm social representation is a product of a peculiarly American political agenda which does not transfer as neatly to the British political situation as the political theory literature would imply. This is because in Britain we have a much stronger tradition of ideological representation than has been the case in the US where functional representation has been more dominant. The arguments and mechanisms for functional representation are more closely aligned to those for social representation that are those for ideological representation.

## REFERENCES

Barrett, Michele (1992) 'Word and Things', in A. Phillips and M. Barrett (eds) *Destabilizing Theory*, Cambridge: Polity Press.

Bashevkin, Sylvia (ed.) (1985) *Women and Politics in Western Europe*, London: Frank Cass.

Benhabib, Seyla (1992) 'The Generalized and the Concrete Other', in *Situating the Self*, Cambridge: Polity Press.

Benhabib, Seyla (1995) 'Feminism and Postmodernism' and 'Subjectivity, Historiography and Politics' in Benhabib, Butler, Cornell and Fraser, *Feminist Contentions*, London and New York: Routledge.

Brown, Wendy (1988) *Manhood and Politics*, Totowa, N.J.: Rowman and Littlefield.

Brown, Wendy (1995) *States of Injury: Power and Freedom in Late Modernity* Princeton, NJ: Princeton University Press.

Butler, Judith (1990) 'Subjects of Sex/Gender/Desire', in *Gender Trouble*, New York and London: Routledge.

Butler, Judith (1995), 'Contingent Foundations' and 'For a Careful Reading' in Benhabib, Butler, Cornell and Fraser, *Feminist Contentions*, London and New York: Routledge.

Chodorow, Nancy (1989) 'Feminism and Psychoanalytic Theory', in *Feminism and Psychoanalytic Theory*, Cambridge: Polity Press.

Cixous, Hélène (1986) 'Sorties', in Hélène Cixous and Catherine Clement, *The Newly Born Woman* (trans. Betsy Wing), Manchester: Manchester University Press.

Dahlerup, Drude (ed.) (1986) *The New Women's Movement*, London: Sage

Dean, Jodi (1997) *Feminism and the New Democracy*, London: Sage.

Dietz, Mary (1992) 'Context is All: Feminism and Theories of Citizenship', in Chantal Mouffe (ed.) *Dimensions of Radical Democracy*, London: Verso.

Elshtain, Jean Bethke (1981) *Public Man, Private Woman*, Oxford: Martin Robertson.

Flax, Jane (1987) 'Postmodern and Gender Relations in Feminist Theory', in *Signs: Journal of Women in Culture and Society*, Vol. 12, No. 4, Chicago: University of Chicago.

Fraser, Nancy (1997) *Justice Interruptus*, New York, Routledge

Gilligan, Carol (1982) *In a Different Voice*, Cambridge, Mass.: Harvard University Press, pp. 1–22, 171–4.

Gutmann, Amy (ed.) (1994) *Multiculturalism*, Princeton, NJ: Princeton University Press.

Jaggar, Alison (1989) 'Love and Knowledge: Emotion in Feminist Epistemology', in *Inquiry* 32, pp. 151–76.

Jones, Kathleen B. (1993) *Compassionate Authority*, New York: Routledge

Larrabee, Mary Jeanne (ed.) (1993) *An Ethic of Care*, New York and London: Routledge.

Lovenduski, Joni (1997) 'Gender Politics: A Breakthrough for Women?', *Parliamentary Affairs*, 50, 4, 705–19.

Lovenduski, Joni and Norris, Pippa (eds) (1993) *Gender and Party Politics*, London: Sage.

Lovenduski, Joni and Norris, Pippa (1995) *Political Recruitment: Gender, Race and Class in the British Parliament*, Cambridge: Cambridge University Press.

Lovenduski, Joni (1996) 'Sex, Gender and British Politics', *Parliamentary Affairs*, Vol. 49, No. 1.

McBride Stetson, Dorothy and Mazur, Amy (1995) *Comparative State Feminism*, Newbury Park, Cal: Sage.

Mies, Maria and Shiva, Vandana (1993) *Ecofeminism*, London: Zed Books.

Millett, Kate (1970) *Sexual Politics*, London: Jonathan Cape.

Morgan, Robin (ed.) (1970) *Sisterhood is Powerful: an Anthology of Writing from the Women's Liberation Movement*, New York: Random House.

Mouffe, Chantal (1992) *Dimensions of Radical Democracy*, London: Verso.

Mouffe, Chantal (1992a), 'Feminism, Citizenship and Radical Democratic Politics', in Judith Butler and Joan Scott (eds) *Feminists Theorize the Political*, London and New York: Routledge.

Mouffe, Chantal (1993) *The Return of the Political*, London: Verso.

Norris, Pippa (1996) 'Women Politicians Transforming Westminster?', in *Parliamentary Affairs*, Vol. 49, No. 1, January: 89–103.

Norris, Pippa and Marsh Michael (1997) 'Political Representation in the European Parliament', *European Journal of Political Research*, Vol 32, No. 2, October.

Okin, Susan (1989) *Gender, Justice and the Family*, New York: Basic Books.

Pateman, Carole (1970) *Participation and Democratic Theory*, Cambridge: Cambridge University Press.

Peterson, V. Spike and Runnyan, Anne Sisson (1993) *Global Gender Issues*, Oxford: Westview Press.

Phillips, Anne (1991) 'Paradoxes of Participation', in *Engendering Democracy* Cambridge: Polity Press.

Phillips, Anne (1995) *The Politics of Presence*, Cambridge: Polity Press.

Riley, Denise (1988) *Am I That Name?* London: Macmillan.

Ruddick, Sara (1980) 'Maternal Thinking', in *Feminist Studies* 6.2 (Summer).

Scott, Joan (1988) 'Gender: a Useful Category for Historical Analysis', in *Gender and the Politics of History*, New York: Columbia University Press.

Stanley, Liz (1990) 'Recovering Women in History from Feminist Deconstruction', *Women's Studies International Forum*, Vol. 13.

Stephenson, Mary Anne (1996) 'Winning Women's Votes: the Gender Gap in Voting Patterns and Priorities', London: Fawcett Society.

Tolleson Rinehard, Sue (1992) *Gender Consciousness and Politics*, New York: Routledge.

Tronto, Joan (1993) *Moral Boundaries: a Political Argument for an Ethic of Care*, New York: Routledge.

Walby, Sylvia (1997) *Gender Transformations*, London: Routledge.

Wilkinson, Helen and Mulgan, Geoff (1994) *Freedom's Children*, Demos pamphlet.

Wilkinson, Helen and Diplock, Shelagh (1996) *Soft Sell or Hard Policies*, Demos pamphlet.

Wilson, Elizabeth (1993) 'Is Transgression Transgressive?', in Joseph Bristow and Angela Wilson (eds) *Activating Theory: Lesbian, Gay and Bisexual Politics*, London: Lawrence and Wishart.

Yeatman, Anna (1994) *Postmodern Revisionings of the Political*, London: Routledge.

Yeatman, Anna (1997) 'Feminism and Power', in Mary Lyndon Shanley and Uma Narayan (eds) *Reconstructing Political Theory: Feminist Perspectives,* Cambridge: Polity Press.

Young, Iris (1990) 'The Ideal of Impartiality and the Civic Public', in *Justice and the Politics of Difference*, Princeton, NJ: Princeton University Press.

# 11 Sexing Political Behaviour in Britain

Joni Lovenduski

The 'breakthrough' by Labour women in the 1997 general election brought Britain to around 20th place in the world league tables of women's representation. It is a recent and late manifestation of changing patterns of women's political behaviour that began in Northern Europe in the 1970s and are apparent in most democratic countries. Differences between women's and men's political behaviour have been eroded and levels of women's representation have risen. While it would be difficult to argue effectively that all these changes are directly caused by the rebirth of feminism and the growth of women's movements, it would make little sense to explain the changes without reference to contemporary feminism.

The issue of the political representation of women has changed substantially since they first secured the franchise. When nineteenth-century feminists sought the right to vote they also wanted the right to stand in elections because they were convinced that changes in women's condition would come about only when women themselves became members of elected legislatures. In contrast, during the 1960s and 1970s many second-wave feminists were cynical about political institutions and electoral politics, preferring the political autonomy they found in new social movement organisations. By the early 1980s, however, there had been a reconsideration of the importance of mainstream politics and many feminists became active members of political parties.

This raises the question of what we mean by political representation. In democratic societies, the representation of a group's interests has at least two meanings: the presence of its members in decision-making arenas and the consideration of its interests in the decision-making process. An implication of the first meaning is that, to be democratic, the composition of the elected assemblies should mirror the composition of the society it serves. But the second meaning implies that it is enough that an assembly takes into account the interests of all its electors. There have been intense theoretical arguments about which of the two formulations should prevail and these arguments have been reflected in debates amongst feminists who have disagreed sharply about the nature of women's interests and the political strategies required to press them (Phillips, 1991). Another feminist concern in the representation debate is about the extent to which women may be thought of as a group. There are differences between women that are at least as

Table 11.1   Women in Parliament, 1979–97

| Year | Labour | Con. | Lib Dem | Other | Total | % |
|------|--------|------|---------|-------|-------|------|
| 1979 | 11 | 8 | – | – | 19 | 2.9 |
| 1983 | 10 | 13 | – | – | 23 | 3.5 |
| 1987 | 21 | 17 | 1 | 2 | 41 | 6.2 |
| 1992 | 37 | 20 | 2 | 1 | 60 | 9.2 |
| 1997 | 101 | 13 | 3 | 3 | 120 | 18.2 |

important as differences between women and men. Divisions of class, race, ethnicity, region, age, and so forth determine women's interests but are not experienced in the same way as similar divisions between men. When devising policy and appeals to voters, it is important to ensure both that account is taken of such divisions and that the divisions are not assumed to affect women and men in the same way. For feminist advocates gender is a lens through which other salient social divisions should be viewed.

In discussions of women's political concerns a useful distinction may be made between women's issues and women's perspectives. Women's issues mainly affect women, either for biological reasons (for example, breast cancer screening, the use of reproductive technology and other reproductive rights), or for social reasons (for example, equal pay and childcare policy). Women's perspectives are women's views on all political concerns. Some commentators argue that although broadly the same issues are significant for both women and men, women perceive those issues in a different way from men. Thus, in 1996, the Fawcett Society published a survey of voters that showed that women and men both prioritised economic issues, but women were more concerned about part-time work, low pay and pension rights, while men were more concerned about unemployment. (Fawcett Society, 1996).

The demands women have made to be represented in party politics reflect both programmatic and organisational concerns and have been justified in terms both of women's issues and women's perspectives. Thus parties have been under pressure to promote policies to attract women voters, to undertake campaigns to recruit women members, to promote women into key positions in the party organisation and to nominate women candidates. To take into account new understandings of gender and power, party programmes have been revised and expanded.

The challenge of including women in British politics has been formidable. Despite the many years of rule by a strong and highly feminine woman politician, political image and discourse maintained a stubborn bias in which the 'normal' citizen is male. Arguably the preferred citizen is also male. In this chapter I examine recent strategies to include women in British

politics. The chapter is organised in three parts. First, a comparative introduction places the British experience in its appropriate context of the
European and Anglo-American democracies. Then, the British case is examined in detail, in a discussion of two important and related areas of political
change among British women – voting and political representation. For
reasons that become apparent in the discussion, I concentrate on Labour
Party politics. I conclude by acknowledging that the evidence that the two
phenomena are linked is circumstantial but still convincing.

## CROSS-NATIONAL TRENDS

Although women are more than one half of citizens in most democracies and
despite the widespread passage of legislation guaranteeing equal citizenship,
women are nowhere the political equals of men in terms of political representation. Moreover, there is considerable evidence that the political behaviour of women and men is differently motivated. In terms of formal politics
women are demonstrably less participant, less politically active, less likely to
be members of political elites than men. Such differences are commonly
referred to as 'gender gaps'. A 'gender gap' occurs when the measurable
behaviour of women and men differs. In politics the term most often refers to
differences in voting behaviour or intentions, but it is also used to describe
differences in political attitudes, language and style.

Women's political representation in democracies takes place in a range of
different councils, committees and social milieux, including elected assemblies, public and private organisations, political parties, social movements,
voluntary groups, and so forth. In this chapter I concentrate on the place of
women in national elected assemblies as it is a good indicator of how a
society values the political contribution of women. Patterns of women's and
men's political representation vary widely, but two common trends are
apparent. First, women are everywhere less well represented in legislatures
than men but, second, in most democracies, the proportion of women in
elected office is rising, a trend which became evident in the Nordic states
in the early 1970s and elsewhere during the 1980s. By the early 1990s women
were around 40 per cent of deputies in Sweden and Norway, but below 10
per cent in Britain, France and Greece.

To explain such differences is a major undertaking which includes attention to political processes and organisations as wide-ranging as established
political parties, government equality offices, trade unions and traditional
and autonomous women's movements as well as to constitutional provisions
such as regulations about the financing of elections and the operation of the
electoral system. Typically women have achieved increased representation by
making claims on political systems working especially in political parties but

also in NGOs such as women's associations, the voluntary and charitable groups and interest organisations of various kinds.

Not much research attention has been given to the analysis of these activities, with the exception of some recent work on political parties. Gradually campaigns for equality of representation gained support, putting three kinds of pressure on political parties. Research on contemporary Scandinavian, German, Italian, British and French politics shows that improving the power of women requires a combination of pressure from women's movements and from women organised in political parties. First women drew attention to the male dominance of public life and made direct demands for the representation of women. Second, women within political parties organised to secure reforms. Thirdly women voters began to penalise parties for masculine biases and for failure to prioritise women's concerns.

That women are more conservative in their voting preferences than men was established as conventional wisdom in the 1950s when a cross-national study of women and politics found consistent differences between women and men voters in a number of European countries including Italy, Norway, France and Germany (Duverger, 1955). Such evidence as was available in the 1960s suggested that this pattern continued. Female conservatism was commonly explained by varying patterns of religiosity and women's greater longevity. Since the 1980s changing patterns of voting have been apparent in a number of countries. Gender gaps in favour of the Right, that is, in which women have traditionally been more likely to vote for conservative parties than for parties of the Left, began to reverse amongst some women in a number of countries. Thus women in the USA became more likely to vote Democrat than men, and similar shifts occurred in Scandinavia. In Britain, Italy and France the pattern has been more mixed, but in each case significant groups of women became more likely to vote for parties of the Left than they had been in the past (Norris, 1996).

These changing patterns appear to be associated with changing patterns of women's employment, levels of education and their involvement in childrearing all of which impact on women's attitudes to politics. Changing attitudes have not been well or systematically studied in Europe. The best available data are the difficult to interpret Eurobarometer surveys of attitudes which show striking cross-national variations in which women are more left-wing than men in some countries, about the same in some and more right-wing than men in others. These data show a generation effect in which younger women are more likely to be left-wing than younger men with the pattern reversed in older generations (Norris, 1996). The evidence thus suggests that shifts in men's and women's voting patterns may continue.

When political parties notice such shifts they are likely to begin to alter their behaviour to court potential women voters, creating the possibility for women's movements to use the gender gap to advance a women's agenda, a development which may now be taking place in Britain where, during the 1990s, Labour has courted the women's vote by offering cabinet status to a women's minister, targeted campaigns on women's issues and concerted attempts to feminise its image, both in terms of campaigning language and style and by nominating more women candidates for winnable seats.

Although in the party's interest, Labour's new women-friendliness did not come about without considerable intervention by women. The 1997 Labour women's breakthrough resulted from *political* action, largely as a result of organised efforts in the party at a time when the drive for modernisation created opportunities to bring about change. The use made of such opportunities illustrates well the sophistication of women's interventions inside the Labour Party. Their 'interventions' were typical of a pattern that was apparent in virtually all democratic party systems. Women's organisations placing pressure on parties to improve the representation of women were joined by women who were already established in their parties who made claims for parity of political representation. The struggle for equal pay was a watershed. Once parties became committed to the policy of equality at work it was only a matter of time before more substantial demands for equal political representation than 'one person, one vote' were made. During the 1980s support for getting more women into politics grew in most democratic political systems. There was a shift in the agendas of both the parties and their women members.

In short, political parties became a major site of women's activity. There was a clear challenge to parties by women who claimed a voice in decision-making and pressed for changes in the political agenda. Women demanded and secured party reforms with varying degrees of success. In some countries this led to the appearance of new issues in party programmes, new systems of candidate selection, new means of policy-making, and the establishment of new structures of government such as ministries for women, equal opportunities ombudspersons and publicly funded women's committees. In response to pressure from women activists, members and voters, gender became an explicit issue for many political parties. This took place in contexts affected by different kinds of party politics. The extent and the manner of party accommodation of gender has been influenced by increased party competition via the entry of new parties and/or the decline of established parties, the erosion of established coalitions, modernisation strategies devised to replace or renew declining constituencies, system-level constitutional change and altered party–state relationships.

As the data in Table 11.2 suggest, demands for women's representation have had the most dramatic success in Scandinavia. Norway is a good example of sustained progress. Norwegian feminists were early in advocating the integration of women into the existing party structure as a strategy of empowerment. It has now been more than 20 years since the 'women's coup'

*Table 11.2* Women as a proportion of elected representatives in democratic legislatures (lower chambers) in the mid-1990s

| Country | Date of election | % Women |
|---|---|---|
| Sweden | 1994 | 40.4 |
| Norway | 1993 | 39.4 |
| Finland | 1995 | 33.5 |
| Denmark | 1994 | 33.0 |
| Netherlands | 1994 | 31.3 |
| Austria | 1995 | 26.8 |
| Germany | 1994 | 26.2 |
| Iceland | 1995 | 25.4 |
| Spain | 1996 | 24.6 |
| Switzerland | 1995 | 21.0 |
| Luxembourg | 1994 | 20.0 |
| Canada | 1993 | 18.0 |
| Australia | 1996 | 15.5 |
| Portugal | 1995 | 13.0 |
| USA | 1996 | 11.7 |
| Italy | 1996 | 11.1 |
| UK | 1992 | 9.5 |
| France | 1993 | 6.4 |
| Greece | 1996 | 6.3 |

*Source*: Inter-parliamentary Union.

overturned agreed party preferences on candidates lists for local authority elections and returned three local councils with a majority of women. The implications of this initial display of women's solidarity were understood rapidly by parties and the progress that Norwegian women have made since then is remarkable. The representation of women grew from below 10 per cent of elected representatives in the 1960s to about 25 per cent in local and national assemblies by the end of the 1970s, and 35 per cent in the early 1980s. At least 40 per cent of the members of every Norwegian government since 1986 have been women. Moreover, much of the women's agenda that has emerged in other countries is complete or well advanced in Norway where a new and wider ranging equality agenda has developed (Skjeie, 1993).

Near the other end of the scale is Britain, where demands for equity in women's representation came later, gathering force in the opposition parties only in the early 1980s and becoming a feature of the then ruling Conservatives' strategies of representation as late as the early 1990s. By 1992 women were fewer than 10 per cent of members of the House of Commons. Of course, the timing of demands for representation is only part of the story. The Norwegian and British political systems present different possibilities for women. In general the rules of the game in Norway favour the representation of women, whilst in Britain they do not. Norway is characterised by all of the features that favour women's representation: an electoral system based on proportional representation and party lists in which elections may be won and lost at the margins, thus forcing political parties to attend to new political groups; a political culture that places a high value on social equality and a large, well-integrated, and politically sophisticated women's movement mobilised to promote women's representation. Britain, on the other hand, has a simple majority, single-member constituency system, a highly fragmented women's movement and a marked lack of tolerance for equality measures such as quotas or other forms of positive action (Lovenduski, 1997).

## THE BRITISH EXPERIENCE

### Women and Voting

Despite their potential importance, gender gaps are not well understood by political scientists, and we are largely reliant on the insights afforded by research on the US which is where most studies have been undertaken. Prior to the 1997 general election campaign, gender gaps in British politics received remarkably little analytical attention from political scientists, journalists or pollsters. In common with studies in other countries, much of the research on women and voting between 1945 and 1979 was very perfunctory, what there was tended to rest on untested popular psychological assumptions about women and politics and implicit beliefs about appropriate behaviour. Very little attention was given to differences between women or to the development of gendered theories of political participation. Neither psephologists nor political scientists were interested in the woman voter, who was mainly ignored. When she was present, the woman voter was categorised in relation to an implicit and unitary male norm, as more traditional and right-wing, temperamentally unsuited to male styles of political activity, unquestioning in her adoption of her husband's political allegiances, more swayed by candidates than issues, more moralistic, more emotional, less politically knowledgeable and interested than men (Goot and Reid, 1975). During the 1980s and 1990s the stereotype of women voters was challenged by a growing number of feminist scholars, whose work slowly won some attention but not full acceptance from the mainstream of political science (Lovenduski and Hills, 1991; Lovenduski and Norris, 1993; Norris, 1996).

  I have long suspected that the lack of psephological interest in women's views about different issues stems partly from the fetishisation of indicators that comes to characterise established datasets such that new questions do not get asked and old questions do not get reinterpreted. In commercial polling the aim of producing newspaper stories shapes election polling. Questions are focused on what is traditionally considered to be newsworthy.

Polling professionals develop considerable faith in their indicators and techniques and resist pressures for change until they become overwhelming. Such attitudes spread throughout the polling community and appear to have effects on private party polling techniques as well as on commercial and academic survey instruments.

Moreover, the tendency in commercial polling is towards smaller samples and fewer questions. Thus the polling regime is antithetical to good gender analysis, which is not part of established polling concerns. Women do not generally get asked by pollsters what they think about political issues in a way that would show up many possible differences with men. Thus recognition of different men's and women's perspectives has been slow to develop and has not found its way into mainstream polling. However, in the run-up to the 1997 election a number of special polls were commissioned to probe women's perspectives and a number of additional surveys were made, giving us some idea of women's concerns at that time. Wilson and Diplock found that men and women cared about the same issues but think about them in different ways, a vindication of the perspectives/issues distinction (Wilkinson and Diplock, 1996). They also found differences amongst women. Older women in their survey were more concerned about pension provision and the availability of public transportation, working women were most interested in the minimum wage and provision for part-time workers. Mothers were most interested in levels of child benefit, which is more important to their incomes than tax cuts. Younger women wanted reassurances about policies aimed at balancing work and family life such as childcare provision.

A study by Adcock of 10,000 respondents to a self-selecting survey conducted in 1996 found strong support by women for equal pay and pension provision, social rights, access to childcare and rights for part-time workers (Adcock, 1997). A series of studies commissioned by the Fawcett Society found similar patterns (Stephenson, 1998). These 'snapshot' surveys were interesting, but have not yet led to a reconsideration of explanations of women's voting. Such a reconsideration requires the use of good quality time-series data, in an analysis that disproves the conventional wisdom. In Britain this means making careful use of the British Election Study (BES) data, which has been collected for every election since 1964. These data allow attention to subgroups, party differences and regional differences, and are generally regarded as the most reliable indicators of British voting behaviour.

Since the mid-1980s Pippa Norris, a British academic who now works at Harvard, has written extensively about women voters in Britain. Her work challenges stereotypes by examining data on political behaviour, presenting evidence about men and women and challenging traditionalists to substantiate their claims. In a series of essays she notes that there is no available evidence on the preferences of different groups of British voters prior to 1945. From that date commercial poll evidence became available and from the 1960s good quality academic studies of voting intentions and political attitudes were made for each election in successive British Election Studies. This evidence indicates that there were significant differences in preferences between women and men voters, that a gender gap in voting choice was characteristic of British politics, but that gap varies significantly among different groups of voters.

Comparing the best available evidence on women's and men's voting between 1945 and 1997, Norris confirmed a gender gap in British voting. So significant was the gap between 1945 and 1979 that, had women not had the vote, there would have been an unbroken succession of Labour govern-ments until 1979. The Conservative advantage among women voters peaked in the 1950s (see Table 11.3), during the 1960s and 1970s it fluctuated, but overall decreased. In 1987 it closed to insignificance, reopening in 1992 and becoming smaller in 1997.

In her most recent account, which uses the 1997 BES data, and therefore includes analysis of Labour's 1997 landslide victory. Norris argues that the long-term trend in aggregate women's and men's voting suggests a gradual convergence between the sexes in voting choice and indicates that the asso-ciation between sex and voting choice has declined to insignificance (Norris, 1998). At 4 percentage points in favour of the Conservatives, the 1997 gender gap was statistically insignificant. The long-term trend of weak ening links between gender and party preference had continued. However, when the 1997 data were disaggregated, they indicated rather different

*Table 11.3* Women's and men's voting and the gender gap 1945–97

|      | Conservative | | Labour | | Liberal | | Gender |
|      | Men | Women | Men | Women | Men | Women | Gap |
|------|-----|-------|-----|-------|-----|-------|-----|
| 1945 | 35 | 43 | 51 | 45 | 11 | 12 | −14 |
| 1950 | 41 | 45 | 46 | 43 | 13 | 12 | −7 |
| 1951 | 46 | 54 | 51 | 42 | 3 | 4 | −17 |
| 1955 | 47 | 55 | 51 | 42 | 2 | 3 | −17 |
| 1959 | 45 | 51 | 48 | 43 | 7 | 6 | −11 |
| 1964 | 40 | 43 | 47 | 47 | 12 | 10 | −4 |
| 1966 | 36 | 41 | 54 | 51 | 9 | 8 | −8 |
| 1970 | 43 | 48 | 48 | 42 | 7 | 8 | −11 |
| 1974 | 37 | 39 | 42 | 40 | 18 | 21 | −3 |
| 1974 | 35 | 37 | 45 | 40 | 16 | 20 | −8 |
| 1979 | 45 | 49 | 38 | 38 | 15 | 13 | −3 |
| 1983 | 46 | 45 | 30 | 28 | 23 | 26 | −2 |
| 1987 | 44 | 44 | 31 | 31 | 24 | 23 | −1 |
| 1992 | 46 | 48 | 37 | 34 | 17 | 18 | −6 |
| 1997 | 29 | 31 | 53 | 51 | 18 | 19 | −4 |

*Note*: The gender gap is calculated as the difference in the Con–Lab lead for women and men. A negative gender gap indicates a greater conservative vote by women.
*Source*: Norris (1998). Calculated from Gallup Polls, 1945–59, and BES, 1964–97.

patterns of support by women and men that appeared to cancel each other out. Age was very strongly related to women's votes: the majority (55 per cent) of younger women preferred Labour by comparison to younger men (44 per cent). In the older generation 39 per cent of women voted Conservative, but only 31 per cent of older men (Norris, 1998) (Table 11.4).

With the exception of education which predicted women's votes better than it does men's, other traditional indicators of political preference proved better predictors of men's than women's choices. Social class, housing tenure and current union membership were more reliable predictors of men's votes (Norris, 1998). Thus although the political behaviour of women and men appears to be converging, the explanations for their behaviour are not. This pattern is consistent with Norris's findings in studies of previous elections (Norris, 1996) and with the analysis done by the Fawcett Society of their specially commissioned Gallup poll conducted during the run up to the 1997 general election (Stephenson, 1998). These findings have significant implications for the ways in which political parties should attempt to mobilise voters. Norris's analysis shows how differences between younger and older women whereby younger women are more 'feminist' in the sense of support for women's rights and sex equality policy do not map onto patterns of party preference, apparently because the parties are not seen as particularly differentiated on such issues. Taken together the various studies conducted of the last election suggest that a reconsideration of how men's and women's voting is understood and explained is overdue. It seems that women and men have different experiences and possibly degrees of belonging to the polity, that they are different kinds of citizens.

*Table 11.4*   The Con–Lab gender generation gap, 1964–97

| Year | Under 25 | 25–44 | 45–65 | 65+ |
|------|----------|-------|-------|------|
| 1964 | 26 | −3 | −11 | 0 |
| 1966 | 23 | −14 | −8 | −5 |
| 1970 | −6 | −7 | −5 | −30 |
| 1974 | −5 | −7 | 7 | −10 |
| 1974* | −17 | −3 | −10 | −2 |
| 1979 | 22 | −6 | 1 | −11 |
| 1983 | 2 | 1 | −2 | −4 |
| 1987 | 6 | −3 | 1 | 3 |
| 1992 | 23 | −3 | −5 | −19 |
| 1997 | 14 | −5 | −12 | −13 |

*The first general election in 1974 was in February; a second general election was held in Octorber 1974.
Source: Norris (1998).

## Party Politics and the Gender Gap

The gender gap in British voting favours the Conservative Party. Although the British gender gap is small, its effects are amplified in three ways: there are more women in the electorate than men (51.7 per cent of the electorate in 1997 were women); over most of their life course women are more likely to vote than men (80.1 per cent of eligible women but only 76.9 per cent of eligible men voted in 1997 – about 2 million more women than men); and there are many more women than men in the oldest age group, a group in which women have both high turnout rates and a distinct Conservative bias). In short, Labour has had a problem with women voters, but a pattern of gender de-alignment made women voters more available to Labour during the 1990s. The manner in which Labour responded to this opportunity tells quite a lot both about gender biases in the party and about the implications for women of the modernisation project.

Despite many attempts to alert Labour to the significance of women's votes, it was only after determined efforts were made by party women to draw attention to the significance of women's votes that the attention of the leadership was gained. A combination of leadership changes, changes in electoral strategy and a widespread reluctance to acknowledge the importance of constituencies of women to party electoral fortunes meant that such efforts had to be repeated many times to ensure that key groups of women voters were targeted.

After the 1987 general election two prominent Labour women, Deborah Mattinson and Patricia Hewitt, published an influential pamphlet arguing that the party's traditional masculine images were costing it support from women (Mattinson and Hewitt, 1989). They were invited to present their results to a meeting of Neil Kinnock's shadow cabinet, who agreed that more attention should be paid to feminising the party's appeal. The decision made good sense. Party modernisation, the strategy devised to change the party in order to replace Labour's shrinking working-class constituency, was by then well underway. Changes in women's lives had apparently resulted in attitudes and policy preferences that should have been favourable to Labour. Within the party, women were organising to promote women as candidates and into official internal party positions. From 1979 onwards women from feminist movement backgrounds joined the Labour Party and organised within it. A similar process was taking place in the trade unions. The revival of party women's sections and politicisation of the women's conference led to widespread changes in party policy on women's representation and to the promotion of women throughout the party organisation (Lovenduski and Randall, 1993).

The agreement to foreground women in the 1992 election campaign turned out to mean little, and only weak mechanisms were established to address party electoral appeals to women. Also apparent was a media reluctance to publicise the appeals the party did make, a response that probably reflected the dependence of journalists on party briefings and informants. Campaigning on women was largely due to the efforts of Labour women organised in 'women's campaigns' in a number of areas. Subsequent studies of Labour's 1992 campaign (in which Hewitt played an important strategic part) found the usual predominance of male politicians and masculine appeals. After the election Angela Eagle, MP commented: 'It was like a glass trapdoor opened up and all of a sudden, all the women disappeared' (quoted in Stephenson, 1998, p. 7).

John Smith, elected leader after Kinnock's resignation in 1992, was very supportive of efforts to feminise the party (Perrigo, 1996; Short, 1996). The office of the party women's officer was upgraded, as was the Shadow Ministry for Women, which got shadow cabinet status and a promise of a place in the cabinet when Labour eventually won a general election. When Clare Short became Shadow Minster for Women in 1995 she became interested in the gender gap in voting and soon instigated a number of activities designed to highlight the problem and indicate strategies to deal with it. She found it very difficult to persuade party pollsters and strategists to take the Conservative advantage among women voters seriously. It was, for example, almost impossible to commission adequate gender analysis of party polls. This proved to be the case even when a poll to explore the gender gap was specially commissioned by the shadow minister and financed from the party's women's budget.

Yet the stakes were high. By this time spectacular Labour leads were being reported in all the opinion polls. But experts inside and outside the party considered Labour's lead to be fragile. Finally, Clare Short and Deborah Lincoln (Labour's women's officer) arranged for Sharon Witherspoon to re-analyse Labour's polls. Her paper confirmed the gender gap and identified the economy, party image and discourse as important underlying causes of Labour's failure with women. As a result, Clare Short and some prominent Labour women agreed to form a group to tackle the problem of the diffidence of women voters towards Labour. Together with Philip Gould they set up the 'Winning Words' group, which met through 1995 and 1996. The group was joined by academics, by women members of Tony Blair's office and by a representative of Labour's advertising agency. Gould was influential in Labour's campaign and polling office and was in a position to get past some of the ambivalence Labour strategists had about targeting women voters. Having worked for the Clinton campaign in 1992, Gould was well aware of the potential importance of gender to voting and receptive to arguments that the gender gap was important and needed to be tackled.

The group re-analysed polls and funded and analysed focus groups. Its task, it became clear, was not only to educate the party, but also to convince the shadow cabinet that a gender gap existed, that it was important and that success in the coming election depended upon reversing it. 'Winning Words' research found that women were attracted to Labour's policies but repelled by its presentation. The strategies proposed by the group were to adopt more women-friendly language, styles, images, media and other political appeals. Such messages were more appealing to all voters, a point that was made repeatedly by the members of the group. Presentations were made at party conferences and to a meeting of the shadow cabinet which agreed its recommendations. The advice was incorporated into campaign literature for candidates and into party training programmes. For example, a presentation was made at the National Women's Training Conference at Blackpool in 1996 and material for making similar presentations at branch and constituency level was circulated and widely used. One of the biggest problems for the 'Winning Words' group was resistance to the very idea of the gender gap by Labour's polling experts and the absence at that time of much public discussion of the nature of the gender gap (see above).[1]

The British media, taking its lead from party and independent pollsters and informants, were remarkably silent on gender differences revealed by the polls; these were infrequently reported and rarely analysed. The conventions of press coverage of the polls (newspapers generate stories by commissioning regular polls from competing polling organisations) simply did not include coverage of the gender gap. Before the long campaign leading to the 1997 general election, press references to Britain's gender gap were infrequent, even at election time, although coverage was given to gender differences in American voting, presumably reflecting press coverage there as much of the British newspaper copy on American politics is simply lifted form the American press. The gender gap in voting in 1992 was discussed in 16 stories between the beginning of the campaign and the discussions of results that immediately followed it. In 1993 there were two stories and one letter; in 1994 the total was seven, in 1995 one story appeared. In 1996 there were 21 stories on the gender gap in the national British press and 17 of those were part of the Tony Blair haircut story.[2]

Inside the party, the gender gap phenomena has been put to good use by feminist advocates who used it as a basis for arguments that more should be done for women. Prior to and during the 1997 election, women's advocates brought the gender gap into greater prominence, using it to campaign about getting more women in parliament and getting more priority for women's issues. By the time the 'Winning Words' group was wound up in February 1997, women's advocacy groups such as the Fawcett Society, the Women's Communication Centre were publicising the gender gap. The strategy was also used inside the Labour Party and is described in detail in a number of recent publications (Eagle and Lovenduski, 1998; Lovenduski, 1996).

**Women's Political Representation**

It is a well-known truth of British politics that voters vote for political parties rather than individual candidates, whose effect on turnout and preference is small and only rarely significant. This gives party selectors rather than voters the real choice of who a constituency's MP will be. It also determines the nature and setting of tactical arguments about women's representation (Lovenduski and Norris, 1993; Norris and Lovenduski, 1995). Although there is an intuitive link between women's voting and women's representation, it is difficult to demonstrate empirically. Supporters of women's representation made good use of the phenomenon in their campaign to improve women's share of candidacies in winnable seats. They argued that increasing the numbers of women candidates was an important part of ridding the party of its unappealing images of traditional masculinity. However, although there are clear resonances and associations with the arguments about representation and the way in which mobilisation around the gender gap took place, they were unable, finally to prove their case.

This returns us to the question raised above about how to explain the breakthrough for women in 1997. As I show below, essentially the explanation is political, a matter of skilful operation by women's advocates within the Labour Party. The increase in women's representation was the result of Labour Party efforts; Labour returned 101 women MPs. The minor landslide of the Liberal Democrats returned only three women, while the Conservative complement of women dropped from 20 to 13.

Policies to increase women's candidacies were a preoccupation of Labour Party women's advocates from the 1970s when a number of campaigns began to increase the power of women in the party. At the beginning of the 1980s the Women's Action Committee initiated campaigns to increase the power of party women, but its association with the Left impeded the success of its ideas about representation. Later, the Labour Women's Network took up the issue of women candidates, not only campaigning to increase their numbers, but also offering training and other support to women who wished to stand for elected office. In 1993 EMILY was founded to offer direct support to Labour women who sought party nomination for elected office.

By the end of the 1980s a number of feminists' voices in different parts of the party were claiming power for women. Their success was notable. In 1989 conference resolved to introduce quotas of 40 per cent for elections at every level. The 1990 conference passed a resolution calling on the NEC to establish a programme whereby, ten years hence, at least 40 per cent of all party decision-making committees had to be women. Conference gave the party three general elections to bring the proportion of women in the PLP up to 50 per cent. It also called for a quota of women on the NEC of 40 per cent. In the same year, following a proposal from the Tribune group, a quota was introduced in the shadow cabinet whereby ballot papers had to include votes for three women in order to be valid. The size of the shadow cabinet was increased by three from a membership of 15 to one of 18 so that no male 'losers' were created by the new policy.

The 1991 conference amended the party constitution to establish quotas of women on most party councils. The NEC accepted the radical principle that a quota place would remain vacant if no woman came forward for it. Thus, in the early 1990s party branches and constituency associations had to ensure that 40 per cent of their officers were women and the General Secretary had to ensure that all policy-making bodies and all committees were composed of at least 40 per cent women. Response to the policy varied and there was great support in many parts of the party but considerable opposition in traditional Labour areas. Nevertheless the forward march of women continued. The significant exception to a widespread initial acceptance of quotas was in the selection of parliamentary candidates. On this matter policy was weak, consisting of a rule that where a woman had been nominated she had to be included on the shortlist for constituency selection and regular exhortation by party leaders and officials that more women should be selected. And more women were selected. Table 11.5 shows that the number of women nominated increased at every election. But these nominations were overwhelmingly in unwinnable or marginal seats and in 1992 Labour returned only 37 women, some 14 per cent of the PLP.

It was clear that, without some mechanism to secure improvement, progress in women's representation would be glacial. But the British electoral system offered no easy way of making rapid improvements. The first-past-the-post system without term limits and with its overwhelming numbers of safe seats offered few vacancies. Each constituency selection was a zero-sum game in which insiders had a huge advantage. For the most part, the insiders were men. Repeated changes in selection rules failed to change the selection successes of women. Those who sought to implement the decision to feminise the PLP had little option but to devise a form of compulsory quota and overcome local resistance to central interference in selection processes.

After the 1992 election the responsibility for devising the policy fell to Clare Short, who was then chair of the NEC women's committee. After

*Table 11.5*   Labour women MPs and candidates, 1979–92

|      | *PPCs* | *MPs* | *Success rate* |
|------|--------|-------|----------------|
| 1979 | 52     | 11    | 21.2           |
| 1983 | 78     | 10    | 12.8           |
| 1987 | 92     | 21    | 22.8           |
| 1992 | 138    | 37    | 26.8           |

consultation with a number of senior party women she concluded that the only realistic policy was to group constituencies regionally and to require that half of the vacant safe and winnable seats were selected from an all-women shortlist. There was considerable pressure from party feminists to require all-women shortlists in all vacant and winnable seats. The compromise decision to require women's selection in only half of such seats was taken because it was felt that the interests of popular male candidates who had fought a seat previously should be protected.

The new selection policy was supported by Gordon Colling, then chair of the Organisation Committee, and by John Smith, who attended the meeting of the NEC women's committee that debated the options. In the wake of a disappointing selection of women for the 1994 European elections the proposal was taken to the 1993 conference where it was carried. (The vote was linked to the controversial OMOV vote which removed the constituency electoral colleges. The OMOV vote dominated the conference and was won by the leadership only because the MSF so strongly supported an increase of women's representation that it abstained rather than cast its votes against OMOV which it opposed.) (Lovenduski and Norris, 1994; Short, 1996).

The decision passed almost unnoticed at the time of the conference but, as selections began to take place under the new policy, all-women shortlists received considerable and hostile press coverage. The policy was successfully challenged in the courts by two disgruntled male aspirants who claimed their right to be considered for employment, protected by the prohibition on positive discrimination of the Sex Discrimination Act of 1975, was breached by the policy. Although the Sex Discrimination Act specifically excluded political parties from its provisions, the Industrial Tribunal at Leeds accepted that the selection procedure by a political party facilitated access to employment and was therefore subject to the Act. Decisions made by Industrial Tribunals are specific to the case on which they are made. The judgment (*Jepson and Dyas-Elliott* v *The Labour Party and Others*, 8 January 1966) did not bind other selectors and did not make all-women shortlists illegal. But it might as well have. To confirm or overturn the decision it was necessary to appeal, a process that may have entangled the party in court action that went all the way to the European Court of Justice. Anxious to complete its selections in good time for the general election and concerned not to jeopardise the positions of women already selected under the quotas policy Labour's National Executive Committee decided not to appeal the tribunal decision, but to discontinue the policy. The result was that selections were completed, women did less well than they had done under the all-women shortlist policy and the legal status of party polices to establish quotas of women candidates was not clarified.

*Table 11.6*   Labour candidates by type of seat

|                              | *Women* | *Men* | *Total* | *% Women* |
|------------------------------|---------|-------|---------|-----------|
| Returned Labour incumbents   | 36      | 199   | 235     | 15.3      |
| Labour retirements           | 11      | 21    | 32      | 34.4      |
| Key seats                    | 43      | 42    | 85      | 50.6      |
| Unexpected gains             | 11      | 55    | 66      | 16.7      |
| **Total MPs**                | **101** | **317** | **418** | **24.2** |
| Unwinnable seats             | 57      | 166   | 223     | 25.6      |
| **Total candidates**         | **158** | **483** | **641** | **24.6** |

*Source*: Eagle and Lovenduski (1998).

Although controversial, all-women shortlists were very successful. To measure its success it is necessary to distinguish between four types of seats: (1) party seats already held by women who in 1997 retained their seats; (2) inheritor seats, regarded as safe seats in which a Labour MP was retiring; (3) key or target seats the party needed to win in order to be certain of victory – these seats were to be privileged in terms of campaign resources; (4) other seats which the party did not expect to win. At the general election Labour retained all of its existing seats, gained 85 key seats and 66 other seats. Most of the new women came in key seats. Thirty-six women were re-elected, 11 were returned in the 32 inheritor seats, 43 were elected in key seats and 11 were elected in the 66 other seats. Their success was largely the result of a selection mechanism – compulsory all-women shortlists – which gave local parties no choice but to select a woman. This policy began in 1993, was controversial throughout its lifetime, and was ultimately dropped in January 1996. These two years saw the selection of many women candidates.

Labour's achievement was not an indication of a popular enthusiasm within the party for the selection of women candidates, a condition implicitly recognised by party managers and leaders. The suspension of the policy was followed by a search for other means of guaranteeing the selection of women. In the cases of the new Scottish parliament and Welsh assembly, quotas are to be introduced through a system of constituency pairing whereby women will be assured one half of Labour seats. In other assemblies however, the representation of Labour women may well fall over the next electoral cycle. Current levels of women's representation were achieved when Labour was at a peak of electoral success. Not only was the 1997 landslide at Westminster a record victory, but the 1994 European elections were Labour's best ever and Labour has a record number of local councillors, whilst the Conservatives 'local government base virtually disappeared during the 1980s and 1990s.

Likely electoral developments mean that opportunities for new candidates at Westminster, in Europe and at local level will arise only where retirements take place, a prospect that suggests slow change at the best of times. Historically there are few Westminster retirements and seats replacing retiring MPs are the hardest fought because they are the safest. At the next general election, by almost all predictions, Labour will lose seats and there will be fewer retirements because of the high proportion of youthful Labour MPs.

To make further progress, deliberate and careful policy is needed. In its bid to feminise the party, to win women's votes and to nominate women candidates Labour initiated a process of competition on women's representation that has been joined by other political parties. The Liberal Democrats and the Conservatives are currently lagging well behind, but are aware of the need to take action. Labour's strong action over selection methods in Wales and Scotland shows some determination to secure and maintain good levels of women's representation. The squeeze on Westminster places in the next election will be a crucial test. The party will need clear and carefully thought out selection policies to maintain progress at Westminster.

In practice the many links between women representatives, women's representation and women voters are being made in the current parliament but these have not yet found a secure place in government. There is evidence that women MPs raise women's issues in debate and feel an obligation to represent women.[3] Following the examples of other European democracies, the government has, reluctantly it appears, established a women's unit and a cabinet sub-committee on women's issues. A Minister for Women with cabinet status has been appointed. Predictably, the ministry has experienced teething problems. These include both the inevitable difficulties faced by any new government structure and apparent internal confusion about the appropriate role of the unit. At the time of writing (summer 1998) the unit appears to be planning to prioritise women's issues such as childcare and domestic violence policies, but has made little headway on women's perspectives. Yet bringing women's perspectives into the policy machinery is one of the main aims of such a unit. Arguably, it is too soon to expect such developments and enough that, at the national level of politics, linkages between women's political representation and public action are becoming apparent, even if only scattered evidence about their meaning and effect is available.

## CONCLUSIONS

The evidence on voting, attitudes, policy and issues is not an adequate basis on which to make strong statements about the relationship between levels of women's representation and women's voting behaviour. Nor is it possible to state with confidence that the rebirth of feminism has brought major changes in women's political behaviour by comparison to men's. However, patterns of both the voting and political representation of British women have changed and it is likely that feminism is implicated in such developments. The patterns of social change in work, education, marriage, fertility, family structure and childcare practices that are normally associated with feminism are also associated with other changes in women's behaviour. There is little evidence that party positions on particular 'women's issues' directly influence women's votes. But there is evidence that women's perspectives on a range of issues incline them to Labour and that Labour's attention to its appeal to women voters in 1997 enabled it to gain from that advantage, at least among younger and better educated women. Undoubtedly the other parties will adjust their appeals in the light of Labour's experience and future elections will see the Conservatives, Liberal Democrats and Nationalists making considerable efforts to win the support of women voters.

## NOTES

1. Such resistance is itself worthy of study, it is also characteristic of the academic community and has much to do with the power of established indicators used by pollsters and other electoral analysts. Similar resistances have been observed in the US.
2. Lexis search results.
3. Such evidence has been assembled by two graduate students who are writing doctoral dissertations on women's representation in Britain, Lucy Peake at Southampton University and Sarah Childs at Kingston University.

## REFERENCES

Adcock, Charlotte (1997) *What Women Want on Politics*, London: Women's Communication Centre.

Duverger, Maurice (1955) *The Political Role of Women*, UNESCO.

Eagle, Maria and Lovenduski, Joni (1998) *High Time or High Tide for Labour Women?* Fabian Pamphlet 585, London: Fabian Society.

Fawcett Society (1996) *Winning Women's Votes: The Gender Gap in Voting Patterns and Priorities*. London: Fawcett Society.

Goot, Murray and Reid, Elizabeth (1975) *Women and Voting Studies: Mindless Matrons or Sexist Scientism*. Beverly Hills: Sage.

Lovenduski, Joni (1997) 'The Integration of Feminism into West European Politics', in Martin Rhodes, Paul Heywood and Vincent Wright (eds) *Developments in West European Politics*. Basingstoke: Macmillan.

Lovenduski, Joni and Hills, Jill (1981) *The Politics of the Second Electorate*. London: Routledge and Kegan Paul.

Lovenduski, Joni and Norris, Pippa (eds) (1993) *Gender and Party Politics*. London: Sage.

Lovenduski, Joni and Norris, Pippa (1994) 'Labour and the Unions', *Government and Opposition*, 29, 2, 201–17.

Lovenduski, Joni and Randall, Vicky (1993) *Contemporary Feminist Politics*. Oxford: Oxford University Press.

Hewitt, P. and Mattinson, D. (1989) *Women's Votes: The Keys to Winning*, London: Fabian Society.

Norris, Pippa (1996) 'Mobilising the Women's Vote: Gender–Generation Gap in Voting Behaviour' *Parliamentary Affairs*.

Norris, Pippa (1998) 'A Gender Generation Gap?' in Geoffrey Evans and Pippa Norris (eds) *Critical Elections: Voters and Parties in Long-Term Perspective*, London: Sage.

Norris, Pippa and Lovenduski, Joni (1995) *Political Recruitment: Gender Race and Class in the British Parliament*. Cambridge: Cambridge University Press.

Phillips, Anne (1991) *Engendering Democracy*. Cambridge: Polity Press.

Perrigo, Sarah (1996) ' Women and Change in the Labour Party 1979–1995', *Parliamentary Affairs*, 49, 1, 116–29.

Short, Clare, MP (1996), 'Women and the Labour Party', *Parliamentary Affairs*, 49, 1, 17–25.

Skjeie, Hege (1993) 'Ending the Male Political Hegemony: The Norwegian Experience', in Joni Lovenduski and Pippa Norris (eds) *Gender and Party Politics,* London: Sage.

Stephenson, Mary-Ann (1998) *The Glass Trapdoor*, London: Fawcett Society.

Wilkinson, Helen and Diplock, Shelagh (1996) *Soft Sell or Hard Policies: How Can the Parties Best Appeal to Women?* London: Demos.

# Index